Understanding Digital Marketing

SECOND EDITION

Understanding Digital Marketing

Marketing strategies for engaging the digital generation

Damian Ryan
and Calvin Jones

KoganPage

LONDON PHILADELPHIA NEW DELHI

Publisher's note

Every possible effort has been made to ensure that the information contained in this book is accurate at the time of going to press, and the publishers and authors cannot accept responsibility for any errors or omissions, however caused. No responsibility for loss or damage occasioned to any person acting, or refraining from action, as a result of the material in this publication can be accepted by the editor, the publisher or either of the authors.

First published in Great Britain and the United States in 2009 by Kogan Page Limited
Second edition 2012
Reprinted 2012 (three times), 2013 (twice)

120 Pentonville Road
London N1 9JN
United Kingdom
www.koganpage.com

1518 Walnut Street, Suite 1100
Philadelphia PA 19102
USA

4737/23 Ansari Road
Daryaganj
New Delhi 110002
India

© Damian Ryan and Calvin Jones, 2009, 2012

The right of Damian Ryan and Calvin Jones to be identified as the authors of this work has been asserted by them in accordance with the Copyright, Designs and Patents Act 1988.

ISBN   978 0 7494 6427 1
E-ISBN   978 0 7494 6428 8

British Library Cataloguing-in-Publication Data

A CIP record for this book is available from the British Library.

Library of Congress Cataloging-in-Publication Data

Ryan, Damian.
   Understanding digital marketing : marketing strategies for engaging the digital generation / Damian Ryan, Calvin Jones. – 2nd ed.
     p. cm.
   ISBN 978-0-7494-6427-1 – ISBN 978-0-7494-6428-8   1. Internet marketing.   2. Social media.
3. Strategic planning.   4. Marketing–Management.   I. Jones, Calvin.   II. Title.
   HF5415.1265.R93 2012
   658.8'72–dc23
                                                                                          2011040583

Typeset by Graphicraft Limited, Hong Kong
Print production managed by Jellyfish
Printed and bound by CPI Group (UK) Ltd, Croydon, CR0 4YY

CONTENTS

PREFACE: WELCOME TO A BRAVE NEW WORLD

The world of digital media is changing at a phenomenal pace. Its constantly evolving technologies, and the way people are using them, are transforming not just how we access our information, but how we interact and communicate with one another on a global scale.

It's also changing the way we choose and buy our products and services.

People are embracing digital technology to communicate in ways that would have been inconceivable just a few short years ago. No longer the preserve of tech-savvy early adopters, digital technologies are today being seamlessly integrated by ordinary people into their everyday lives.

From SMS updates on their favourite sports teams to a free video call with relatives on the other side of the globe, to collaborative online gaming and much, much more: ordinary people – your customers – are starting to use digital media without giving it a second thought.

The global online population was around 2.1 billion at the end of March 2011 (Internet World Stats). In the developed world, internet access is becoming practically ubiquitous, and the widespread availability of always-on broadband connections means that people are now going online daily to do everything from checking their bank statement to shopping for their groceries, to playing games.

What makes this digital revolution so exciting is that it's happening right now. We're living through it, and we have a unique opportunity to jump in and be part of this historic transition.

In the pages that follow we'll take you on a journey into the world of digital marketing. We'll show you how it all started, how it got to where it is today, and where thought leaders in the industry believe it's heading in the future. Most important of all, we'll show you – in a practical, no-nonsense way – how you can harness the burgeoning power of digital media to drive your business to the crest of this digital marketing wave, and how to keep it there.

This book will:

- help you and your business to choose online advertising and marketing channels that will get your ideas, products and services to a massive and ever-expanding market;
- give you that elusive competitive edge that will keep you ahead of the pack;
- future-proof your business by helping you to understand the origins of digital marketing and the trends that are shaping its future;

- give you a concept of the scale of the online marketplace, the unfolding opportunities and the digital service providers who will help your business to capitalize on them;
- provide practical, real-world examples of digital marketing successes – including leading brands that have become household names in a relatively short space of time;
- offer insight through interviews, analysis and contributions from digital marketing experts;
- ultimately, give you the tools you need to harness the power of the internet to take your business wherever you want it to go.

We set out to unravel the mysteries of digital marketing by taking you on a journey. As we travel into this digital world we'll reveal how leading marketers in sectors as diverse as travel, retail, gambling and adult entertainment have stumbled on incredibly effective techniques to turn people on to doing business online, reaping literally millions as a result. We'll show you how to apply their experience to transform your own digital enterprise.

Whether you're looking to start up your own home-based internet business, work for a large multinational or are anywhere in between, if you want to connect with your customers today and into the future, you're going to need digital channels as part of your marketing mix.

The internet has become the medium of choice for a generation of consumers: the first generation to have grown up taking instant access to digital information for granted. This generation integrates digital media into every facet of their daily lives in ways we could never have conceived in even the recent past. Today this generation of digital natives is entering the workplace and is spending like never before. This is the mass market of tomorrow, and for businesspeople and marketers the challenge is to become fluent in this new digital language so that we can talk effectively to our target audience.

Television froze a generation of consumers to the couch for years; now digital media are engaging consumers and customers in ways that the early architects of the technology could never have dreamed. The advent of 'two-screen' or even 'three-screen' marketing is now becoming a real consideration – just look at what Channel 4 is doing with *Million Pound Drop* – an on-air game that encourages couch-based users to join in the fun online.

When the Apple Mac came along it opened up the art of publishing, and as a result print media boomed. Today the same thing is happening online, through the phenomenon of user-generated content (UGC) and social networking: ordinary people are becoming the directors, producers, editors and distributors of their own media-rich content – the content they, their friends and the world want to see. But that's only the start.

Prime-time television audiences are falling, print media are coming under increasing pressure to address dropping circulation figures – and while the old school sits on the sidelines, bloated and slowly atrophying, digital media have transformed themselves into a finely tuned engine delivering more power, opportunity and control than any other form of media could dream of.

In other words – it's time to follow the smart money!

Over the last 18 years I've had the absolute pleasure and pain of working at the coalface of these burgeoning and insistent new media. I've met lots of smart people and spoken to literally hundreds of organizations with massively diverse and challenging agendas. The one common factor was a hunger for data and knowledge: anything that would give their particular brand that elusive competitive edge.

When putting this book together we wanted to make it as informative and practical as possible. Each chapter begins with a summary of its content, so you can easily browse through the chapters and select the one that addresses the topic you're interested in. We've purposely left out the jargon – and where technical terms have been absolutely necessary we supply a clear definition in the text, backed up by a complete glossary at the back of the book that explains in plain English all of the terms we use. The result, we hope, is a book that is clear, informative and entertaining, even for the complete digital novice.

In your hands you hold what independent marketers around the world have been crying out for: a book that shows you how to successfully use the internet to sell your products or services. We begin with the origins of the medium and take you through the various disciplines of digital marketing campaigns. We travel around the world collecting facts, figures, comment and opinion from acknowledged experts, brands and organizations in different fields, getting them to spill the beans on how the net delivered the goods for them.

We'll look in detail at areas like search marketing and affiliate marketing, we'll delve into e-mail marketing, creative online executions, and look at various digital marketing strategies, some moral, some less so.

Digital marketing has its sinister side too – while many marketers play above board, some have been tempted by the dark side of the force and find more return on investment by using unscrupulous tactics to undermine their rivals and gain competitive advantage. The book will examine the world of 'black-hat marketing'.

It took television 22 years to reach 50 million households; it took the internet just five years to achieve the same level of penetration. Things are progressing at an unbelievable rate, and we're approaching a pivotal point in marketing history – a time when digital marketing will overtake traditional mass media as the medium of choice for reaching the consumer of tomorrow.

In the summer of 1993 I interviewed Jerry Reitman, head of direct marketing for Leo Burnett in Chicago, for my magazine, *goDirect*. During our conversation Jerry pointed at the computer on his desk and said: 'And that... that's where it's going.' I wondered what he was talking about.

Eighteen years on and practically the entire population is online. Consumers have grown tired of mass-media marketing, and are turning instead to the internet. They want more engagement, more interaction. They're starting to spend most of their leisure time in a digital world, and creative digital marketing is the way your business will reach them.

Welcome to our world...

Damian Ryan, Chiswick

CASE STUDY Nokia push snowboarding to new heights with the N8

FIGURE 0.1 To launch its most ambitious handset to date, Nokia launched its most ambitious campaign ever – it set out to revolutionize snowboarding

The challenge

To launch the innovative Nokia N8, the Swedish mobile company needed to do something ambitious, to create buzz around its new flagship device. It wanted to demonstrate the innovation, power and openness of the new N8.

Target audience

There were two clearly defined target audiences for the campaign. First there were the developers and technology geeks: hackers, modders and developers who love to collaborate, explore, break down and rebuild things. They fully embraced the open-source nature of the project and the fact that Nokia was inviting them to participate in the product development process in a way they'd never experienced before.

The second target was snowboarders and mass armchair sports fans who love consuming entertaining sporting content. They often embrace new and exciting technologies and enjoy finding new ways to enhance their sporting experiences.

Action

There were three key elements to this ambitious campaign:

- a new sports technology, created by agency Hypernaked and built around the Nokia N8;

- openness and collaboration: the development took place in public, and was fuelled by input from the 'crowd';

- the fact that the product development process actually formed the marketing for the Nokia N8.

At the project's heart was the Push Snowboarding kit. Working in partnership with snowboard manufacturer Burton, the team incorporated a series of sensors into the snowboarder's equipment. Built from, and around, the Nokia N8, these sensors record and track a large amount of data generated as the user rides, including speed, airtime, foot pressure, orientation, heart rate, and galvanic skin response – what the team liked to call 'rush'.

All the information was relayed live via multiple Bluetooth streams to an application on the Nokia N8, allowing riders to track, compare and improve on their runs.

Launched first on social media platforms, followed by events, online and above the line (ATL), Push Snowboarding gained a cult following of fans that contributed to and helped fuel the discussion as it spread around the globe from niche tech blogs to top snowboarding magazines and even a six-minute film played on TV news channels around the world from CNN to Sky Sports.

Results

Push Snowboarding significantly surpassed all of its pre-campaign KPI targets. With almost no media spend it reached over 300 million people around the world, and gained coverage in more than 15 languages. Based on equivalent media value the campaign delivered almost 18 times more value than the original invested.

On Twitter alone the campaign reached 8.2 million people, and recorded over 35,000 hours of video views on YouTube. Transworld Sport ran a six-minute film about the project that was syndicated to 249 million people on TV channels around the globe.

In terms of perception of the Nokia N8 and the brand, there was a 14 per cent jump in favourability for the Nokia N8 and dramatic shifts in Nokia brand favourability and metrics related to perceptions of innovativeness. These shifts were consistently strong across the four markets in which the research was conducted.

Conversation around the project was also positive with sentiment at 94 per cent favourable. Ultimately the project succeeded in reinvigorating a connection with and admiration for the Nokia brand and its newest products.

Some of the consumer feedback received included: 'This is Nokia's comeback.' 'Nokia = magic.' 'Makes me love Nokia again.' 'This technology couldn't happen on an iPhone.'

The Push Snowboarding campaign so excited snowboarding legend Terje Haakonsen that he invited Nokia to trial it at his event, the Arctic Challenge, testing it himself on the slope-style course.

'We've made people love Nokia,' he said, 'and we're on our way to revolutionizing snowboarding and enhancing the sport for both pros and amateurs alike.'

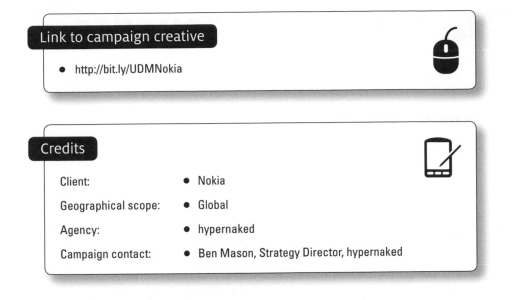

Link to campaign creative

- http://bit.ly/UDMNokia

Credits

Client:	• Nokia
Geographical scope:	• Global
Agency:	• hypernaked
Campaign contact:	• Ben Mason, Strategy Director, hypernaked

ACKNOWLEDGEMENTS

Damian Ryan

Just like the digital marketing industry, this book continues to evolve. This new edition contains a re-write of most of the original 11 chapters. However we have replaced the creative chapter with a mobile marketing chapter. Why? Well because creative speaks for itself doesn't it? So why not just share with you a collection of some of the most amazing digital marketing campaigns from around the world rather than rabbit on about 'how to be creative', a question we still struggle to answer in any case!

Also the increased level of activity in mobile marketing meant a chapter was required this time round to reflect the importance of mobile as it moves rapidly towards centre stage in the digital marketing spectrum.

As usual I have a list of people to thank for their input, advice and support.

Alexandra O Brien helped us pull together the case studies for this edition and our deepest thanks go to her for a brilliant job well done.

Keeping us all sane was Barry Flaherty, my colleague at Mediaventura. Barry got stuck into some desk research during times when business became too important and the book got shoved into second or third place.

Our thanks to Abigail Coften and Ian Hallsworth of Kogan Page – particularly as they helped us celebrate the launch of our other book (*The Best Digital Marketing Campaigns in the World*) back in the summer. Our thanks also go to Colin Lloyd and Marialena Zinopolou from the CAM Foundation who also took part in our launch earlier this year.

Sean Duffy of Emailcenter and Simon Bowker of eCircle for their contributions to the chapter on e-mail marketing.

Adrian Copeland of Webgains made a significant contribution to the chapter on affiliate marketing – Adrian has now headed off to join Trade-Doubler so our best to you Adrian, thanks again.

Once again the writing partnership with Calvin Jones continues to flourish. He is a terrific friend, confidante and collaborator. We have now completed three books together over a five-year period and enjoyed all the distractions that go on around that task – book launches, interviews, conference events and article writing too. Thanks Calvin.

I dedicate this book to my daughters Katie and Alannah Ryan, both already demonstrating extraordinary abilities with technological and creative pursuits. I am such a proud dad – chips off the old block but definitely of the silicon variety!

It has been a wonderful couple of years back in London and a big THANKS to all my new and old friends here: Teresa, Andrew, Nick, Paul, Mick, Tess, Iolo, Amelia, Jo, Jon and Claire and many others, thanks.

Calvin Jones

Creating a book is a collaborative process. I say that not just because Damian and I have worked together on it – the collaboration runs much deeper and is far more extensive than that. Many people have contributed to the content of this book in more ways than there's scope to mention here.

For my part that includes the people who have inspired, motivated and encouraged me over the years, directly and indirectly. This book belongs to them as much as it does to me: they have helped, in no small measure, to shape its evolution.

Damian has already expressed our gratitude to those who have contributed directly to this second edition in terms of both content and research. I'd like to echo his sentiments, and to re-iterate our gratitude to those who helped make the first edition of this book successful. This edition is very much built on the solid foundation that was, in part, provided by their contribution.

To our publishing team – Ian, Abby, Sara and the rest of the gang at Kogan Page in London: thank you for making the entire process so straightforward; it's been a pleasure, as always, working with you.

Of course I have to thank Damian – working with him again has been remarkable in all sorts of ways. I'd love to know where he finds his boundless energy and enthusiasm.

My thanks to Colin and Padraig – for keeping it real, and making sure my feet remained firmly anchored in the reality of West Cork life when my head was spinning in the virtual cloud.

To Ava, Nia and Lana – who keep pestering me to write a children's book next – it's on the to-do list girls, honest!

Finally, huge thanks to Sally Ann – for everything. This is for you!

It's always great to receive feedback from our readers, so please do get in touch:

Damian Ryan: dryan@mediaventura.com, on Twitter @damianryan1 or www.linkedin.com/in/understandingdigital

Calvin Jones: calvin@cjwriting.com, on Twitter @WriterCJ or www.linkedin.com/in/CalvinJones

Or why not share your views with a wider audience by writing an Amazon review.

Going digital – the evolution of marketing

We look at the present through a rear-view mirror. We march backwards into the future. **MARSHALL MCLUHAN**

The press, the machine, the railway, the telegraph are premises whose thousand-year conclusion no one has yet dared to draw.

FRIEDRICH NIETZSCHE

Whoever, or whatever, wins the battle for people's minds will rule, because mighty, rigid apparatuses will not be a match, in any reasonable timespan, for the minds mobilized around the power of flexible, alternative networks.

MANUEL CASTELLS, AUTHOR OF *THE NETWORK SOCIETY*

OUR CHAPTER PLEDGE TO YOU

When you reach the end of this chapter you'll have answers to the following questions:

- How did we reach the dawn of a digital age in marketing?
- What are the similarities between the internet and historical global communications revolutions?
- How many people are on the internet and how quickly is it growing?
- How is digital technology influencing consumer behaviour?

In the beginning...

Etched on a dusty kerbstone amidst the ruins of the ancient Roman city of Pompeii, you'll find an engraved penis, strategically carved to point the way to what, at the time, was one of the most popular brothels in the area. Guides will tell you it's the 'oldest advertisement in the world, for the oldest business in the world'. While the truth of that claim is debatable, the phallic ad is certainly very old.

The Pompeii penis was buried by the eruption of Mount Vesuvius, which destroyed the city on 24 August AD79, but the true origins of marketing go back much further than that. Although, according to business historians, marketing as a discrete business discipline wasn't born until the 1950s, marketing activities have played a fundamental role in the success of businesses from, well, the very first business. There are few certainties in the world of business, but one thing's for sure: if you don't let customers know about your business, you won't stay in business for very long.

But this is a book about marketing in the digital age – the present, and the future

That's true. We're here to talk about the exciting new world of digital marketing as it emerges from relative obscurity into the mainstream. We're going to look at how businesses just like yours can harness the power of this online revolution to connect with a new wave of consumers: consumers who take this pervasive technology and integrate it seamlessly into their everyday lives in ways we could never have conceived as recently as a decade ago.

This book is about the future of marketing. So why are we starting it by looking backwards?

In his 1960s classic, *Understanding Media: The Extensions of Man*, Canadian communications theorist and philosopher Marshall McLuhan notes: 'It is instructive to follow the embryonic stages of any new growth, for during this period of development it is much misunderstood, whether it be printing or the motor car or TV.' As is so often the case, having a basic grasp of the past can help our understanding of the present, and ultimately illuminate our view of the future.

So buckle your seatbelt as we take a whistle-stop tour of how marketing has evolved over the years, and how advertising and technology have converged to define a new marketing landscape that is just beginning to mature, and is still gravid with opportunity.

The changing face of advertising

Advertising can be intoxicating. The spin, the story, the message, the call to action, the image, the placement, the measurement, the refinement. It all adds up to a powerful cocktail that can ultimately change the world. At its core, advertising is all about influencing people – persuading them to take the action we want, whether that's choosing a particular brand of toothpaste, picking up the phone, filling in a mailing coupon or visiting a website. Done well, the power of advertising can achieve amazing things, and if you're in business you're already doing it, and will continue to do so.

Advertising through the ages

Advertising, an essential component in the marketing of any business, has been around for a long time. The Pompeii penis is positively modern compared to some of the advertising relics archaeologists have unearthed in ancient Arabia, China, Egypt, Greece and Rome. The Egyptians used papyrus to create posters and flyers, while lost-and-found advertising (also on papyrus, and often relating to 'missing' slaves) was common in both ancient Greece and Rome. Posters, signs and flyers were widely employed in the ancient cities of Rome, Pompeii and Carthage to publicize events like circuses, games and gladiatorial contests.

People have been trying to influence other people since the dawn of human existence, utilizing whatever means and media they had at their disposal at the time. The human voice and word of mouth, of course, came first. Then someone picked up a piece of stone and started etching images on a cave wall: enduring images that told stories, communicated ideas and promoted certain ways of doing things.

The first advertising? That's debatable, but these images, some of which are around to this day, certainly demonstrate an early recognition of the power images and messages have to influence the perception and behaviour of others.

The development of printing during the 15th and 16th centuries heralded a significant milestone in advertising, making it more cost effective for marketers to reach a much wider audience. In the 17th century, adverts began to appear in early newspapers in England, and then spread across the globe. The first form of mass-media advertising was born.

The 18th and 19th centuries saw a further expansion in newspaper advertising, and alongside it the birth of mail-order advertising – which would evolve into the massive direct mail/direct response industry we know and love today. It also saw the establishment of the first advertising agency, set up in Boston in 1843 by the pioneering Volney Palmer. Initially ad agencies acted as simple brokers for newspaper space, but before long they developed into full-service operations, offering a suite of creative and ad-placement services to their clients.

The 20th century saw the dawn of another new advertising age, with the advent of radio offering a completely new medium through which advertisers could reach out to prospective customers. Then came television, which shifted the advertising landscape yet again, and towards the end of the century a new force – the internet – began moving out of the realm of 'techies' and early adopters to become a valuable business and communication tool for the masses. The era of digital marketing was born.

Technological advances have punctuated the evolution of advertising throughout history, each fundamentally altering the way businesses could communicate with their customers. Interestingly, however, none of these ground-breaking developments superseded those that came before. Rather they served to augment them, offering marketers more diversity, allowing them to connect with a broader cross section of consumers. In today's sophisticated age of paid search placement, keyword-targeted pay-per-click advertising and social networking, you'll still find the earliest forms of advertising alive and well.

Stroll through any market, practically anywhere in the world – from the food markets of central London to the bazaars of North Africa, to the street markets of India – and you'll be greeted by a cacophony of noise as vendors use their voices to vie for the attention of passing customers. The human voice, the first marketing medium in history, still going strong in the digital age.

The technology behind digital marketing

As we've already mentioned, developments in technology and the evolution of marketing are inextricably intertwined. Technology has underpinned major milestones in the history of marketing since its inception. The process tends to go something like this:

- New technology emerges and is initially the preserve of technologists and early adopters.

- The technology gains a firmer foothold in the market and starts to become more popular, putting it on the marketing radar.

- Innovative marketers jump in to explore ways they can harness the power of this emerging technology to connect with their target audience.

- The technology migrates to the mainstream and is adopted into standard marketing practice.

The printing press, radio, television and now the internet are all examples of major breakthroughs in technology that ultimately altered the relationships between marketers and consumers forever, and did so on a global scale. But of course marketing isn't about technology, it's about people: technology is only interesting, from a marketing perspective, when it connects people with other people more effectively.

There are plenty of examples of technology through the ages having a significant impact on various markets – technology that may seem obscure, even irrelevant today. Remember Muzak – the company that brought elevator music to the masses back in the 1930s? The technology for piping audio over power lines was patented in 1922 by retired Major General George O Squier, and exclusive rights to the patent were bought by the North American Company. In 1934, under the corporate umbrella of Muzak, they started piping music into Cleveland homes.

Muzak seemed to have hit on a winning formula, but the advent of free commercial radio sounded the death knell for the company's chosen route to market. With free music available on their shiny new wirelesses, households were no longer prepared to pay for the Muzak service. Undeterred, the company focused its efforts on New York City businesses. As buildings in New York soared skywards, the lift/elevator became practically ubiquitous. Musak had found its niche, and 'elevator music' was born.

'So what?' you might think.

It's true that, compared to behemoths of contemporary media like radio, television and now the internet, elevator music is small potatoes. But back in its heyday this was cutting-edge stuff, and it reached a lot of people. Muzak had the power to sway opinions and influence markets, so much so that for music artists of that era, having your track played on the Musak network practically guaranteed a hit.

The point is that technology has the ability to open up completely new markets, and to radically shake up existing ones. The mainstream adoption of digital technology – the internet, the software applications that run on it, and the devices that allow people to connect to both the network and each other whenever, wherever and however they want to – promises to dwarf all that has come before it. It heralds the single most disruptive development in the history of marketing.

Whether that disruption represents an opportunity or a threat to you as a marketer depends largely on your perspective. We hope the fact that you're reading this book means that you see it as an opportunity.

The first global communications network: 'the highway of thought'

To understand the explosive growth of the internet, we need to look back at how early communications technology evolved into the global network of interconnected computers that today we call the internet. The story of electronic communication begins with the wired telegraph – a network that grew rapidly to cover the globe, connected people across vast distances in a way that seemed almost magical, and changed the world forever.

In his book, *The Victorian Internet*, Tom Standage looks at the wired telegraph and draws some astonishing parallels between the growth of the world's first electronic communications network and the growth of the modern-day internet. Standage describes the origins of the telegraph, and the quest to deliver information from point to point more rapidly in the days when speedy communication relied on a fast horse and a skilled rider:

On an April day in 1746 at the grand convent of the Carthusians in Paris, about 200 monks arranged themselves in a long, snaking line. Each monk held one end of a 25-foot iron wire in each hand connecting him to his neighbour on either side. Together the monks and their connecting wires formed a line over a mile long. Once the line was complete, the abbot, Jean-Antoine Nollet, a noted French scientist, took a primitive battery and, without warning, connected it to the line of monks – giving all of them a powerful electric shock.

These 'electric monks' demonstrated conclusively that electricity could transmit a message (albeit a painful one) from one location to another in an instant, and laid the foundation for a communications revolution.

In 1830 Joseph Henry (1797–1878), an eminent US scientist who went on to become the first director of the Smithsonian Institute, took the concept a step further. He demonstrated the potential of the electromagnet for long-distance communications when he passed an electric current through a mile-long cable to ring an electromagnetic bell connected to the other end. Samuel Morse (1791–1872), the inventor of Morse code, took Henry's concept a step further and made a commercial success of it: the electronic telegraph was born.

In 1842 Morse demonstrated a working telegraph between two committee rooms in Washington, and congress voted slimly in favour of investing $30,000 for an experimental telegraph line between Washington and Baltimore. It was a very close call: 89 votes for the prototype, 83 against and 70 abstentions by congressmen looking 'to avoid the responsibility of spending the public money for a machine they could not understand'.

Despite the reservations of the congressmen, the new network was a huge success. It grew at a phenomenal rate: by 1850 there were more than 12,000 miles of telegraph line criss-crossing the United States, two years later there was more than twice that, and the network of connected wires was spreading rapidly around the globe.

This spellbinding new network delivered news in moments rather than the weeks and months people were used to. It connected people over vast distances in ways previously inconceivable, and to many remained completely incomprehensible.

Governments tried and failed to control this raw new communications medium, its advocates hailed it as revolutionary, and its popularity grew at an unprecedented rate. Newspapers began publishing news just hours rather than weeks after the event, romance blossomed over the wires, couples were married 'online', gamblers used the new network to cheat on the horses, and it transformed the way business was conducted around the world. In the space of a generation the telegraph literally altered the fabric of society.

Does any of this sound familiar?

A *New York Times* article published on Wednesday 14 September 1852 describes the telegraph network as 'the highway of thought'; not much of a stretch from the 'information super-highway' label we apply to our modern-day revolutionary network. If anything, the communications revolution instigated by the telegraph must have represented more of a cultural upheaval than the explosive growth of the internet today.

For the first time people grasped that they could communicate almost instantly with people across continents and even oceans. They felt a sense of closeness, a togetherness that simply hadn't been possible before. The telegraph system was hailed by some as a harbinger of peace and solidarity: a network of wires that would ultimately bind countries, creeds and cultures in a way hitherto unimaginable. Others, of course, used the network to wage war more efficiently. The sheer expansion of ideas and dreams that ensued must have been truly staggering, the opportunities and potential for change bewildering.

For rapid, long-distance communications the telegraph remained the only game in town until 1877, when two rival inventors battled to be the first to patent another new technology set to turn the world of electronic communications on its head. Its name, the telephone; the inventors, Elisha Grey and Alexander Graham Bell. They submitted their patent applications within hours of one another – but Bell pipped Grey to the post, and a now famous legal battle ensued.

The first words ever transmitted into a telephone were uttered by Bell, speaking to his research assistant, Thomas Watson, in the next room. He simply said: 'Mr. Watson – come here – I want to see you.'

Early networks

The internet story really starts in 1957, with the USSR's launch of the Sputnik satellite. It signalled that the United States was falling behind the Russians in the technology stakes, prompting the US government to invest heavily in science and technology. In 1958, the US Department of Defense set up the Advanced Research Projects Agency (ARPA) – a specialist agency established with a specific remit: to make sure the United States stayed ahead of her cold war nemesis in the accelerating technology race.

In August 1962 a computer scientist called Joseph Carl Robnett Licklider (1915–90), vice president at technology company Bolt Beranek and Newman, wrote a series of memos discussing the concept of an 'Intergalactic Computer Network'. Licklider's revolutionary ideas, amazingly, encompassed practically everything that the internet has today become.

In October 1963, Licklider was appointed head of the Behavioral Sciences and Command and Control Programs at ARPA. During his two-year tenure he convinced the agency of the importance of developing computer networks, and although he left ARPA before work on his theories began, the seed for ARPANET the precursor to the internet – had been sown.

In 1965 researchers hooked up a computer at Massachusetts Institute of Technology's (MIT) Lincoln Lab with a US Air Force computer in California. For the first time two computers communicated with each other using 'packet'-based information transmitted over a network.

ARPA (since renamed DARPA – **www.darpa.mil**) started the ARPANET project in 1966, claiming that it would allow the powerful computers owned by the government, universities and research institutions around the United States to communicate with one another and to share valuable computing resources. IBM and other large computer companies at the time were sceptical, reportedly claiming that the network ARPA proposed couldn't be built.

ARPA ploughed on, and on 21 November 1969 the first two computers were connected to the fledgling ARPANET, one at University of California Los Angeles, the other at Stanford Research Institute. By 5 December the same year the network doubled in size as they were joined by two other computers: one at University of California Santa Barbara, the other at University of Utah's graphics department.

The new network grew quickly. By 1971, 15 US institutions were connected to ARPANET, and by 1974 the number had grown to 46, and had spread to include overseas nodes in Hawaii, Norway and London.

You've got mail

E-mail, which is still often described as the internet's 'killer application', began life in the early 1960s as a facility that allowed users of mainframe computers to send simple text-based messages to another user's mailbox on the same computer. But it wasn't until the advent of ARPANET that anyone considered sending electronic mail from one user to another across a network.

In 1971 Ray Tomlinson, an engineer working on ARPANET, wrote the first program capable of sending mail from a user on one host computer to another user's mailbox on another host computer. As an identifier to distinguish network mail from local mail, Tomlinson decided to append the host name of the user's computer to their user login name. To separate the two names he chose the @ symbol.

'I am frequently asked why I chose the "at" sign, but the "at" sign just makes sense,' writes Tomlinson on his website. 'The purpose of the "at" sign (in English) was to indicate a unit price (for example, 10 items @ $1.95). I used the "at" sign to indicate that the user was "at" some other host rather than being local.'

E-mail, one of the internet's most widely used applications – and one of the most critical for internet marketers – began life as a programmer's afterthought. Tomlinson created e-mail because he thought it 'seemed like a neat idea' at the time. 'There was no directive to "go forth and invent e-mail". The ARPANET was a solution looking for a problem. A colleague suggested that I not tell my boss what I had done because e-mail wasn't in our statement of work,' he said.

From ARPANET to internet

The term 'internet' was first used in 1974 by US computer scientist Vinton Cerf (commonly referred to as one of the 'fathers of the internet', and now a senior executive and internet evangelist with Google). Cerf was working with Robert Khan at DARPA on a way to standardize the way different host computers communicated across both the growing ARPANET and between the ARPANET and other emerging computer networks. The TCP

(Transmission Control Program) network protocol they defined evolved to become the TCP/IP (Transmission Control Program/Internet Protocol) protocol suite that's still used to pass packets of information backwards and forwards across the internet to this day.

In 1983 the ARPANET started using the TCP/IP protocol – a move that many consider to signal the true 'birth' of the internet as we know it. That year, too, the system of domain names (.com, .net, etc) was invented. By 1984 the number of 'nodes' on the still fledgling network passed 1,000 and began climbing rapidly. By 1989 there were more than 100,000 hosts connected to the internet, and the growth continued.

Making connections – birth of the web

It was in 1989 that Tim Berners-Lee, a British developer working at CERN (the European Organization for Nuclear Research) in Geneva, proposed a system of information cross-referencing, access and retrieval across the rapidly growing internet based on 'hypertext' links. The concept of a hypertext information architecture was nothing new, and was already being used in individual programs running on individual computers around the world. The idea of linking documents stored on different computers across the rapidly growing internet, though, was nothing short of revolutionary.

The building blocks for the world wide web were already in place – but it was Tim Berners-Lee's vision that brought them together. 'I just had to take the hypertext idea and connect it to the TCP and DNS ideas and – ta-da! – the World Wide Web,' Berners-Lee comments on the W3C (World Wide Web Consortium) website.

The first web page on the internet was built at CERN and went online on 6 August 1991. It contained information about the new world wide web, how to get a web browser and how to set up a web server. Over time it also became the first ever web directory, as Berners-Lee maintained a list of links to other websites on the page as they appeared.

The wild wide web – a new frontier

Up to this point, the internet had been the realm of technologists and scientists at research institutions. But the advent of the web changed the landscape, making online information accessible to a much broader audience. What happened next was explosive. Between 1991 and 1997 the web grew at an astonishing 850 per cent per annum, eclipsing all expectations. With more websites and more people joining the online party every day, it was only a matter of time before innovative tech-savvy marketers started to notice the web's potential as an avenue for the marketing message.

The mid 1990s saw an explosion in new online ventures as pioneering entrepreneurs, grasping the burgeoning potential of this exciting new medium, scrambled to stake their claim on this virtual new frontier. In August 1995 there were 18,957 websites online; by August 1996 there were 342,081 ('15 years of the web, internet timeline', **www.bbc.co.uk**).

Silicon Valley was awash with venture capital as investors bet big bucks on the net's next big thing – some with viable business plans, others with charismatic founders riding on the coat-tails of the prevailing net mania. New ventures sprang up almost daily, selling everything imaginable – or selling nothing at all. Fledgling companies spent vast amounts of money growing quickly, with scant regard for turning a profit, betting their future on building strong online brands that could win the hearts and minds of net consumers. The profits would come later... at least, that was the theory. Some of these companies were destined to become household names in a few short years; others would vanish into obscurity just as quickly.

These were heady, almost euphoric times. The internet had acquired the mythical Midas touch: a business with .com in its name, it seemed, was destined for great things. Initial Public Offerings (IPOs) of dot.com companies made millionaires of founders, and made the headlines, fuelling further mania. It was an era that saw the birth of some of today's best-known online brands: sites like Amazon, Yahoo!, eBay... and, in September 1998, Google Inc.

Boom, boom... bang!

For a time it seemed like the halcyon days of the late 1990s would continue forever, that the dot.com bubble was impervious to bursting. Fuelled by speculative investment and high-profile high-tech IPOs, the Nasdaq Composite stock index continued to rocket upwards. Each new dot.com success fuelled the fervour for technology stocks, blowing the bubble up a little more. On 10 March 2000 the Nasdaq index hit an intra-day high of 5,132.52 before settling to an all-time closing high of 5,046 points.

And then it went into free fall.

What happened to the railways in the 1840s, radio in the 1920s and transistor electronics in the 1950s had finally hit the dot.com boom. Between March 2000 and October 2002 some US$5 trillion in all was wiped off the market value of technology stocks. Speculative investment suddenly stopped, venture capitalists were less cavalier with their cash, and high-risk start-ups with dubious business plans ran out of places to source funding. With profits still a distant dream, even for high-profile internet start-ups, the coffers soon began to run dry. It signalled the end of the road for many.

Despite the occasional 'blip', both the stock market index and the fortunes of internet businesses continued to wane until 2003, when, slowly but surely, the tide turned and things started to look up. Although there had been some high-profile closures, mergers and acquisitions in the wake of the crash, the reality is that, for the internet industry as a whole, the inevitable 'readjustment' had a positive impact. It essentially cleared the decks – sweeping away a plethora of unviable, poorly conceived and poorly managed businesses – and served as a poignant reality check to those who remained.

Yes, there were casualties, but overall the industry emerged stronger, more focused and both optimistic and, crucially, realistic about its future.

Two other critical elements helped fuel the recovery, and to some extent the public fascination with the internet: one was the meteoric rise of Google from relative obscurity to dominate the world of internet search, the other was the accelerated roll-out of high-speed, always-on broadband access for residential users.

People could suddenly find what they were looking for online – could get access to what they wanted, when they wanted it – without having to go through the frustrating rigmarole of a dial-up connection. It transformed the online experience, turning it from a passing curiosity into a useful every-day tool for a much wider demographic of users. And the more people used the internet, the more indispensable it became.

Enough technology... let's talk about people

If you're non-technical, the world of digital marketing may seem a bit daunting at first. All that technology must be really complicated... right? Not necessarily.

One of the key things to remember if you're new to digital marketing is this: digital marketing isn't actually about technology at all; it's all about people. In that sense it's similar to traditional marketing: it's about people (marketers) connecting with other people (consumers) to build relationships and ultimately drive sales.

Technology merely affords you, the marketer, new and exciting platforms that allow you to connect with people in increasingly diverse and relevant ways. Digital marketing is not about understanding the underlying technology, but rather about understanding people, how they're using that technology, and how you can leverage that to engage with them more effectively. Yes, you have to learn to use the tools at your disposal – but understanding people is the real key to unlocking the potential of digital marketing.

A huge and growing market

Although internet companies suffered bruised finances and a tarnished public image in the wake of the dot.com crash, the internet itself never stopped growing, both in terms of the number of websites online, and, crucially from a marketing perspective, the number of people with internet access. In March 2000, when the dot.com bubble burst, there were an estimated 304 million people in the world with internet access. By March 2003 that figure had doubled to 608 million, and in December 2005 the global online population passed one billion. As of March 2011 the figure sits at 2.1 billion people. That's about a third of the global population... and it's still climbing (Internet World Stats, **www.internetworldstats.com**). See Figure 1.1.

FIGURE 1.1   The global distribution of the world's 2.1 billion internet users by region (according to Internet World Stats, March 2011)

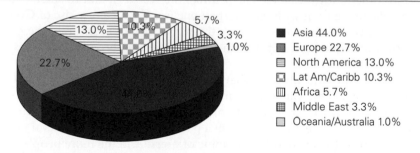

■ Asia 44.0%
■ Europe 22.7%
▤ North America 13.0%
▨ Lat Am/Caribb 10.3%
▥ Africa 5.7%
▦ Middle East 3.3%
☐ Oceania/Australia 1.0%

SOURCE: Internet World Stats – www.internetworldstats.com/stats.htm

BASIS: 2,095,006,005 Internet users on March 31, 2011

Copyright © 2011, Miniwatts Marketing Group

As global and local online populations have spiralled upwards, so too have the levels of broadband penetration, which means that not only are there more people online, but they're also online more often, for much longer periods of time and can do much more with that time. All of which means the market penetration of digital channels is growing rapidly. As the potential audience grows, so too does the allure of digital marketing. Marketers around the world are sitting up and taking notice, and big-name brands are starting to take the internet and other digital marketing channels seriously: loosening the purse strings and redistributing their advertising spend.

According to online market research specialist eMarketer, US online advertising spend for 2002 stood at US$6 billion; by 2005 it had more than doubled to US$12.5 billion. In 2004, 2005 and 2006 online advertising spend enjoyed unprecedented growth of over 30 per cent per annum.

'It's been a long time since any medium had three years in a row of 30 per cent-plus ad spending increases,' commented eMarketer senior analyst David Hallerman. 'With a 34 per cent gain in 2006, as new research from IAB/PwC shows, the internet now matches cable TV from 1983 to 1985 and broadcast TV from 1952 to 1954 for such strong, long-term spending increases.'

Unsurprisingly growth slowed during the global recession, but digital is leading the charge as economies around the world bounce back. Current e-Marketer projections estimate that US digital advertising spend will surpass US$28 billion in 2011, and will continue double-digit growth year-on-year to hit a whopping US$40.5 billion in 2014.

'It may seem ironic, but marketers' economic concerns are leading them to spend more for online advertising,' said Hallerman. 'This trend reflects how most forms of internet advertising are now seen as more of a "sure thing" than most traditional media.'

That's reflected in the market share figures from both the United States and the UK, where online continues to gain ground. 2010 figures from the UK's

Internet Advertising Bureau (iabuk.net) show that online advertising claimed 25 per cent of the £16.65 billion UK ad spend market last year, almost matching TV at 26 per cent, and eclipsing press display at 18 per cent.

Introducing Consumer 2.0

Unless you've been hiding under a rock in the Outer Hebrides since about 2004 you'll be familiar with the Web 2.0 (pronounced two-point-oh) moniker. It's bandied about with alacrity by the web-savvy elite, but what exactly does it mean?

Let's start off with what Web 2.0 is not: it's not a new version of Web 1.0. Web 2.0 is not a revolution in technology, it's an evolution in the way people are using technology. It's about harnessing the distributed collaborative potential of the internet to connect and communicate with other like-minded people wherever they are: creating communities and sharing knowledge, thoughts, ideas and dreams.

If you've ever shared photos on Flickr, read and commented on a blog, looked for friends on Facebook, watched a video clip on YouTube, tried to find your house on Google Maps, video-called friends or family abroad using Skype or looked up an article on Wikipedia, then you've used Web 2.0 technologies.

Suddenly it seems we've been inundated with version 2.0 of anything and everything as different sectors of society seek to demonstrate that they're current and progressive. We have Business 2.0, Government 2.0, Education 2.0, Careers 2.0... and, of course, Marketing 2.0. Well, not to be outdone, we'd like to introduce you to the new, improved, Consumer 2.0.

Once upon a time, consumers were quite happy to sit in front of passive broadcast media, accepting whatever was being peddled their way by editors and programme schedulers. Yes, there was an element of choice – you could buy a different newspaper, listen to a different station or choose a different channel – but the ultimate decision in terms of the content available to you rested with somebody else.

Then along came the web, and changed all the rules. Now, with Web 2.0, broadband and rich media content, today's consumers are in control like never before. They can choose the content they want, when they want it, in the way that they want it... they can even create their own and share it with their friends, their peers and the world for free.

'Consumers are becoming better informed, better connected, more communicative, and more in control than ever,' highlights Julian Smith, an analyst with Jupiter Research writing for the ClickZ network. 'They're better informed through the increased ability to access and sift an abundance of information any time, anywhere. They're better connected through the ability to instantaneously communicate with others across time zones and social strata. They're more communicative through the ability to publish and share their ideas and opinions. They're more in control through the ability not only to personalize their information and entertainment consumption, marketing messages, and the products and services they buy, but also to gain satisfaction on demand.'

Analysts at Jupiter Research identified seven key ways in which the increasingly widespread adoption of technology is influencing consumer behaviour:

- **Interconnectivity**: networked digital technology is enabling consumers to connect with each other more readily, be it through e-mail, IM, mobile messaging, or web-based social networking platforms such as Facebook, MySpace and LinkedIn – or more likely a combination of all of these platforms. Consumers are interacting with like-minded people around the world, paying scant regard to trifling concerns like time zones or geography. Peer-to-peer interaction is reinforcing social networks, and building new virtual communities.

- **Technology is levelling the information playing field**: with digital technology, content can be created, published, accessed and consumed quickly and easily. As a result the scope of news, opinion and information available to consumers is broader and deeper than ever. Consumers can conduct their own unbiased research, comparing and contrasting products and services before they buy. Knowledge is power… and digital technology is shifting the balance of power in favour of the consumer.

- **Relevance filtering is increasing**: with such a glut of information available to them, digital consumers are, through necessity, learning to filter items relevant to them and ignore anything they perceive as irrelevant. Increasingly, digital consumers look to have their information aggregated, categorized and delivered (whether through e-mail or RSS feeds). They use personalization features to block out irrelevant content and increasingly employ software solutions to exclude unsolicited commercial messages.

- **Niche aggregation is growing**: the abundance and diversity of online content allow consumers to participate in and indulge their specialist interests and hobbies. Aggregations of like-minded individuals congregate online; the homogeneous mass consumer population is fragmenting into ever-smaller niche groups, with increasingly individual requirements.

- **Micropublishing of personal content is blossoming**: digital media's interactive and interconnected nature allows consumers to express themselves online. Publishing your own content costs little more than a bit of time and imagination, whether through discussion forums, message boards, feedback forms, voting platforms, personal photo galleries or blogs. Users are posting their opinions online for all to see, and are consulting the opinion of their online peers before making purchasing decisions. How often do you check an online review before booking a table at an unknown restaurant, a weekend break at a hotel, or even buying a new car?

- **Rise of the 'prosumer'**: online consumers are getting increasingly involved in the creation of the products and services they purchase, shifting the balance of power from producer to consumer. They're letting producers know what they want in no uncertain terms: the level of interaction between producer and consumer is unprecedented. Individuals are more involved in specifying, creating and customizing products to suit their requirements, and are able to shape and mould the experiences and communications they receive from producers. Traditional mass-production and mass-marketing concepts are rapidly becoming a thing of the past.

- **On-demand; any time, any place, anywhere**: as digital technology becomes more ubiquitous in people's lives, the corresponding acceleration of business processes means that consumers can satisfy their needs more quickly, more easily and with fewer barriers. In the digital economy, trifling concerns like time, geography, location, and physical store space are becoming irrelevant. It's a world of almost instant gratification – and the more consumers get of it, the more they want it… now, now, now!

For marketers this evolution of the marketplace and the shift in consumer mindset that it heralds present a plethora of new challenges. As consumers increasingly embrace new ways of communicating, take greater ownership of the information and entertainment they consume, and aggregate in increasingly specialized niche online communities, marketers must shift their approach if they want to connect with them.

And that's what the rest of this book is all about.

CASE STUDY Malaria charity exposes horror of real bloodsuckers online

I remember watching a premiere of *Twilight* getting a hysterical reaction from a young crowd, and thought there is a genuine horror story taking place in the world today that should be getting this attention.

Charlie Mawer, Executive Creative Director, Red Bee Media

The challenge

Malaria No More UK wanted to reach out to a non-traditional audience with its anti-malaria message, engaging the British public and spurring them to take action to help the charity reach its goal of ending malaria-related deaths in Africa by 2015.

The challenge: to produce an innovative, engaging, surprising, effective and measurable integrated social media campaign on a minimal budget.

FIGURE 1.2 'Malaria No More UK' taps into the burgeoning popularity of horror films within the target demographic by taking a blood-curdling look at the world's number-one serial killer

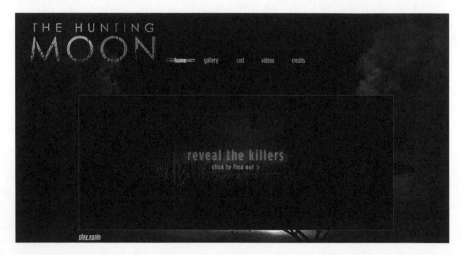

Target audience

The target audience was defined as 16–45-year-old vampire movie/*Twilight* fans.

Action

The creative team decided that the brief offered a great opportunity to tap into the core audience's burgeoning obsession with horror. They centred the campaign around a fictitious horror film: *The Hunting Moon*. The film would star four British students on an exciting adventure in Africa, but their once-in-a-lifetime trip takes a dark and sinister turn when they discover they're surrounded by bloodsucking creatures that come out to feed after dark, killing people in their thousands.

Red Bee Media created and produced a dramatic 90-second cinematic-style trailer for *The Hunting Moon*, which went live on the film's micro-site, **www.thehuntingmoon-movie.com**, on 25 October 2010. It was simultaneously seeded on YouTube and through selected blogs and social media platforms by viral distribution specialist 7th chamber.

On arriving at the site, viewers could watch the trailer, enjoy behind-the-scenes content and view cast biographies. It was content typical of any new movie release. The twist came at the end of the trailer, when the viewer was delivered a call to action prompting them to click to 'reveal the killers'.

The trailer then played again, but this time highlighting key facts about malaria that were subtly referenced in the original. The voiceover reveals the scale of the malaria problem: a preventable disease, malaria claims the life of a child every 45 seconds in Africa. Sky News anchor Lukwesa Burak, who grew up in Zambia, has first-hand experience of the disease, and who features in the news broadcast on the original trailer, narrated the voiceover for the reveal.

The Hunting Moon audience was then prompted to sign up to the fight against malaria by entering a competition for exclusive prizes, including a tennis racquet used and signed by British tennis ace Andy Murray, and a limited-edition mosquito-design locket created by luxury jeweller Stephen Webster, who is a Special Ambassador for Malaria No More UK.

Results

- The trailer reached 19.5 million people across 127 countries through YouTube, the microsite, Twitter and blogs, and gained extensive coverage in the traditional media.

- The campaign won a Bronze Creative Circle Award 2011 for best multimedia campaign.

- It also won a Gold Promax Europe Award.

- Opinion polls showed that awareness of Malaria No More UK more than doubled during the campaign period.

- More than 66 per cent of the British public now view malaria as an important issue.

Link to campaign creative

- http://bit.ly/UDMMalaria

Credits

Client:	• Malaria No More UK
Geographical scope:	• Global
Agency:	• Red Bee Media
Campaign contact:	• Arabella Gilchrist, Director of Communications for Malaria No More UK; Executive Producer of the Hunting Moon campaign

02 | Strategic thinking

> "*The most dangerous strategy is to jump a chasm in two leaps.*
> **BENJAMIN DISRAELI**

> "*Perception is strong and sight weak. In strategy it is important to see distant things as if they were close and to take a distanced view of close things.* **MIYAMOTO MUSASHI**

> "*Simplicity is the ultimate sophistication.* **LEONARDO DA VINCI**

OUR CHAPTER PLEDGE TO YOU

When you reach the end of this chapter you'll have answers to the following questions:

- What is a digital marketing strategy and why do I need one?
- How do I know if digital marketing is right for my business?
- How do I formulate a digital marketing strategy?
- How do I convince decision makers that now is the time to invest in digital marketing?
- Are my customers ready for digital marketing?

Why you need a digital marketing strategy

Why do you need a digital marketing strategy? The simple answer: because without one you'll miss opportunities and lose business. Formulating a digital marketing strategy will help you to make informed decisions about your foray into the digital marketing arena, and ensure that your efforts are focused on the elements of digital marketing that are most relevant to your business. It's a crucial first step towards understanding how the constantly evolving digital marketplace relates to you, and how it affects the relationship between your business or brand, and your customers and prospects.

It doesn't matter what business you're in, it's a fairly safe bet that an increasing number of your target market rely on digital technology every day to research, evaluate and purchase the products and services they consume. Without a coherent strategy of engagement and retention through digital channels, your business is at best missing a golden opportunity, and at worst could be left behind, watching your competitors pull away across an ever-widening digital divide.

Unlike conventional forms of mass media marketing, the internet is unique in its capacity to both broaden the scope of your marketing reach and narrow its focus *at the same time*. Using digital channels you can transcend traditional constraints like geography and time zones to connect with a much wider audience. At the same time, digital technology allows you to hone your marketing message with laser-like precision to target very specific niche segments within that wider market. Implemented effectively, it can be an incredibly powerful combination.

It's often stated that the internet puts consumers in control like never before. But it's important to remember that the internet also delivers an unprecedented suite of tools, techniques and tactics that allow marketers to reach out and engage with those same consumers. The marketing landscape has never been more challenging, dynamic and diverse.

And therein lies the crux of our need for a cohesive digital marketing strategy. If you're going to harness the power of digital marketing to drive your online business to dizzying new heights, you need a thorough understanding of your market, how your customers are using digital technology, and how your business can best utilize that same technology to build enduring and mutually rewarding relationships with them.

As digital channels continue to broaden the scope available to us as marketers, so they add to the potential complexity of any digital marketing campaign. Having a clearly defined strategy will help to keep you focused, ensure that your marketing activities are always aligned with your business goals, and, crucially, that you're targeting the right people.

Your business and digital marketing

Whether or not your business is suited to digital marketing depends very much on the nature of that business, where it is now, and where you want it to go in the future. If, for example, you're a dairy farmer in rural Ireland, have a fixed contract to supply milk to the local cooperative, and have little, if any, scope or ambition to diversify and grow your business year on year, then digital marketing probably isn't for you. Likewise, if you're a local butcher with an established client base in a thriving market town in the English Peak District and simply want to maintain the status quo, then again you'll probably do just fine without digital marketing.

If, however, you're a Peak District butcher looking to diversify your product offering, broaden the scope of your business and start selling your quality organic produce to restaurants and hotels around the country... well then, welcome to the world of digital marketing.

In truth there are very few businesses today that can't benefit from at least some degree of digital marketing – even if it's just providing a basic online brochure telling people what you do and sending out the occasional update to existing customers via an e-mail newsletter or RSS feed (RSS: Really Simple Syndication – a way to automatically retrieve updated posts/ articles from a website).

Whether you're running a home-based 'lifestyle' business selling hand-embroidered cushion covers, are a small-scale artisan food producer, an up-and-coming restaurateur or managing a large multinational corporation, a growing proportion of your customer base is already online, with more joining them every day. Obviously, the more your target market comes to rely on these online channels for its information, research and purchasing needs, the more critical digital marketing will become to the ongoing success of your business.

Digital marketing – yes or no

There are really only two key questions you need to answer when it comes to deciding whether or not your business needs a digital marketing strategy. They are:

- **Is my audience online; is it going to be online?** If your customers use digital technology to research and/or purchase *the products and services you provide*, then you absolutely need to embrace digital marketing now to engage with them and retain them. If they don't, then you don't. It really is that simple. Just bear in mind that as the next generation of consumers start to become your new customers, they're likely to demand more digital interaction from your business. If you're not in a position to deliver that, they could well choose to spend their money elsewhere.

FIGURE 2.1 Are your customers online? Figures from the Pew Internet & American Life Project, December 2010, showing the proportion of US adults now online, and a breakdown of their demographic make-up

---

Demographics of internet users

Below is the percentage of each group who use the internet, according to our December 2010 survey. As an example, 76% of adult women use the internet.

% who use the internet

Total adults	**77**
Men	78
Women	76
Race/ethnicity	
White, Non-Hispanic	80
Black, Non-Hispanic	69
Hispanic (English- and Spanish-speaking)	66
Age	
18–29	90
30–49	84
50–64	76
65+	46
Household income	
Less than $30,000/yr	63
$30,000–$49,999	79
$50,000–$74,999	92
$75,000+	96
Educational attainment	
Less than High School	40
High School	69
Some College	89
College+	93
Community type	
Urban	78
Suburban	80
Rural	68

SOURCE: The Pew Research Center's Internet & American Life Project, November 23–December 21, 2010 Social Side of the Internet Survey. N=2,303 adults, 18 and older, including 748 reached via cell phone. Interviews were conducted in English and Spanish.

- **Are my products/services/brands suited to digital marketing?** This can be a tricky one – but the answer is usually yes. Typically it doesn't matter what your product, service or brand is; as long as you've established that there's a viable online audience for it (see the first question), then you should be promoting it online. While some products and services are obviously more suited to online purchase and fulfilment than others (digital files, like e-books or music, spring to mind), you'll also find plenty of items being marketed effectively through digital channels that few people would ever dream of actually purchasing over the internet. Consumers go online to research, evaluate and compare their choices. They make purchasing decisions based on the quality of their online experience, then head to a bricks-and-mortar store to hand over their cash. Boats, cars, houses, apartments, horses, tractors – you name it – they're all being actively and successfully marketed online.

Defining your digital marketing strategy

Once you've decided that you do, in fact, need to pursue some form of digital marketing, the next step is to actually sit down and define your strategy. Unfortunately there is no 'one size fits all' strategic panacea here. We don't have a magic recipe to ensure your digital marketing success, and neither does anybody else (despite some of the online hyperbole you may read on the subject). Basically every business needs to 'bake' its own unique strategy based on its own particular set of circumstances. While the available ingredients are the same (and we'll cover the major ones later in the book), the resulting strategies can be radically different.

It's common sense really. If you sell apples to local grocers by the truck load your strategy will bear little resemblance to that of a company selling downloadable e-books and reports on financial trading, which will in turn be very different from the strategy adopted by a sports clothing manufacturer who wants to cut out the middleman and sell directly to consumers over the web.

Different products, different markets, different needs... different solutions.

What it ultimately boils down to is this: the best people to define your digital marketing strategy, curiously enough, are the people who best know your business.

Laying strong digital foundations

The good news is that you've almost certainly already started the process of defining your digital marketing strategy. Before even picking up this book you've probably been thinking about digital marketing in the context of your business, about what your competitors are doing online and why, about how your customers and prospects are integrating digital technology into their lives, and about how you can best exploit these new and exciting digital channels to foster longer, more productive relationships with them. These are the components that will form the foundation of your digital marketing strategy:

- **Know your business**: is your business ready to embrace digital marketing? Are your products/services suited to online promotion? Do you have the right technology/skills/infrastructure in place? How will digital marketing fit into your existing business processes; do those processes need to change; and are you and your staff ready to accommodate those changes?

- **Know the competition.** who are your main competitors in the digital marketplace? Are they the same as your offline competitors? What are they doing right (emulate them), what are they doing wrong (learn from them), what aren't they doing at all (is there an opportunity there for you?) and how can you differentiate your online offering from theirs? Remember, competition in the digital world can come from just around the corner or from right around the globe. The same technologies that allow you to reach out to a broader geographical market also allow others to reach in to your local market. When you venture online you're entering a global game, so don't limit your analysis to local competition.

- **Know your customers**: who are your customers and what do they want from you? Are you going to be servicing the same customer base online, or are you fishing for business from a completely new demographic? How do the customers you're targeting use digital technology, and how can you harness that knowledge to engage in a productive and ongoing relationship with them?

- **Know what you want to achieve**: if you don't know where you're going, there's a pretty fair chance you'll never get there. What do you want to get out of digital marketing? Setting clear, measurable and achievable goals is a key part of your digital marketing strategy. Are you looking to generate online sales, create a source of targeted sales leads, improve your brand awareness among online communities, all of the above or perhaps something completely different? Your goals are the yardsticks against which you can measure the progress of your digital marketing campaigns.

- **Know how you're doing**: the beauty of digital marketing is that, compared to many forms of advertising, results are so much more measurable. You can track everything that happens online and compare your progress against predefined goals and key performance indicators (KPIs). How is your digital campaign progressing? Are certain digital channels delivering more traffic than others? Why is that? What about conversion rates: how much of that increased traffic results in tangible value to your business? Measure, tweak, refine, re-measure. Digital marketing is an ongoing iterative process.

The process of formally defining your digital marketing strategy forces you to sit down and analyse the market in which you're operating with a critical eye, and to really think about the different components of your business and how digital marketing can help you to achieve your business goals.

Don't get too bogged down in the technical details – remember, digital marketing is about people communicating with other people; the technology is just the bit in the middle that helps it to happen. Your strategy should provide you with a high-level framework – a bird's-eye view of the digital marketing landscape with your business centre stage – the details will come later.

Understanding the digital consumer

There is a notion that pervades marketing circles today, a notion of mysterious ethereal creatures who exist in a hyper-connected, multifaceted cyberworld of their own. They are an enigma: they speak a different language, communicate in ways we don't understand, and they're turning the world of marketing on its head. These are the ephemeral, wraith-like 'digital consumers', who slip effortlessly through the marketer's grasp. Digital consumers are different, we're told… but are they really?

The digital consumer revealed

The first thing to realize about digital consumers is that there's basically no such thing. The customers and prospects you encounter online are the very same people who walk into your store every day, call you on the telephone, or order something from your mail-order catalogue. There's nothing dark, sinister or mysterious about them. They're people – like everybody else.

'There is no great mystery about how [digital consumers] think and what they want,' maintains interactive marketing expert Giles Rhys Jones of Interactive Marketing Trends (**http://interactivemarketingtrends.blogspot.com**). 'These consumers are doing exactly what people have been doing for thousands of years – communicating with each other.

'The fact that technology is enabling them to communicate with each other faster, over distance, over mobiles and in 3D worlds is being perceived as something dangerous, unique and extraordinary, something that needs to be controlled and pinned down. People talk to each other – they always have. They are talking the same language and saying the same things, they are just not necessarily sitting in the pub talking to one or five people, but doing it online to 15 or 5,000.'

Making the web their own

Consumers, whatever their 'flavour', don't care about the way marketers define what they do. Concepts like 'above the line', 'through the line', 'below the line', 'digital', 'traditional', 'experiential', 'linear', 'analogue', 'mobile', 'direct', 'indirect' or any other box we care to slip our marketing endeavours into are completely meaningless to them. All consumers care about is the experience – how the marketing available to them can enhance the experience and help them to make more informed decisions.

People are the single most important element in any form of marketing. That's just as true in the digital space as it is in any other sphere of the discipline. As a marketer you need to understand people and their behaviour – and here's where the notion of the digital consumer does carry some weight, because consumer behaviour is changing, and it's changing because of the pervasive, evocative and enabling nature of digital technology.

'The majority of today's consumers are actively personalizing their digital experiences and sampling niche content and video with increasing frequency,' said Dave Friedman, president of the central region for Avenue A | Razorfish, writing in an article for *Chief Marketer* (**www.chiefmarketer.com**).

In July 2007, Avenue A | Razorfish surveyed 475 US consumers across all demographics and geographies in an effort to understand their desires, frustrations and digital consumption habits. The results showed that US consumers are adopting digital technology across the board, and are harnessing its power to filter, organize and personalize the content they consume in an increasingly information-intensive world.

'We've reached a collective digital tipping point as a majority of consumers are tapping into a variety of emerging technologies and social media to increasingly personalize their digital experiences,' said Friedman. 'From recommendation engines, to blogs, to customized start pages, today's "connected consumer" navigates a landscape that is much more niche and personalized than we ever expected.'

The practice of broadcasting generic advertising messages to the mass market is rapidly being usurped by specifically targeted, narrow-cast marketing, through digital channels, to an increasingly diverse and segmented marketplace. Even, ultimately, to a target market of one. Digital marketing allows us to build uniquely tailored ongoing relationships with individual customers. This is a conversation, not a lecture. Marketing in the digital age has been transformed into a process of dialogue, as much about listening as it is about telling.

I don't know you and you don't know me

Perceived anonymity is another online trait that can have a profound effect on consumer behaviour. It liberates consumers from the social shackles that bind them in the real world; online they are free to do and say as they please with scant regard for the social propriety that holds sway in 'real life'. In a bricks-and-mortar store, shoppers will wait patiently for service, and will often endure a less than flawless shopping experience to get what they want. Online they won't; they demand instant gratification and a flawless customer experience. You have to deliver, first time, every time. If you fail to engage, retain and fulfil their expectations on demand, they're gone, vanishing into the ether of cyberspace as quickly as they came, the only trace a fleeting, solitary record on your web server's log file...

And then they'll tell all their online friends about their less than stellar experience.

Key traits of the online consumer

We're all familiar with the old road rage analogy of the congenial, neighbourly man or woman who suddenly becomes a raving speed demon when they get behind the wheel of a car. Well, there's something about the immediacy and anonymity of the digital experience that has a similar effect on people.

It's always risky to generalize and make assumptions about people – especially in a field as dynamic and fast moving as this one. The only real way to know your market intimately is to conduct original research within your particular target group. That said, a lot of research work has been done (and continues to be done) on the behavioural traits of online consumers, and a broad consensus has emerged around the key characteristics that epitomize the digital consumer:

- **Digital consumers are increasingly comfortable with the medium**: many online consumers have been using the internet for several years at this stage – and while the user demographic is still skewed in favour of younger people, even older users are becoming increasingly internet savvy. 'It's almost like a piano player who plays faster once they know the instrument. In the beginning people "pling, pling, pling" very carefully, and then they move on to playing symphonies,' said web usability guru Jacob Nielsen in an interview with the BBC. As people become more comfortable with the medium they use it more efficiently and effectively. Which means they don't hang around for long: your content needs to deliver what they want, and it needs to deliver quickly.

- **They want it all, and they want it now**: in the digital world, where everything happens at a million miles per hour, consumers have grown accustomed to getting their information on demand from multiple sources simultaneously. Their time is a precious commodity, so they want information in a format that they can scan for relevance before investing time in examining the detail. Designers and marketers need to accommodate this desire for 'scanability' and instant gratification when constructing their online offering.

- **They're in control**: the web is no passive medium. Users are in control – in the Web 2.0 world more than ever before. Fail to grasp that simple fact and your target audience won't just fail to engage with you, they will actively disengage. We need to tailor our marketing to be user centric, elective or permission based, and offer a real value proposition to the consumer to garner positive results.

- **They're fickle**: the transparency and immediacy of the internet don't eradicate the concept of brand or vendor loyalty, but they do erode it. Building trust in a brand is still a crucial element of digital marketing, but today's consumer has the power to compare and contrast competing brands literally at their fingertips. How does your value proposition stack up against the competition's around the country and across the globe? Your brand identity may be valuable, but if your *overall* value proposition doesn't stack up you'll lose out.

- **They're vocal**: online consumers talk to each other... a lot. Through peer reviews, blogs, social networks, online forums and communities they're telling each other about their positive online experiences...

and the negative ones. From a marketing perspective this is something of a double-edged sword – harness the positive aspects and you have incredible viral potential to propagate your message; get it wrong, and you could just as easily be on the receiving end of an uncomfortable online backlash.

The rise of the digital native

It's 7 am. Janet wakes up to the sound of her smartphone, sitting in its cradle across the room, playing a random song from an album she set to download last night. As she gets out of bed her phone trills… a text has arrived from her college friend, Simon. It's about last night's party.

Janet stabs at the mobile keypad with one hand, deftly firing off a reply, then she switches to the social media dashboard on her smartphone: a one-stop shop where she can check what's happening across her various social networking accounts. A cursory glance shows her that there's nothing major going on among her circle of friends. She heads over to her desk and opens up her laptop – while she can do pretty much everything she wants on her phone these days, there are some times when you just need more screen real estate.

She fires up her webmail account and simultaneously opens up her feed-reader, scanning both to see what's new. In the background her smartphone picks another song at random from her music collection and continues to play.

As the 20 or so messages sent to her overnight jostle for position in her prioritized e-mail inbox, Janet's mobile trills again – it's Simon, replying to her message and arranging to meet her before lectures start. She checks the clock widget on her desktop and fires off a quick confirmation – she'll meet him outside the library in an hour and a half. A quick scan of her incoming mail reveals most of it to be newsletter subscriptions. She'll take a cursory glance through them later, but one from her friend, Amy, catches her eye. She reads it, and is about to reply when she notices that Amy is signed in to her IM account, so she sends her an instant message instead.

They chat for a few minutes… mainly about last night's party and what to do after college today. Janet checks the weather in another sidebar widget – there's rain forecast for later. They agree on the cinema. A quick visit to the theatre's website reveals what's on, they check out some online peer reviews to see what's hot, agree on a show, and pre-book the tickets. Job done.

Janet glances at the clock… it's 7:15 am, time for a shower, then breakfast.

Welcome to the world of the digital native – a hyper-connected, high-octane world of instant access and gratification with digital technology at its core. To young people today these aren't merely digital tools, they are essential, seamlessly integrated elements of their daily lives. These are digital consumers, the net generation, generation Y… call them what you will. They are insistent, impatient, demanding, multi-tasking information junkies. They are the mass market of tomorrow – and it's absolutely imperative that we, as marketers, learn to speak their language today.

Using influencers to help spread the word

There is one particular category of users online that warrants a special mention when it comes to defining your digital marketing strategy. Dubbed 'influencers', these early adopters are the online opinion leaders. Through blogs, podcasts, forums and social networks they harness the power of the web to extol the virtues of products and brands that they like, and equally to denigrate those they find unsatisfactory.

Why are influencers important to you as a marketer? Because they have the virtual ear of the online masses. People read and listen to what they have to say; they value their opinion and trust their judgement. These online influencers have already won the pivotal battle for the hearts and minds of online consumers. Engage positively with them and you essentially recruit a team of powerful online advocates who can have a potentially massive impact on a much wider group of consumers. This is the online equivalent of word-of-mouth marketing on steroids. Of course, give them a negative experience and... well, you can guess the rest.

But how exactly will you recognize these online influencers?

A December 2006 report by DoubleClick ('Influencing the influencers: how online advertising and media impact word of mouth') defined an influencer as a person who 'strongly agreed' to three or more of the following statements:

- They consider themselves expert in certain areas (such as their work, hobbies or interests).
- People often ask their advice about purchases in areas where they are knowledgeable.
- When they encounter a new product they like, they tend to recommend it to friends.
- They have a large social circle and often refer people to one another based on their interests.
- They are active online, using blogs, social networking sites, e-mail, discussion groups, online community boards, etc to connect with their peers.

Identifying the influencers within your market sector, analysing their behaviour and tailoring part of your digital campaign to target this small but influential group can result in disproportionate knock-on benefits. Don't neglect your core market, of course – but certainly consider targeting influencers as part of your overall digital marketing strategy.

Mind your Ps

You might be asking yourself how all this new-fangled digital 'stuff' fits into the traditional marketing mix: the venerable four Ps of product, price, promotion and place. Well, it breaks down something like this:

Place

Let's start with the obvious one: it's the internet. It's the 2 billion-plus people around the world who have decided it's better to be connected... whether accessed through a computer, a mobile device, IPTV or whatever else might come along. That's really it.

Price

Pricing is critical online. You have to be competitive: this is the internet, and pricing is transparent. You don't necessarily have to be the cheapest – but to compete you need to make sure your overall value proposition to the customer is compelling. Overprice your product and a host of price-comparison sites will soon highlight the fact, as will the countless peer review communities where consumers actively debate the relative merits (or otherwise) of everything from financial products to wedding stationery.

FIGURE 2.2   MoneySupermarket.com, billed as 'the UK's leading finance price-comparison website and a leading UK travel price comparison website'

Product

This is what you have to offer – your unique value proposition to your customers. A good product, of course, is the cornerstone of all successful marketing, but it's particularly crucial in the digital arena. A product that delivers tangible benefits and fills a real need in the marketplace – something that leaves the customer with a genuine perception of value – gives marketers the scope they need to do their job effectively. When you're promoting something viable, it's much easier to engage with consumers and to convince them to buy.

Conversely, the best marketing minds in the world will struggle to promote a product that doesn't deliver the goods. And this is where the all-pervading, viral nature of the internet can really come back to bite you. If you promote a product online and that product doesn't deliver, you'd better be prepared for the backlash.

Digital consumers are no wallflowers – they are vociferous and well connected. They won't keep the shortcomings of your product or business to themselves – they'll shout about it from the tallest building in cyberspace, and others will quickly pick up the cry. Once that happens you can pretty much shelve your marketing ambitions and go back to the drawing board.

So it's important to make sure your product and the entire customer value chain associated with it are right from the start. You need a solid foundation if you're going to build a sustainable online business, and that all starts with a sound product.

Promotion

Promotion is everything you do, online and offline, to get your product in front of your prospects, acquire new customers and retain existing ones. Examining those options will form the bulk of the rest of this book: in the following chapters we'll discuss the major forms of online promotion available now, and will go on to look at emerging and future trends. Here we summarize the main elements to whet your appetite:

- **Your website:** your website is the hub of your digital world – and perhaps the most important element in your whole digital marketing strategy. It's a vital piece of online real estate to which all of your other online activity will direct your prospects. A lot of the digital marketing techniques discussed in this book are about generating traffic to your website – but traffic in itself is worthless. To become valuable, traffic must be converted – and that's essentially what your website should be: a conversion engine for the traffic being directed to it.

- **Search engine optimization (SEO):** part and parcel of the website is SEO, or the process of aligning content on your website to what your prospects are actively searching for, and presenting it in a manner that makes it accessible to both people and search engines. The organic or natural search results (the results in the middle of the search engine results page) is *the* place to be if you want to increase targeted traffic to your website.

- **Pay-per-click search advertising (PPC):** pay-per-click advertising offers you a way to buy your way onto the search results pages for chosen keywords or key phrases. Depending on your business and what keywords you want to rank for, this can be an extremely effective way of generating search engine traffic quickly, although as the medium continues to gain in popularity more competitive keywords are becoming prohibitively expensive for smaller businesses.

- **Affiliate marketing and strategic partnerships**: how to partner with other organizations and websites in mutually beneficial relationships to promote your products or services.
- **Online public relations**: using online channels like press releases, article syndication and blogs to create a positive perception of your brand and/or position you as an authority in your particular field.
- **Social networking**: a relatively new marketing opportunity, but one that can potentially offer highly targeted advertising to niche social groups based on profile information they volunteer through sites like Facebook, Twitter and others.
- **E-mail marketing**: the granddaddy of internet marketing, suffering something of a crisis in the wake of perpetual spam bombardment, but still an important tool in the digital marketer's arsenal, particularly when it comes to maintaining ongoing relationships with existing customers and prospects who've 'opted in' to receive information.
- **Mobile marketing**: the up-and-coming star of digital... mobile is finally poised to deliver on the latent potential that's been promising to erupt for years. With smartphone penetration growing and fast mobile internet becoming almost ubiquitous, at least in urban centres, mobile means your customers now have access to your content any time, any place, anywhere!
- **Customer relationship management**: retaining existing customers and building mutually rewarding relationships with them are another important element of digital marketing. Digital technology makes developing an enduring connection with your customers more straightforward and effective than ever before.

Eyes on the prize

Another crucially important area of your digital marketing strategy is setting realistic goals. Your strategy should explicitly define the business goals you want your digital marketing efforts to help you achieve. As with any other journey, you can only plan an effective route if you have a clear, unambiguous destination in mind from the start. Or to put it another way, you might be the world's best archer – but if nobody gives you a target to aim at what good will it do you?

To measure your progress towards those goals, you also need to set milestones along the way, consistently measuring your achievements and steering your digital campaign towards your ultimate destination. Here again the digital realm offers a raft of tools and techniques to help marketers reap a better return from their investment.

We'll be examining the topic of web metrics and website intelligence in Chapter 5, but the crucial thing to remember here is that digital marketing is an iterative process of continuous improvement and refinement. You can monitor and analyse the effectiveness of your digital marketing campaigns in practically real time. You can measure everything, and even run alternative ads and strategies side by side to see what works best before committing to a given course: test, refine, retest and then decide where to make your investment based on real data from real customers.

Tracking accountability

When a computer or mobile phone – in fact, let's call it a digital media device – hits a site, a record is created in the web server's log file based on the unique IP address of that user and tracks their navigation through the site. Software on the web server also sends a small, unobtrusive file to the user's browser, known as a 'cookie', which essentially allows the web server to recognize the same user when they come back to the site again.

Based on information in the log file, marketers can tell a surprising amount about the user's activity on the site:

● We know the broad geographical location based on the digits in the IP address.

● We know when they arrived and from where.

● We know what type of browser and operating system they're using.

So far we know very little but we can already start to be more accountable. For example, we can now order our advertising and marketing messages to be delivered only to people with a Mac who live in Ireland and don't like working before lunchtime but are seriously interested in sports.

Now let's make things a little more interesting.

By adding specific 'page tags' to our website (with the help of a website developer, webmaster and analytics partner), we can start to do some very clever things – following website visitors to the purchase point and beyond.

For example, say we choose to run a banner ad campaign. We can detect not only the people who click on the banner and go through the site to become purchasers, we can also detect those people who do *not* click on the banner, but then go ahead and buy the product anyway a few weeks later. This is really exciting stuff for marketers because ultimately it dispenses with our whole fascination with the value of the click-through.

Not long ago digital marketing metrics were all about clicks, clicks, clicks. Today, while clicks remain an important guideline, ultimately they are about as useful as saying 230 people noticed your ad today – isn't that great? Well, in a word, no.

Today's online marketing investment is about tangible returns, it's about conversion and ROI; ultimately it is about the accountability of the brand, the price, the ad campaign and the job of the marketer

Which scenario would you prefer: a warm post-campaign glow when the research company pats you on the back and says 'Well done' for achieving a 10 per cent increase in brand recall among 18–24-year-olds, or 1,293 enquiries about your product and the names and addresses (e-mail of course) of the 233 new customers who now own your product?

Online marketing is very like direct marketing in that regard. You invest, you sell, you weigh up your ROI, you learn, you adapt, you move on. Except that online the process is much accelerated. Yes, of course there's still value in brand-based advertising. The drum-playing gorilla who makes you want to eat Dairy Milk or the girl on the bench who makes you want to whistle the Nokia tune and give her your Coca-Cola... it's all good brand-building stuff, and the kind of advertising that's sure to remain with us. The big problem with it is its lack of accountability.

The truth is that digital is simply more accountable. You have far more control and can make far more informed decisions based on the feedback and information the technology provides. It's easy to control the pace and flow of your marketing budget, to turn it up or down and to channel it in different directions.

If you are selling holidays, for example, you already know enough about your customers to realize that certain times of the year (holiday season) are less effective for advertising than others (freezing winter days). But how cool would it be if you could target your holiday advertising so that your ads start to run when the temperature drops below 10 degrees in a particular region? What about being able to advertise your currency exchange services based on the performance of the markets? Well, in the digital world, you can do that. The potential is boundless.

Bringing it all together

There's a lot to think about when defining your digital marketing strategy but in the end the process is about researching, analysing and understanding three things that are crucial to your success: your business, your competition and your customers. Your strategy lays the foundation for everything you'll do as a digital marketer, and will guide the decisions you make as you implement some of the techniques outlined in the coming chapters – and choose not to implement others, precisely because they don't fit with your chosen strategy.

Effective digital marketing is about boxing clever. You pick and choose the elements that are specifically relevant to your business. Going through the process of defining a clear strategy, based on a thorough analysis of where your business is now, and where you want digital marketing to take it, puts you in the ideal position to know what's likely to work for you, and just as important, what probably won't.

CASE STUDY Cats with Thumbs

FIGURE 2.3 Ever wondered why cats stare when you're pouring milk? Now imagine what might happen if they possessed the manual dexterity that people take for granted…

Campaign budget

£12 million total media spend.

The challenge

In 2011, agency Wieden + Kennedy was briefed to create a new campaign for Cravendale, a leading UK dairy producer. Cravendale wanted to maintain the brand's dominance in the filtered milk market. The main challenge was to come up with a campaign that would jolt people out of their milk-buying inertia and encourage more of them to consciously switch from buying standard fresh milk to Cravendale's premium product.

Target audience

Although the primary target audience was mums who tend to make the grocery purchasing decisions for UK households, the campaign needed to appeal to the whole family, from little kids to parents and even grandparents.

Action

By dramatizing Cravendale's superior taste and quality in the brand's familiarly light-hearted way, the aim was to encourage people to switch from standard fresh milk to buy Cravendale's premium milk product. Cravendale is passionate about milk and the 'Cats with Thumbs' campaign was created to remind consumers of that passion.

The campaign featured cats with a subtle evolutionary difference – they had developed opposable thumbs. What might happen if cats had the same level of manual dexterity as humans do?

Before the main TV ad spot was released, the team seeded an unbranded video featuring Jimmy – a cat equipped with opposable thumbs – to generate buzz around the idea of polydactyl cats. The film went viral with more than a million views in just four days. Then the TV element of the campaign broke, featuring a posse of cats with opposable thumbs preparing to get their dextrous hands (paws?) on the Cravendale milk they craved.

The idea was to drive awareness and love for the brand across all generations, through an idea that consumers would notice and talk to their friends about online and offline.

The lead feline character in the TV spot, Bertrum, is a wily creature intent on world domination. Throughout the campaign, his character was active on social networks, interacting and engaging with consumers in real time, and adding a new element of depth to the thumbcat narrative.

Results

Success for this cross-platform campaign was measured principally through sales uplift, monitoring brand buzz and view metrics for online elements of the campaign:

- TVC received more than 2 million hits on YouTube in less than three weeks.

- Cravendale buzz on Twitter increased by 2,226 per cent as a result of the campaign.

- Bertrum attracted more than 4 million impressions on Facebook in three weeks.

- The Cravendale brand experienced an 8 per cent sales uplift as a result of the campaign.

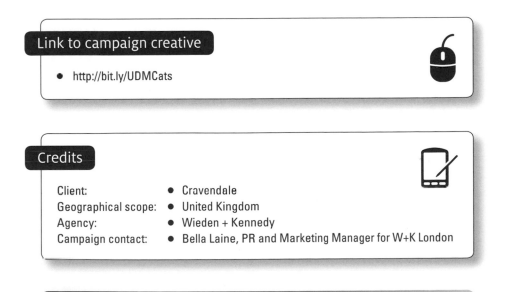

Link to campaign creative

- http://bit.ly/UDMCats

Credits

Client:	• Cravendale
Geographical scope:	• United Kingdom
Agency:	• Wieden + Kennedy
Campaign contact:	• Bella Laine, PR and Marketing Manager for W+K London

03 Your window to the digital world

> *I feel I'm able to serve my customer by knowing what she or he wants. One of the ways I'm able to do this is through my website and e-mail: people give me great ideas, tell me what they want, what they don't want. It's really instrumental, and helps me stay in touch with people.*
>
> **KATHY IRELAND**

> *If you do build a great experience, customers tell each other about that. Word of mouth is very powerful.* **JEFF BEZOS**

> *Small opportunities are often the beginning of great enterprises.*
>
> **DEMOSTHENES (384–322 BC)**

OUR CHAPTER PLEDGE TO YOU

When you reach the end of this chapter you'll have answers to the following questions:

- Why is my website so important?
- How do I build an effective website?
- How should I structure the information on my website?
- What is usability, and why should I care?
- Why are accessibility and web standards important?
- How do I create compelling web content?

Your website – the hub of your digital marketing world

Your website is your place of business. You may have all sorts of campaigns out there, tapping the far-flung reaches of cyberspace for a rich vein of new customers, but ultimately everything will be channelled back through a single point: your website. That makes your website incredibly valuable. In fact, it's the single most valuable piece of digital real estate you'll ever own. Get your digital marketing strategy right, and who knows, it could well end up being the most valuable piece of real estate you own: period.

We can't stress this point enough. In an uncertain and constantly evolving digital world, your website is the one thing over which you have complete and explicit control. You can change anything and everything on your website; you can tweak it, tune it and manipulate it in any way you want; you can build in ways to track and measure *all* of the activity on your website. You own it, it's yours, and it's the yardstick by which your entire online business will be measured.

A conversion engine for traffic

All of the digital marketing techniques we'll discuss in the coming chapters have one thing in common: they're designed to drive targeted, pre-qualified traffic to your website. But *traffic on its own does nothing but consume internet bandwidth*. It's your website that converts that traffic into prospects and customers – taking the numbers and transforming them into something of tangible value to your business.

Your website is *not* just an online brochure to let people know who you are and what you do. Granted, some of the information you provide on your site will serve that purpose – but only in a peripheral capacity. Nor is it there simply to garner search engine 'mojo' and generate huge volumes of traffic. Think of your website primarily as a *conversion engine* for the traffic you garner through all of your other digital marketing endeavours.

Yes, you need to provide information about your business, products and services – but always with your conversion goals in mind. Everything on your website should be geared towards achieving those conversion goals, either directly (products and service information, online ordering/sales functionality, sales-focused copy and calls to action, enquiry forms, newsletter sign-up, etc) or indirectly (business and brand information that builds trust, content that encourages repeat visits and/or establishes your authority/reputation in your field).

Your conversion goals could be anything from an actual online purchase (a sales transaction) to an online query (lead generation), to subscribing for your online newsletter (opt-in for future marketing)… or whatever else you decide is important for your business and appropriate for your customers. You can, of course, have multiple, tiered conversion goals. Your primary goal might be an online sale or booking, your secondary goal could be online lead generation and your tertiary goal could be to harvest opt-in e-mail addresses for your mailing list.

It doesn't matter what your goals are, or whether your website is a small information/brochure-type site or a huge online store; the important thing is that you keep them in mind when you design (or redesign) your website. Remember, conversion is the key to digital marketing success; your website and the user experience you deliver through it are what will ultimately drive that conversion.

Building an effective website

An effective website is essentially about the convergence of two things: your business goals and the needs of your target market. Build something that aligns the two and you'll end up with an effective website. Broken down like that it sounds simple, but achieving that convergence can be a tricky process – and a quick surf around the web will soon demonstrate that it's easier to get it wrong than to get it right.

You'll note we used the word 'effective' rather than 'successful'. For a website to be successful, people need to be able to find it (which we'll cover in the next chapter, on search), but if you build your site to cater for the right people's needs you significantly increase the chance that, once they arrive, they'll become more than just a passing statistic.

First, let's state here and now that this isn't a definitive guide to website development. This is a book about digital marketing. In this chapter we'll be exploring how to approach your website with digital marketing in mind. Our focus is to maximize the effectiveness of your website with a view to your digital marketing endeavours.

What follows is a high-level overview of the important elements to consider when designing your website from a digital marketing perspective. It is not meant to be an exhaustive guide. Most of the topics we touch on here would warrant an entire book to themselves. In fact, if you surf on over to Amazon you'll find a swathe of titles available in each category. You'll also find an avalanche of relevant (and of course irrelevant) information on the web.

Here, our aim is to arm you with the high-level knowledge you'll need to make informed decisions about your website design in a digital marketing context, and to communicate exactly what you need to engage with your web design partners when it's time to construct your digital hub.

The main steps of building your website

Different businesses will follow different processes involving different groups of people when designing, developing and implementing a website, but regardless of the approach you choose to take, how formal or informal the process, there are a number of key stages that generally form part of any web development project:

- **Planning**: establish your goals for the site; analyse the competition; define who your target market is, how they'll find you online and what they're going to be looking for when they arrive; map out a schedule and decide who's going to do what and when.
- **Design**: decide on the 'look and feel' of the site: colours, graphics, information architecture,[1] navigation, etc.
- **Development**: putting it all together, taking the agreed design and constructing the actual pages of the site, crafting the content, links and navigation hierarchy.
- **Testing**: making sure everything works the way it should before you let it out onto the big bad internet.
- **Deployment**: your new site becomes live on the internet for the whole world to find... or not, as the case may be.

Before you start

Know why you're building a website

'What is my website for?'

It's a simple enough question, yet you'd be amazed how many businesses have never asked it. They have a website because everyone else has one and it seemed like a good idea at the time. The result is a site, invariably an isolated little island in the backwaters of cyberspace, that brings nothing to the business but the expense of annual hosting and maintenance.

Ideally you should have a clear idea of exactly what it is your organization wants to achieve from a website *before* you start to build it.

Know who your website is for

Knowing who exactly you're creating your website for is also crucial to its success. Yet, surprisingly, it's another thing that's often overlooked in the process. Far too many websites end up being designed to appeal to the committee of executives who ultimately sign off on the project, instead of the people who will actually be using them. Don't fall into that trap. For your website to succeed it needs to appeal to one group of people, and one group of people only: your target market.

Think about how your users will access your website. What will they want to find when they get there, and how can your site fulfil those needs? Put yourself in their shoes, or better still, ask them directly what they'd like to see/do on your website. Try conducting some informal market research with people who would potentially use your website (online and/or offline). The results may be illuminating, and could be the difference between a successful website and an expensive online experiment.

Build usability and accessibility into your website design

Usability and accessibility are central to good web design... and yet both are frequently ignored, or at least are not given the weighting they warrant when it comes to making design decisions. They are about making sure that your site content can be accessed by the widest possible audience, and delivering the information and functionality users want in a way they're comfortable and familiar with.

Usability

The theory behind web usability is straightforward enough: simple, elegant and functional design helps users to achieve what they want to achieve online more effectively. It's about taking the frustration out of the user experience, making sure things work intuitively, eliminating barriers so that users accomplish their goals almost effortlessly. Your goal is to help the user to do what they want to do in the most efficient and effective way possible. Everything else is just web clutter. Achieving a simple, elegant design that delivers what the user wants with a minimum of fuss isn't easy, but putting in the effort can pay huge dividends.

For a step-by-step guide to usability, and a comprehensive downloadable e-book of research-based web design and usability guidelines, check out the US government's usability website at **www.usability.gov**.

Accessibility

The term 'accessibility', in relation to the web, refers to the process of designing your website to be equally accessible to everyone. A well-designed website should allow all users equal access to the information and functionality it delivers. By adhering to accessibility guidelines when designing your site, you're basically making sure that it's useful to as broad a cross section of your target audience as possible.

If your site complies with accessibility guidelines it will work seamlessly with hardware and software designed to make the internet more accessible to people with disabilities. For example, by making sure you include descriptive text alternatives to images and multimedia content on your website, you can help visually impaired or even completely sightless visitors to access your site through special text-to-speech software and/or text-to-Braille hardware. How stringently you choose to adhere to these accessibility guidelines will depend on several factors, including the nature of your site, your target audience and, in some circumstances, the requirements of local accessibility legislation.

With both accessibility and usability, very small and simple steps can make a big difference; even something as small as ensuring that the text on your website resizes according to the user's browser preferences can have a huge impact on some people's ability to use your site effectively.

You'll find a more detailed look at website accessibility, including all of the most current accessibility standards and guidelines, on the W3C website at **www.w3.org/WAI/**.

A word about the W3C and web standards

The World Wide Web Consortium (W3C, **www.w3.org**) is the gatekeeper of web standards. Its mission: 'to lead the World Wide Web to its full potential by developing protocols and guidelines that ensure long-term growth for the Web'.

Since its inception in 1994 the consortium has published more than 110 of these standards, which it calls W3C Recommendations. These open standards are primarily designed to ensure what the W3C calls the 'interoperability of the web' – or basically to make sure that all of the different computers, platforms and technologies that make up and access the web can work together seamlessly.

In practice it's a good idea to make sure that your website is designed and implemented to be web standards compliant. A standards-compliant website is much more likely to work consistently across the different browsers and operating systems used by your target market. It also future-proofs your site to some extent, reducing the need for maintenance. Standards-compliant sites should (in theory at least) continue to work consistently with new browser versions (which *should* be backward compatible with the standards), while a non-compliant site may not.

Maintaining a standards-compliant site is also more straightforward, because the code that makes up the pages is – you guessed it – *standard*. It makes it easier for a web developer to pick up and maintain somebody else's code – which could be important if you decide to change your web designer or to bring the entire process in house in the future.

In general you should aim to make sure your site is as standards compliant as possible while still achieving what you need. Make sure your web designer knows you're aware of web standards, and that you want your site to adhere to them. All of the standards are available on the W3C site, and there are online validators that will screen your pages for compliance. You can even download a little 'badge' to display in the footer of your standards-compliant website to prove to the world that your pages validate.

Words make your website tick

The world of the web is dominated by words. Audio, video, flash and animation may seem to be everywhere online, but even in an era where multimedia content seems to be taking over, at its core the web is still all about text, and the connections between different words and phrases on and between websites. As a digital marketer, some of those words and phrases are more important to you than others, and knowing which words are relevant to your business is essential to building an effective website.

These are your keywords or key phrases, and in the search-dominated world of the digital marketer they are – in a word – key. Exactly what they are will depend on your business, the digital marketing goals you defined as part of your overall strategy, and on the online behaviour of your target market. But you need to know what they are.

Keywords are practically synonymous with search, so we cover the basics of keyword research and selection in the search chapter (Chapter 4). But it's a very good idea to have your list of target keywords in mind from the very beginning. It's much easier to optimize a site for search engines as you build it than it is to retrofit search engine optimization after the fact. Your keywords will help to guide everything, from your site design to your information architecture and navigation, right down to the content you put on the individual pages of your website.

Know your competition

Identifying your competition, analysing what they're trying to achieve with their websites, where they're succeeding and where they're failing can be a great way of getting ideas and looking at different ways you can compete online. Take the keyword phrases you've identified for your website and type them into leading search engines – the sites that rank highly for your keywords are your online competition.

What are they doing well, and how easy would it be for you to emulate and improve on those things? Put yourself in the user's shoes. What sort of user experience are the sites offering? How could it be improved upon? What about the content?

A thorough analysis of your online competition can reveal a lot, not just about them and what they offer online, but about the direction you choose to take with your website in order to compete effectively with them.

Choosing your domain name

Every website on the internet has a unique address (a slight simplification, but we don't need to get into the complexities here). It's called an IP address, and it's not very interesting, informative or memorable to most humans. It consists of a series of numbers something like 209.85.143.99 (type that address into your browser and see where it takes you).

While that's fine for computers and the occasional numerically inclined tech-head, it's not much use to the rest of us. So, back in the early days of the internet, the domain name system was developed to assign human-readable names to these numeric addresses. These domain names – things like digitalmarketingsuccess.com, google.com, wikipedia.org or harvard.edu – are naturally much more useful and memorable to your average human than the IP addresses they relate to.

You need your own domain name

If you don't have your own domain name, you're going to need to register one. As a business, if you want to be taken seriously online, piggybacking on someone else's domain is completely unacceptable. An address like **www.mysite.someothersite.com** or **www.someothersite.com/mysite/** looks unprofessional, makes your web address difficult to remember, won't do you any favours with search engines and generally tarnishes your business image wherever you publicize it, online and offline.

The good news is that registering a domain is cheap (less than US$10 per year, depending on the domain registrar you choose) and easy. It may be included as part of the package offered by your website developer, or you can easily register a domain yourself. You can check availability, select your domain and register it in minutes online. (The registrar we used to register the domain associated with this book is **www.mydomain.com**. There are plenty more to choose from; just type 'domain registration' into your favourite search engine and you'll be presented with plenty of options.)

While most domains operate on a first-come-first-served basis, some country-specific domains (such as Ireland's .ie domain) have special eligibility conditions that need to be satisfied before the registration is confirmed. Check with the relevant country's domain name authority to see if any country-specific conditions apply to the domain(s) you're interested in.

Some things to bear in mind when choosing your domain name are:

- **Make it catchy, memorable and relevant**: choose a catchy, easily identifiable domain name that's relevant to your business and *easy for people to remember*.

- **Use a country-specific top-level domain (TLD)[2] to appeal to a local audience**: if your market is local, it often pays to register the local version of the domain (.co.uk or .ie, for example) instead of (or as well as) the more generic .com, .net or .org. If you're appealing to an international audience, a generic TLD may serve you better. Of the generic TLDs, .com is by far the most universally accepted and popular – making it the most valuable one to secure.

- **You can buy multiple domain names**: there's nothing to stop you buying more than one domain to prevent others from registering them. You can then *redirect* the secondary domains to point to your main website. Another option is registering country-specific domains to give yourself an online 'presence' in each country you do business in. You can then deploy a regionally tailored version of your website to each of those domains (the preferable option), or redirect them to a localized section on your main website.

- **Keywords in a domain name can be beneficial**: you may decide to incorporate one of your keyword phrases into your domain name. Opinion varies on the significance of this in terms of its impact on your search engine ranking, but it may help both search engines and users to establish what your site is about right from the start.

Hosting – your website's home on the internet

The other bit of housekeeping you'll need to take care of before your site goes live is hosting. Your finished site will consist of files, applications and possibly a database, all of which sit on a computer that's permanently connected to the internet. This computer is your web server, and will be running special software that will accept requests from users' web browsers and deliver your web pages by return. It's a bit more complicated, but basically that's what it boils down to.

Unless you belong to a large organization with its own data centre that has a permanent connection to the internet backbone, it's highly unlikely that you'll host your site in house. A much more likely scenario is that you'll arrange a hosting solution through a specialist hosting provider.

Different types of hosting

There are basically three different types of hosting offered by web-hosting companies – all of which are perfectly acceptable for your business website. Which option you choose will depend largely on your budget, how busy you anticipate your website will be (in terms of visitor traffic), and the amount of control you want over the configuration of the server (whether you'll need to install your own custom software, change security settings, configure webserver options, etc).

A word of warning here: avoid 'free' hosting accounts. While they may be tempting for a small business site to begin with, they tend to be unreliable, often serve up annoying ads at the top of your site, don't offer the flexibility or functionality of a paid hosting account, may not support the use of your own domain name, offer limited (if any) support, and present a greater risk that you'll be sharing your server with some less-than-desirable neighbours – which can hurt your search engine rankings.

Shared hosting accounts

With shared hosting you are essentially renting space on a powerful server where your website(s) will sit alongside a number of other websites (typically hundreds, sometimes thousands on a single server). Each hosting account has its own, secure virtual space on the server where you can upload your site's files. A dedicated control panel for account administration offers some degree of control over server configuration and usually provides access to a suite of additional software and tools to help you (or your webmaster) manage your website(s). All of the websites on a server typically share system resources like CPU, RAM, etc.

Shared hosting is the most common and cheapest form of hosting, and it's how the majority of websites – particularly for small-to-medium-sized businesses – start out. Most shared hosting accounts have space restrictions and a monthly bandwidth cap. They are ideal for small-to-medium-sized businesses and websites with average levels of traffic. In most instances this is the most cost-effective form of hosting.

Virtual dedicated hosting

With virtual dedicated hosting a single server is 'split' into a number of virtual servers. Each user feels like they're on their own dedicated computer, when in fact they're sharing the resources of the same physical machine. The users will typically have complete administrative control over their own virtual space. This is also known as a virtual private server or VPS. While virtual dedicated hosting offers complete flexibility in terms of the administration, software and configuration options available, you're still sharing server resources with other users/websites.

Dedicated hosting

Dedicated hosting solutions provide a dedicated, high-powered server for your website(s), and your website(s) alone. You don't share space or system resources with anybody else – which means you don't share the cost either... making dedicated hosting comparatively expensive.

Dedicated servers offer much more power and flexibility, because changes made to the server affect only your website(s). That means that you (or your webmaster/technical team) have complete control over server configuration, security, software and settings. They also typically offer much more capacity in terms of space and bandwidth than shared hosting – making them suitable for high-traffic sites.

Because of the flexibility and control offered by dedicated hosting solutions (complete control over the host computer), they tend to require more technical ability to administer than shared hosting environments.

Server co-location

Co-location is essentially the same as dedicated hosting, except that instead of the hosting company providing a preconfigured dedicated server for your website, you buy and configure your own server, which is then hosted at their dedicated hosting facility. This offers perhaps the ultimate in flexibility, because you have complete control not only over the software and setting on the server, but also over the hardware specification, operating system, software, security… everything. Co-location is essentially the same as hosting your own server in your own office – except that your server is plugged into a rack in a dedicated hosting facility with all of the bells and whistles you'd expect.

Cloud-based hosting

Cloud-based hosting is different from traditional hosting models in that you pay for your hosting based on the resources you use, rather than paying for a fixed hardware resource and monthly allowance of space and bandwidth. Essentially when you're hosting in the 'cloud', your webserver is a virtual entity, it doesn't exist on a single physical server, it's distributed across multiple clustered servers, sharing resources between them. In theory, cloud-based hosting can be cost effective because you only pay for the resources you use; instantly scalable, because you can tap into practically limitless computing resources on the fly; and inherently reliable, as there's no single point of failure. If one physical machine keels over, the others share the load until another comes onstream to replace it. That's a very simplistic explanation of how cloud computing works… but you get the idea.

Cloud computing, which encompasses cloud-based hosting, isn't without its issues. These largely revolve around data ownership, privacy and security, and the debate, as always, is ongoing. That said, cloud-based hosting is really gaining traction in the marketplace, and increasing numbers of hosting providers are now offering cloud-based 'pay for what you use' options as part of their portfolios. As always, you need to weigh the merits of what's on offer and decide what works best for your business.

Choosing your hosting company

Your website developer will be able to help you decide which web-hosting option is right for you, based on the size, design, functionality and configuration of your website, and your anticipated levels of traffic based on your business goals. They should also be able to recommend a reliable web-hosting company that will serve your needs.

When choosing your web host, bear the following in mind:

- **Choose a host in the country where your primary target market lives:** this is important, because search engines deliver local search results to users based in part on the geographical location of the server on which the web pages reside (which they can infer from the server IP address).

- **Make sure the host is reliable:** do they offer guaranteed uptime/levels of service? Many hosts publish live server statistics that demonstrate the reliability of their services. You should expect a service level approaching 100 per cent from a high-quality hosting service.

- **What sort of support do they offer?**: make sure the hosting you choose includes efficient and effective support 24/7. If your website goes down you need to be confident you can call on your host for assistance whatever time of the day or night.

- **Backup and disaster recovery**: if the worst happens and the server goes belly up, what sort of disaster-recovery options does the host have in place? Ideally your host should take several daily snapshots of your entire account/server, allowing them to restore it and get your site back up and running as quickly as possible, should the worst happen.

- **What do others think?**: find out what other customers think. Read testimonials, and search for discussions on webmaster forums and social media sites relating to the hosts you're considering. Are other people's experiences good or bad? Post a few questions.

- **Shop around**: hosting is an incredibly competitive industry, so shop around for the best deal – but bear in mind that the *cheapest option isn't always the best choice*.

How to choose a web designer/developer

Unless you're a web designer yourself, or have access to a dedicated in-house web development team, you'll need to bring in a professional web-design firm to help you with your website project. You'll find a host of options out there, offering a range of services that will boggle your mind. The good news is, if you've done your preliminary work, you should already have a fair idea what you want out of your website, who it's aimed at and the sort of features you'd like to include. Armed with that knowledge, you can start to whittle down the list of potential designers to something more manageable.

- **Look at their own website**: in trying to assess the relative merits of a web-design company, the best place to start is with their own website. What's their site like? Examine it with a critical eye. Does it look professional? Is it functional? Think about what they're trying to achieve, and how well the site addresses the needs of its target audience (you, in this case). Is it easy to find what you want? Does it meet or exceed your expectations? If not, do you really want the same people working on your website?

- **Examine their portfolio**: practically every web-design firm offers an online portfolio showing recent website projects they've worked on. Look at these – but go beyond the portfolio pages and click through to the actual websites themselves. Again, put your analytical hat on and ask what the sites are trying to achieve, who they're aimed at and how well the designers have achieved those goals. That should give you enough of a steer to produce a reasonable shortlist of potential candidates. Now you can dig a little deeper.

● **Ask their customers for recommendations**: go back to the best of the portfolio sites for your shortlisted designers. Go to the Contact us page and drop them a line by e-mail or pick up the phone to ask for some honest feedback on their web design experience. Would they recommend the firm?

● **What's their online reputation like?**: web forums, online communities and peer review sites are another good place to look for information about your shortlisted web-design firms. Is the online vibe positive or negative? What are people saying about them?

● **Are they designing sites to be found?**: your website is only as good as the quality traffic it gets. Are your shortlisted designers search engine savvy? Go back to the portfolio sites you looked at and pick out some of the keyword phrases you'd expect them to rank for in a search engine. Now go to the search engines and type in those keyword phrases. Have those sites been indexed? Where do they rank on the search results page? Low ranking doesn't necessarily indicate a problem with their web design – there are many components that contribute to search engine ranking (see the next chapter), but it may be something you should ask them to clarify before making your decision.

● **Do they adhere to web standards?**: go to the W3Cs website validation page (**www.w3.org/QA/Tools/**) and run the web addresses of your shortlisted web designers through the MarkUp Validator, Link Checker and CSS Validator. Do the sites validate as web standards compliant? You shouldn't necessarily discount your favourite designers because of this – but it is something else you should ask them about before making your final decision.

By now you should have whittled your shortlist down to a few competent and professional companies you'd like to quote/tender for your website project. The final decision is, of course, up to you.

Arranging your information

Your site structure – the way you arrange and group your information and how users navigate their way around it – can have a massive impact on its usability, its visibility to search engine spiders, its rank in search engine result pages (SERPs)[3] and its potential to convert traffic once it arrives. Getting your information architecture[4] right is absolutely critical to the success of your website.

It can be difficult to know where to start. You know what information you want on your site, but what's the best way of arranging it so that users can access it intuitively, at the level of granularity they desire, while also providing you with maximum exposure in the search engines for specific keywords? The answer, as is so often the case in digital marketing, is that it depends. It depends on the sort of business you're in, the type of site you're building, your target audience, your business goals and a whole host of other variables.

Start with your keywords

The keywords your potential users are searching on should give you a good indication of both the content they're looking for and the search terms you want your site to rank for in the SERPs. Take those keywords and arrange them into logical categories or themes. These themes, along with the staple Home page, About us and Contact us links, give you the primary navigation structure for your site.

Define your content structure

Look at your main themes, the keywords you've associated with each of them and the corresponding information or content you want to include beneath each. Now define a tiered hierarchy of subcategories (your secondary, tertiary, etc navigation levels) within each theme as necessary until you have all of your targeted keywords covered. Arrange your content so that the most important information is summarized at the highest levels, allowing the user to drill down to more detailed but less important information on the specific topic as required. Try not to go too deep in terms of navigation subcategories – it is rarely necessary to go beyond three, in exceptional cases four, levels deep from the home page.

FIGURE 3.1 A simple website information hierarchy

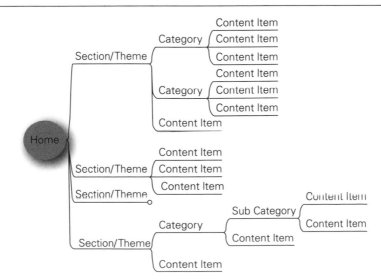

Your home page

The home page is often perceived as one of the most important pages on your site, but is potentially one of the least useful, both to your business and to your site visitors. For a start, home pages tend, by necessity, to be relatively generic. Too generic to answer a user's specific query or to instantly entice the conversion you crave. Indeed, many of your visitors – especially those arriving from a search engine, or by clicking on a link from another website or an online advertisement – will tend to land on a much more focused internal page, one that deals with the specific topic that they've searched for or clicked on. This deeper page should be much better at satisfying their immediate requirements.

Where a home page comes into its own is as a central reference point for navigating your content. A breadcrumb trail or navigation path along the top of your site can tell a user at a glance exactly where they are on your site in relation to a fixed point: your home page. It's also a convenient central location that users can easily return to. No matter where they wander on your site, users are always only one click from home... which reassures them that they can't get lost.

Your home page should be a 'jumping-off point' for the rest of your site, offering intuitive one-click navigation to all of your main sections or themes, and telling people immediately what your site is all about, and how it can help them. It's also a good place to highlight new products and services, special offers, incentives, news or anything else you want to promote on your site.

Avoid splash screens that simply show your company logo and a 'Click here to enter' button – they offer no benefit at all to your users or to your business – they are web clutter at its worst. Likewise flash intros – the 'Skip intro' button is one of the most widely clicked buttons on the web. Remember that you want to make it as easy as possible for your visitors to achieve their goals, so avoid putting obstacles between them and your real content.

Writing effective web content

Now you've defined a structure for your information, you're ready to put together your content.

Stop!

Don't make the mistake that often happens with new websites. You can't simply take your offline marketing collateral and paste the same copy into your web pages and expect it to work.

The golden rule of writing effectively in any medium is to know your audience – the more your writing is tailored to your audience, the more effective it is. It's exactly the same on the web. The difference between effective web writing and effective print writing reflects the core difference in the nature of the audience. Print is a linear medium, the web is random access; people read through printed material from beginning to end, on the web they scan and skip; offline readers are patient, online readers want the information they're looking for now, now, now.

We already know a bit about the characteristics of online users from our look at online consumer behaviour in the last chapter – writing effective web content is about taking what we know about web users in general, and the target audience of our website in particular, and applying that knowledge to deliver our information in a format that meets those readers' needs.

- **Grab attention**: web users are impatient – forget flowery introductions and verbose descriptions; make your writing clear, concise and to the point from the start.
- **Make it scannable**: avoid large blocks of uninterrupted text. Use headings, subheadings and bullet points to break up the text into manageable, scannable stand-alone chunks.
- **Make it original**: unique, original content is a great way to engage your users, establish your relevance and authority, and search engines love it.
- **Use the inverted pyramid**: the inverted pyramid writing style often used for newspaper stories tends to work well on the web. Aim to deliver the most important points of your story first, going on to deliver supporting details in order of decreasing importance down the page. Ideally, the user should be able to stop reading at any point and still get the gist of the content.
- **Be consistent**: use a simple, easy-to-read writing style, and keep things consistent across the site. If you have a number of people creating your content, consider developing a style guide or house style to help maintain consistency.
- **Engage with your reader**: use a conversational style, and write as if you were talking to an *individual* rather than an audience. It will help your writing to engage with the reader on a much more personal level.

Top 10 mistakes in web design

Jakob Nielsen (updated 2007), reproduced with permission

Since my first attempt in 1996, I have compiled many top-10 lists of the biggest mistakes in web design. This article presents the highlights: the very worst mistakes of web design.

1. Bad search

Overly literal search engines reduce usability in that they're unable to handle typos, plurals, hyphens, and other variants of the query terms. Such search engines are particularly difficult for elderly users, but they hurt everybody.

A related problem is when search engines prioritize results purely on the basis of how many query terms they contain, rather than on each document's importance. Much better if your search engine calls out 'best bets' at the top of the list – especially for important queries, such as the names of your products.

Search is the user's lifeline when navigation fails. Even though advanced search can sometimes help, simple search usually works best, and search should be presented as a simple box, since that's what users are looking for.

2. PDF files for online reading

Users hate coming across a PDF file while browsing, because it breaks their flow. Even simple things like printing or saving documents are difficult because standard browser commands don't work. Layouts are often optimized for a sheet of paper, which rarely matches the size of the user's browser window. Bye-bye smooth scrolling. Hello tiny fonts.

Worst of all, PDF is an undifferentiated blob of content that's hard to navigate.

PDF is great for printing and for distributing manuals and other big documents that need to be printed. Reserve it for this purpose and convert any information that needs to be browsed or read on the screen into real web pages.

3. Not changing the colour of visited links

A good grasp of past navigation helps you understand your current location, since it's the culmination of your journey. Knowing your past and present locations in turn makes it easier to decide where to go next. Links are a key factor in this navigation process. Users can exclude links that proved fruitless in their earlier visits. Conversely, they might revisit links they found helpful in the past.

Most important, knowing which pages they've already visited frees users from unintentionally revisiting the same pages over and over again.

These benefits only accrue under one important assumption: that users can tell the difference between visited and unvisited links because the site shows them in different colours. When visited links don't change colour, users exhibit more navigational disorientation in usability testing and unintentionally revisit the same pages repeatedly.

4. Non-scannable text

A wall of text is deadly for an interactive experience. Intimidating. Boring. Painful to read. Write for online, not print. To draw users into the text and support 'scannability', use well-documented tricks:

- subheads;
- bulleted lists;
- highlighted keywords;
- short paragraphs;
- the inverted pyramid;

- a simple writing style;

- de-fluffed language devoid of marketese.

5. Fixed font size

CSS style sheets unfortunately give websites the power to disable a web browser's 'change font size' button and specify a fixed font size. About 95 per cent of the time, this fixed size is tiny, reducing readability significantly for most people over the age of 40.

Respect the user's preferences and let them resize text as needed. Also, specify font sizes in relative terms – not as an absolute number of pixels.

6. Page titles with low search engine visibility

Search is the most important way users discover websites. Search is also one of the most important ways users find their way around individual websites. The humble page title is your main tool to attract new visitors from search listings and to help your existing users to locate the specific pages that they need.

The page title is contained within the HTML <title> tag and is almost always used as the clickable headline for listings on search engine result pages (SERPs). Search engines typically show the first 66 characters or so of the title, so it's truly microcontent.

Page titles are also used as the default entry in the Favourites when users bookmark a site. For your home page, begin the with the company name, followed by a brief description of the site. Don't start with words like 'The' or 'Welcome to' unless you want to be alphabetized under 'T' or 'W'.

For other pages than the home page, start the title with a few of the most salient information-carrying words that describe the specifics of what users will find on that page. Since the page title is used as the window title in the browser, it's also used as the label for that window in the taskbar under Windows, meaning that advanced users will move between multiple windows under the guidance of the first one or two words of each page title. If all your page titles start with the same words, you have severely reduced usability for your multi-windowing users.

Taglines on home pages are a related subject: they also need to be short and quickly communicate the purpose of the site.

7. Anything that looks like an advertisement

Selective attention is very powerful, and web users have learned to stop paying attention to any ads that get in the way of their goal-driven navigation. (The main exception being text-only search engine ads.)

Unfortunately, users also ignore legitimate design elements that look like prevalent forms of advertising. After all, when you ignore something, you don't study it in detail to find out what it is.

Therefore, it is best to avoid any designs that look like advertisements. The exact implications of this guideline will vary with new forms of ads; currently follow these rules:

- Banner blindness means that users never fixate their eyes on anything that looks like a banner ad due to shape or position on the page.

- Animation avoidance makes users ignore areas with blinking or flashing text or other aggressive animations.

- Pop-up purges mean that users close pop-up 'windoids' before they have even fully rendered; sometimes with great viciousness (a sort of getting-back-at-GeoCities triumph).

8. Violating design conventions

Consistency is one of the most powerful usability principles: when things always behave the same, users don't have to worry about what will happen. Instead, they know what will happen based on earlier experience. Every time you release an apple over Sir Isaac Newton, it will drop on his head. That's good.

The more users' expectations prove right, the more they will feel in control of the system and the more they will like it. And the more the system breaks users' expectations, the more they will feel insecure. Oops, maybe if I let go of this apple, it will turn into a tomato and jump a mile into the sky.

Jakob's Law of the Web User Experience states that 'users spend most of their time on other websites'.

This means that they form their expectations for your site based on what's commonly done on most other sites. If you deviate, your site will be harder to use and users will leave.

9. Opening new browser windows

Opening up new browser windows is like a vacuum cleaner salesperson who starts a visit by emptying an ashtray on the customer's carpet. Don't pollute my screen with any more windows, thanks (particularly since current operating systems have miserable window management).

Designers open new browser windows on the theory that it keeps users on their site. But even disregarding the user-hostile message implied in taking over the user's machine, the strategy is self-defeating since it disables the Back button which is the normal way users return to previous sites. Users often don't notice that a new window has opened, especially if they are using a small monitor where the windows are maximized to fill up the screen. So a user who tries to return to the origin will be confused by a greyed-out Back button.

Links that don't behave as expected undermine users' understanding of their own system. A link should be a simple hypertext reference that replaces the current page with new content. Users hate unwarranted pop-up windows. When they want the destination to appear in a new page, they can use their browser's 'Open in new window' command – assuming, of course, that the link is not a piece of code that interferes with the browser's standard behaviour.

10. Not answering users' questions

Users are highly goal driven on the web. They visit sites because there's something they want to accomplish – maybe even buy your product. The ultimate failure of a website is to fail to provide the information users are looking for.

Sometimes the answer is simply not there and you lose the sale because users have to assume that your product or service doesn't meet their needs if you don't tell them the specifics. Other times the specifics are buried under a thick layer of marketese and bland slogans. Since users don't have time to read everything, such hidden info might almost as well not be there.

The worst example of not answering users' questions is to avoid listing the price of products and services. No B2C [business-to-consumer] e-commerce site would make this mistake, but it's rife in B2B [business-to-business], where most 'enterprise solutions' are presented so that you can't tell whether they are suited for 100 people or 100,000 people. Price is the most specific piece of info customers use to understand the nature of an offering, and not providing it makes people feel lost and reduces their understanding of a product line. We have miles of videotape of users asking 'Where's the price?' while tearing their hair out.

Even B2C sites often make the associated mistake of forgetting prices in product lists, such as category pages or search results. Knowing the price is key in both situations; it lets users differentiate among products and click through to the most relevant ones.

Jakob Nielsen is one of the world's leading authorities on web usability and user interface design. You'll find more details and a host of web usability resources on his website, **www.useit.com***.*

Website design summary

- **Establish clear business goals for your website right from the start:** remember the analogy in the strategy chapter: if you don't know where you're heading, you haven't a hope of getting there. What does your business want to achieve with this website? What is it for? We know your website's primary focus is taking the traffic you gain through digital marketing and turning it into something of tangible value to your organization. But what does that mean? Is it about building your brand, direct online selling, harvesting sales leads, building an online customer-centric community... what?

- **Know your target audience:** no surprises here. Like everything else in marketing, knowing what makes your target market tick will help you to design a website that will engage them. What are your potential customers looking for online? How do they look for it and what are the best ways to make sure your website delivers?

- **Know your competition**: what your competition are doing online can provide real insight into what you should be doing. Don't copy them, but do emulate what they do well, enhance it and look for opportunities where you can differentiate your online offering.

- **Use a professional web designer**: unless you're an accomplished web developer in your own right, or have a team of in-house web professionals at your disposal, it always pays to bring in a professional to design and implement your site. Anyone can build a website – but you want a good website… right?

- **Professional look and feel**: your website needs to look professional and it needs to be functional. It doesn't have to look 'pretty' per se, as long as it doesn't look amateur and it gets the job done efficiently and effectively. On the web, function always outranks form, but if you can achieve both, so much the better.

- **Follow standards**: make sure your site is designed to comply with accepted web standards and, where relevant, accessibility standards. Your web designer should be familiar with these standards and should know how to implement them.

- **Keep it simple**: relevant, efficient websites deliver what users want with a minimum of fuss and bother. The most successful websites are often those that do the simplest thing that works effectively to get the desired task done. Of course, achieving simplicity isn't easy, but it's almost always worth the additional effort.

- **Design to be found**: make sure your site is search engine friendly as well as user friendly. Conversion is a function of usability, but getting traffic to convert in the first place is heavily dependent on your search engine rankings. Avoid search engine spider traps (see Chapter 4).

- **Content written for the web**: use clear, concise, scannable, original and compelling content written specifically for your website and your target audience.

- **Test everything**: nothing will erode your online credibility or your search engine ranking like a website that doesn't work. Before putting your site 'live', test it exhaustively to make sure everything works as it should, and that it achieves your original goals. If possible, test on different platforms (operating systems, browsers, etc) to ensure consistency.

- **Hold the initial marketing blitz**: hold off on marketing your new site when it first goes live. Give yourself a few weeks to iron out any kinks… then officially launch it and promote the living daylights out of it!

That's it: your new site is ready, it's live online… it's there for all the world to see, and it looks great. Now all you need is traffic, and in the chapters that follow we'll show you exactly how to get it!

CASE STUDY Italian foodie passion and digital – a perfect match

FIGURE 3.2 Antonio Carluccio and Gennaro Contaldo share their Italian passion for food in their new BBC TV series, the inevitable book, and of course an integrated digital campaign

The campaign was crucial to our brand, with our founder in a new television series for the first time in 11 years. The devil was in the detail of linking all elements of the digital campaign integrating Twitter, search, e-mail and website to give a strong net result.

Paschalis Loucaides, Head of Marketing at Carluccio's

The challenge

To support the Carluccio's brand association with Antonio Carluccio's new BBC2 TV series, *Two Greedy Italians*.

Internationally renowned chefs and old friends Antonio Carluccio and Gennaro Contaldo return to the Italy they left more than 40 years ago to discover what has changed in Italian culture and how that has affected the way Italians eat. The campaign would need to support the show, the accompanying book and the Carluccio brand's national chain of restaurants in the UK. Core objectives were to drive awareness, book sales, restaurant bookings and brand engagement on social channels.

The challenge was heightened when the TV show's air date was brought forward a full three months, putting tremendous time pressure on the creative team.

Target audience

ABC1 consumers who love great Italian food.

Action

The campaign focused around two key touchpoints: the website (full campaign takeover and landing page) and social media activity – predominantly on Twitter, using hashtags and short URLs (containing integrated analytics tracking codes). This was supported on YouTube with campaign takeover, search engine optimization and e-mail promotion to over a quarter of a million subscribers.

Results

Digital is now the fastest-growing area of the business for Carluccio's. Data from Google shows spikes of activity of up to 400 per cent during each episode of the TV show, and Twitter following jumped by almost 20 per cent. The Twitter account is now ranked in the top 2 per cent of all accounts on Twitter, according to Hubspot's Twitter Grader, scoring 98.2 out of 100, and the restaurant has seen a 102 per cent increase in online bookings like for like.

Search marketing delivered page one results for search terms relating to the TV series and the book, competing favourably against bbc.co.uk, guardian.co.uk and amazon.co.uk, and the website's online shop continues to enjoy double-digit revenue growth year on year.

The Carluccio's online store sold more gift-set hampers including a copy of the book (at a higher mark-up) than it did individual book sales.

'The results speak for themselves, but the approach tells a different story from the norm,' said Simon Priddle, Managing Director at Evolving. 'The team took the essence of the brand and the series to its heart, the food, the sense of (re)discovery and long-term friendship.

'When a brand is front of mind and is in your living room, on the TV, on your laptop or on your mobile it's very personal, yet sociable at the same time and this is what we wanted to capitalize on with *Two Greedy Italians*. At the core of our thinking was the growing trend of two-screen living and real-time digital interaction between brand and audience. This delivered some great results – it is only the beginning and I am looking forward to the future.'

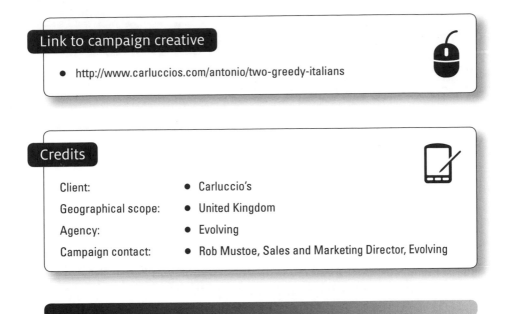

Link to campaign creative

- http://www.carluccios.com/antonio/two-greedy-italians

Credits

Client:	● Carluccio's
Geographical scope:	● United Kingdom
Agency:	● Evolving
Campaign contact:	● Rob Mustoe, Sales and Marketing Director, Evolving

Notes

1 Information architecture: the arrangement or structure of the information contained on a website. The way information is arranged can have a big impact on a site's usability and its perceived relevance and authority both for users and search engines.

2 Top-level domain (TLD): the element of an internet domain name that comes after the 'dot'. For instance, in the domain name digitalmarketingsuccess.com, the top-level domain is com or COM (internet domain names are not case sensitive).

3 Search engine result pages (SERPs): a term in search engine marketing that refers to the result pages returned when a user submits a query to a search engine.

4 Information architecture: the structure of an information system, including the way that information is arranged, and the methods of navigation between the different elements that make up the system.

04. **The search for success**

> If you make a product good enough, even though you live in the depths of the forest the public will make a path to your door, says the philosopher. But if you want the public in sufficient numbers, you would better construct a highway. **WILLIAM RANDOLPH HEARST**

> Learning is the beginning of wealth. Learning is the beginning of health. Learning is the beginning of spirituality. Searching and learning are where the miracle process all begins. **JIM ROHN**

> We've only achieved 2 per cent of what we can do. The world of search will get much, much bigger.
>
> **MARISSA MAYER, VICE PRESIDENT, SEARCH PRODUCTS AND USER EXPERIENCE, GOOGLE INC, SEPTEMBER 2007**

OUR CHAPTER PLEDGE TO YOU

In this chapter you'll discover answers to the following questions:

- Why is search important?
- What is a search engine, and how does it work?
- How big is search?
- How do I optimize my website for the search engines?
- What is paid search marketing?
- What is black-hat SEO and why should I avoid it?

Search: still the online marketer's holy grail

When the first edition of this book was published in 2009 we called search the online marketer's holy grail. Back then search was essentially the panacea that, if harnessed effectively, would drive sustainable waves of targeted traffic to your website, and ultimately generate more revenue for your business. For many businesses it still is.

During the intervening period social media has continued its remarkable surge in popularity, and with an ever-increasing population of always-connected smartphones, mobile has grown to deliver on at least some of its latent promise. Both have been grabbing more than their share of the digital limelight, and have shifted the spotlight away from search marketing.

The stats reflect this shift too. In 2010 more US web users visited Facebook than visited Google (Experian/Hitwise report, December 2010). That's pretty impressive, but it's important to remember that visitor volume is only part of the equation when it comes to choosing an effective platform for marketing your business. When it comes to getting your information in front of a highly targeted audience at the precise moment *when they're looking to buy your products or services*, search engines still reign supreme. To discount their importance to your online business based on the fickle barometer of online 'buzz' would certainly be a mistake.

In the last chapter we discovered how your company's website forms the hub of your digital world. Your website is much more than a shop window to a huge and growing global marketplace: a well-designed and implemented website is a place where you can interact with your customers, a virtual meeting place where you can do real business, with real people, in real time. The commercial potential is, quite simply, unparalleled.

But if you're going to realize even a fraction of that potential then you need to make sure people can *find your site*. Even in this age of rampant online engagement, peer recommendation and reviews, the way the vast majority of people find the things they need online is by typing a phrase into that little empty box on the home page of their favourite search engine.

On the internet there's really no such thing as passing trade. The chances of a potential customer stumbling across your site while randomly browsing the web are approaching negligible. That means your visitors have to learn about your site from somewhere else: by word-of-mouth recommendations (online or offline), through conventional advertising and branding channels, by following a link from another website or (still by far the most likely scenario) by clicking on a link in a search engine results page (SERP).

Think about the way you use the internet. Where do you go when you're looking for information, products or services online? If you're shooting the virtual breeze with your friends you head for Facebook or Twitter, but if you're trying to find something specific you're much more likely to head for your favourite search engine, even if you're using your mobile phone. There are relatively few class-leading online brands (like Amazon.com for books, eBay.com for online auctions, YouTube.com for video) where consumers are likely to remember the web address (URL) to access the site directly; for almost everything else people use search engines.

Search: still a fledgling industry

Can you remember an internet search before Yahoo!, Bing (the search engine formerly known as MSN), Ask and AltaVista... before Google?

Today it feels as though search engines have been with us forever, but Google – the market leader in search by a country mile – was only established in late 1998. In less than 15 years the search company has become a leading global brand to rival the biggest and the best out there, and has changed the way businesses operate forever.

On 8 October 2007, Google's stock passed the US$600 threshold, putting the value of the company at a staggering US$190 billion, a figure that makes it more valuable than long-established global giants like FedEx, McDonald's, Coke, Intel, IBM and Walmart.

Google's incredible growth and the unprecedented rise of search in general are testament to the practically ubiquitous appeal of online search, both to a constantly growing pool of internet users and as a marketing vehicle for businesses large and small. To the user, search engines offer a window to the web – a convenient way for them to sift through the literally billions of pages out there to find valuable, relevant information on what they're interested in at any given time. For marketers, search engines offer a unique opportunity to get their products or services in front of online prospects at the exact moment they're looking for them. It is, perhaps, one of the ultimate forms of targeted, pre-qualified marketing.

The fact that the internet search industry is still a relatively young one, and that it's still growing and evolving so quickly, makes the whole area of search engine optimization (SEO) and paid search advertising an incredibly exciting and challenging one. Because things are changing constantly, you're always shooting at a moving target, and have to tweak your aim accordingly. Search is a fluid and dynamic environment, and nobody has all the right answers, because the nature of the questions keeps changing.

That said, there are a number of widely accepted legitimate strategies, (and some less ethical ones that we'll touch on later) that, if you implement them diligently and consistently, will help your site rise to a more prominent position in the SERPs. Equally, there are plenty of SEO myths out there that won't help your search rankings but will waste your valuable time. We'll reveal some of the more common ones later in this chapter.

Looking forward

Both the increasingly widespread adoption of high-speed internet access in the home and the ever-increasing capability and market penetration of mobile digital devices are opening up a slew of new digital media opportunities for marketers the world over. The rise of social networking sites and the word-of-mouth and viral marketing opportunities that they offer (see Chapter 7) may in time dilute the prominence of SEO and paid search advertising in the digital marketing mix. Likewise, as ever-increasing numbers of web users develop a 'feel' for where they need to go to find the things that they want online, or access branded content directly on the move through dedicated smartphone applications, they are likely to rely less on search for certain things.

While the significance of search may wane for a proportion of people and for certain applications over time, given its current level of importance for both internet users and digital marketers, the propensity of major search engines to innovate and adapt, and the fact that new people are going online and discovering the value of search engines every day, search looks certain to remain a cornerstone of digital marketing for some time to come.

About the engines

Why is search engine marketing so important?

In 2011 US businesses will spend a staggering US$19.3 billion on search marketing (SEMPO/EConsultancy Annual State of Search survey, 2011). Why will they spend so much?

Simple: because search engines give those businesses a prime opportunity to put their products, services or brands in front of a vast and ever-growing market of prospective customers *at the precise time* those customers are looking for exactly what the business is selling. That's a pretty evocative marketing proposition – especially when you consider the volumes involved.

During the month of March 2011, in the United States alone, search engines fielded more than 16.9 billion search queries (comScore qSearch). That's almost two and a half searches for every living person on the planet in a single month!

How do search engines work?

Before you start optimizing your site for the search engines, it makes sense to know how they work. Not the detailed technical 'nuts and bolts' of it all – just a high-level understanding of what makes a search engine tick. Knowing what the search engines are trying to achieve and how they go about doing it is at the heart of good SEO.

The mission of search engines

It's important to understand at this point that search engines are interested, first and foremost, in delivering timely, relevant, high-quality search results to their users. You could say it's their prime directive – their reason for being. The search engines are constantly researching, developing, testing and refining ways to enhance the service that they provide – looking to optimize the relevance and quality of the results they serve back to the user on every single query.

The rationale is simple: the better the search experience for the user, the better the reputation of the search engine and the more users it will attract. The more users a search engine has, the more alluring it is to advertisers, ergo the more ad revenue it can pull in.

Putting users first makes search engines richer... and that makes search engine shareholders happy; QED.

In that respect the internet is no different from traditional marketing channels like commercial television, radio and print publications. It's the viewers, listeners and readers these channels look after first – because it's the audience that brings in the advertisers. Without an audience, they have no advertisers, and without advertisers they have no business.

From a marketer's perspective the search engines' constant quest to improve the search experience for users is something of a double-edged sword. Yes, it means that the best search engines have a bigger pool of potential prospects for your paid search advertising and your organic SEO efforts. But equally, the fact that things keep changing makes the process of optimization a continuous, uncertain and labour-intensive process.

Scouring the web

To deliver accurate, relevant, high-quality search results to their users, search engines need to gather detailed information about the billions of web pages out there. They do this using automated programmes called 'bots' (short for robots) – also known as 'spiders' – which they send out to 'crawl' the web. Spiders follow hyperlinks and gather information about the pages that they find.

Once a page has been crawled by a spider, the search engine stores details about that page's contents and the links both into and out of it in a massive database called an index. This index is highly optimized so that results for any of the hundreds of millions of search requests received every day can be retrieved from it almost instantly.

It's a mammoth task. While nobody knows the real number of unique web pages out there, and search engines typically don't publicize the size of their indices, a post on Google's official blog in July 2008 gave some rare insight into just how big the web is:

> The first Google index in 1998 already had 26 million pages, and by 2000 the Google index reached the one billion mark. Over the last eight years, we've seen a lot of big numbers about how much content is really out there. Recently, even our search engineers stopped in awe about just how big the web is these days – when our systems that process links on the web to find new content hit a milestone: one trillion (as in 1,000,000,000,000) unique URLs on the web at once!

Search engines don't index every one of those trillion URLs, of course. Many contain similar or duplicate information, or aren't really relevant to search (think of a dynamically generated online event calendar, for example, with links to 'next day' and 'previous day' – in theory you could keep clicking forever, but only pages containing event information are of any relevance in search results), so some don't make it into the index.

We don't know how many pages there are on the web, or, for that matter, how many are stored in the search engines' indices (information that's rarely volunteered), but it's safe to assume that we're dealing with some very big numbers.

The list of results for any given search query, which often contains many millions of pages, is then run through the search engine's complex ranking algorithms: special programs that use a variety of closely guarded proprietary formulas to 'score' a site's relevance to the user's original query. The output is then sorted in order of relevance and presented to the user in the SERPs.

Search engines process a huge volume of searches, scanning billions of items and delivering pages of relevant, ranked results in a fraction of a second. To the user the process seems quick, straightforward and seamless; but there's a lot going on behind the scenes. Google and Bing (which, following a 2010 agreement between Yahoo! and Microsoft, now also powers Yahoo! search results) are running some of the most complex and demanding computer applications in the world.

Optimizing your site for the engines

To many, SEO appears to be something of an arcane art. It's a world that's shrouded in high-tech mystery, a complicated world full of secrets that mere mortals haven't a hope of understanding. But according to leading UK-based SEO expert Jason Duke, of Strange Logic, there are no real secrets in SEO. 'The web is a very open place,' he says. 'If a site is riding high in the search engine listings, then you can, with enough persistence, get to see why it ranks so well. Replicate it, and you can join them – it really is as simple as that.'

Matt McGee, an SEO expert who specializes in advising small businesses (**www.smallbusinesssem.com**), concurs with Jason's sentiments. In an interview on the 'Your SEO Plan' (**www.yourseoplan.com**) blog in December 2006, Matt says, 'SEO is not rocket science. It's simple, but it's not easy. There's a difference! There's a small set of basic rules that apply to any web page or website, whether you're a small business or not. Your site has to be crawlable, your content has to be good – and I'd include things like page titles, keyword use, etc under the umbrella of "content" – and you need quality, relevant inbound links. That applies to everyone.'

One of the best places to start for tips on improving your site's ranking with the search engines is with the search engines' own guidelines, tips and resources for website owners. See Table 4.1

TABLE 4.1 Links to webmaster resources for major search engines

Search engine	Resource	URL for webmasters
Google	Webmaster Central	http://www.google.com/webmasters
Bing	Webmaster Tools	http://www.bing.com/toolbox/webmasters/
Yahoo!	Web Publisher Tools	http://tools.search.yahoo.com/about/forsiteowners.html

Make your site easy to crawl

If you're looking to attract search engine traffic, the last thing you want to do is make it difficult for search engines to index your website. Make sure your site design doesn't present unnecessary obstacles to search engine spiders.

Spiders are interested in text, text and more text. They don't see the graphics, clever animations and other flashy bells and whistles that web designers routinely use to make sites look pretty. In fact, over-reliance on some of these things can even hinder spiders, potentially preventing some of them from being indexed at all.

While some 'window dressing' is obviously important to make your site appeal to real people when they arrive, to get enough of them to your site in the first place it's vital that your design doesn't unwittingly alienate search engine spiders. Make sure your site works for both, and that each page includes relevant text-based content; avoid flash-only sites and frames, which are difficult for spiders to crawl effectively; and make sure that every page on your site can be reached via a simple text-based hyperlink.

Words are the key to unlocking the power of search

The key to effective SEO is knowing what people looking for your products, services or information are typing into that little box on the search engine home page. Known as keywords or keyword phrases (which consist of two, three or more keywords), these form the foundation of your SEO efforts.

Find the optimum keywords, follow a few basic SEO guidelines, and when the spiders re-index your site you'll start to see it rise up the organic search rankings for those keywords, and, with a bit of luck, you'll notice a corresponding increase in the level of targeted traffic arriving at your site.

TABLE 4.2 Spider traps: web design features that can hurt your search engine visibility

Website feature	Why it's bad for your SEO
All-Flash website	Difficult for spiders to crawl. While search engines have improved their ability to index text-based content within flash files, excessive dependence on flash is still a bad idea for both SEO and usability.
JavaScript navigation	Spiders often don't activate JavaScript code, so unless you implement an alternative they may struggle to reach other pages on your site via script-based navigation. Make sure you have at least one *regular, text-based hyperlink* to every page on your site.
Frames	Frames are notoriously difficult to implement effectively from a user-experience perspective, are very rarely necessary, and often cause indexing problems for search engine spiders.
Image maps and other non-text navigation	Some spiders may have problems following these links. If you use image maps for navigation on your pages, make sure you have *alternative text-based hyperlinks* leading to the same pages.
Dynamically generated pages	Less of a problem than it used to be, but some spiders can have trouble with very long dynamically generated URLs that contain too many parameters (?W=XYZ). Try to configure your site to use search engine-friendly URLs where possible, or at least restrict dynamic URL parameters to a maximum of three.
AJAX	See notes for JavaScript above.

Choose the wrong keywords, however, and the best SEO in the world won't deliver the results you're looking for.

Choosing effective keywords

So how do you go about choosing the right keywords for site optimization?

Well, a good place to start is with the people you're hoping to attract. Knowing your target audience is a critical component of any marketing campaign – and it's the same here. Put yourself in your prospect's shoes, sitting in front of your favourite search engine, looking for information on the product or service you're selling. What would you type into the box?

These are your 'seed' keywords. They give you a starting point to work from. Take these keywords and play around with them. Imagine the various combinations of search terms your prospects might use to find your site. Type these into the engines and look at the results. Examine the sites that are ranking highly for your chosen keywords. Analyse them and try to work out how they're achieving those rankings.

You can also use a wide range of automated keyword suggestion tools like the free tools provided by Google AdWords (**http://bit.ly/GoogKWTool**) and on the SEO Book website (**http://bit.ly/UDMSEOBook**); or Wordtracker (**www.wordtracker.com**) and Trellian's (**http://bit.ly/KWDiscovery**) keyword tools, both of which offer a free basic service with paid upgrades for a more comprehensive version. These tools typically provide insight into the search traffic volumes for the most popular phrases relating to seed keyword phrases you provide.

There are a lot of different keyword research tools and services available on the web; perhaps the best way to research your options is to look for things like 'keyword research tool' or 'keyword suggestion' in your favourite search engine.

Analyse the competition

Other tools on the web can provide you with insight into how your leading competitors are doing in terms of search engine traffic for particular keywords. Services on sites like SEO Toolset (**www.seotoolset.com**) and Compete (**www.compete.com**) can provide information on which keywords are driving traffic to your competitors' websites from the major search engines, and which of your competitors' sites are ranking for which keyword phrases – all of which can inform the choice of keywords you want to optimize for.

While automated tools are a good guide, don't underestimate the value of people as a source of inspiration for keyword selection. 'Use the automated tools to assist,' advises Jason Duke, 'but please remember that although automated tools are brilliant, nothing is better at understanding the minds of people than people themselves.'

That's good advice. What you believe people will search for and what they actually type into the search box are often two very different things.

Get a group of people together – if possible, representative of your target market – and start brainstorming keywords. The results will probably surprise you.

I have my initial keyword list, now what?

After analysing your keywords and phrases, and examining the competition, you've probably got a list of target keywords as long as your arm. What do you do with them all?

The first thing you'll want to do is narrow your initial list down to a more manageable size. What constitutes a manageable size will depend on your situation – on how much time, money and resources you have available for your SEO effort. Remember, there's nothing wrong with starting small: optimize a few pages for what you believe are your main keywords, monitor the results on ranking, traffic and conversion for those pages. That will give you a solid foundation from which to build your optimization efforts and your SEO expertise.

To whittle your list down to size, start by eliminating all of the words or phrases that are way too general. Broad single-word terms like 'shoes', 'mortgages', 'bottles' or 'computers' tend to be both very difficult to rank for (because they're high-traffic terms that can apply equally to a huge number of sites across the net), and at the same time are far too generic to drive valuable targeted traffic to your site.

Suppose you're an independent mortgage consultant based in Killarney, County Kerry, Ireland. If you choose to optimize a page based on the keyword 'mortgages', you'll find yourself competing with a raft of mortgage providers, mortgage advisers, mortgage brokers, mortgage consultants, mortgage industry news sites, etc from all over the world. Even if (and it's a big if) your page does make it to those coveted elevated positions in the SERPs for that keyword, the chances that people searching for the term 'mortgages' will be looking for an independent consultant in County Kerry are slim at best.

Phrases like 'mortgages in Killarney' or 'mortgage consultant Kerry', on the other hand, are potentially much less competitive, and generate much lower search volumes, but are much more valuable to your business, because the people who search on those terms are far more likely to be interested in the products and services you offer.

In other words, the more general a keyword, the less likely it is that your site will contain what the searcher is trying to find. Effective SEO isn't just about generating traffic volume; it's about finding that elusive balance between keyword search volume and keyword specificity that drives the maximum volume of *targeted traffic* to your site.

'Your target keywords should always be at least two or more words long,' explained search guru Danny Sullivan, in a 2007 article for Search Engine Watch (**www.searchenginewatch.com**). 'Usually, too many sites will be relevant for a single word, such as "stamps". This "competition" means your odds of success are lower. Don't waste your time fighting the odds. Pick phrases of two or more words, and you'll have a better shot at success.'

Single-keyword searches used to be the norm – but not any more. Search users are using more sophisticated search queries to narrow down the results they get back. These days two, three or even more words are becoming increasingly common. Exploiting that trend in your choice of optimization keywords can yield real dividends.

Long-tail versus short-tail keywords

Keywords in SEO fall into two broad categories. Short-tail keywords are simple one- or two-word phrases that are typically very general in nature and attract a large volume of individual search requests. Long-tail keywords, on the other hand, are more complex queries that contain more words, and are much more specific in nature. Individually they attract a much lower volume of search traffic than their short-tail counterparts, but cumulatively these long-tail-type queries account for the lion's share of internet search traffic.

Martin Murray, Head of Global Agency Operations at Google, sums it up like this:

> In any keyword domain there are a small number of highly trafficked keywords or phrases and a large number of low-trafficked keywords or phrases. Often, the keyword domain approximates to the right half of a normal curve with the tail of the curve extending to infinity. Low-trafficked keywords are therefore also known as 'long-tail keywords'.
>
> The highly trafficked [short-tail] keywords have the following characteristics: highly competitive, consist of one or two words, have a high cost per click and may have low conversion rates as they tend to be quite general. Examples from the accommodation sector might include 'hotel', 'London hotel' or 'cheap hotel'.
>
> Low-trafficked [long-tail] keywords are not so competitive, often consist of four, five or more words, have a lower cost per click and can have a higher conversion rate as they are quite specific, indicating that the searcher is further along the online purchasing cycle. Examples might include 'cheap city centre hotel Dublin', 'stag weekend hotel temple bar Dublin' or 'business hotel with gym and spa Wexford'.
>
> Effective search marketing campaigns tend to put a lot of effort into discovering effective long-tail terms, particularly for use in sponsored listings (PPC) campaigns.

Typically it makes sense to take a balanced approach, and work with a mixture of general short-tail keywords and more specific long-tail keywords as part of your organic SEO effort, while focusing on highly specific long-tail search terms is likely to yield a higher return on your investment for pay-per-click (PPC) campaigns (see later).

Focus on one page at a time

The list of keywords you're left with is very important. It essentially provides you with an SEO 'template' for your website.

One of the key things to remember when you're approaching SEO is that you'll be optimizing your site *one page at a time*. While you'll look at some site-wide factors as part of your SEO effort, SEO isn't a straightforward 'one-size-fits-all' operation, and each of the existing pages on your site will need to be optimized independently. It's also highly likely you'll want to create new pages to maximize your potential search engine exposure for as many of your chosen keyword phrases as possible.

Think about it: when a search engine presents results to a user, it's not presenting whole sites, it's presenting the individual pages that, according to its algorithms, best match a user's query. That means each individual page on your website gives you an explicit opportunity to optimize for specific keywords or phrases – and that's important.

'Each page in your website will have different target keywords that reflect the page's content,' says Danny Sullivan. 'For example, say you have a page about the history of stamps. Then "stamp history" might be your keywords for that page.'

Jason Duke of Strange Logic also emphasizes the importance of optimizing individual pages for specific keywords. 'These [keywords] become the structure for your site, with a page for every topic. Laying these foundations and allowing them to grow according to what you, your team and your visitors think are the key to successful opportunities to rank.'

Your goal, then, is to isolate the important keywords and phrases in your particular market, and then to ensure your site includes individual pages with unique, relevant content optimized for a small number (ideally one or two – no more than three) keyword phrases. The more individual pages you have, the more opportunities you have to get your business in front of your prospects in the SERPs... and at the end of the day that's what SEO is all about.

Choose your page <title>s carefully

There's a small but very important HTML tag that lives in the header section of the code on each of your web pages. It's called the 'title' tag, and the text it contains is what appears in the title bar at the top of your browser window when you visit a web page. It's also, crucially, the text that appears as the 'clickable' blue link for a page when it's presented to users in the SERPs.

This means that what you put in the title tag is incredibly important for the following reasons:

- The title tag is one of the most important on-page factors used by the search engines to rank your page. At this stage most, if not all, SEO

FIGURE 4.1 Screenshot showing title tag and meta description as they appear in HTML source code, and the same page as it's rendered in the Firefox browser, showing the start of the same title tag in the active tab

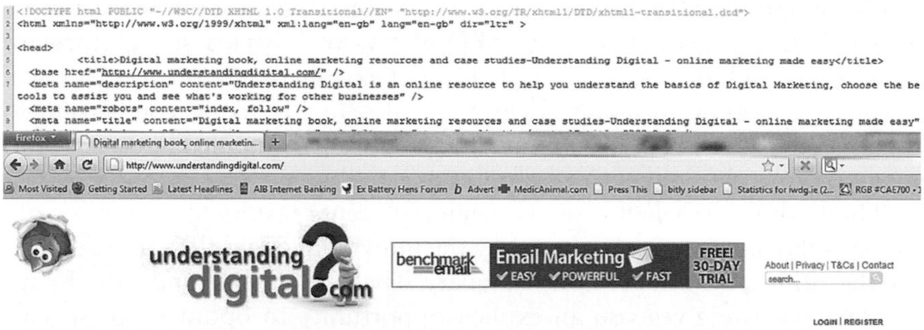

experts agree that appropriate use of the title tag is a key factor in ranking well in the SERPs, and advise weaving your primary keyword(s) for a page into the title tag whenever possible. Just remember not to sacrifice readability for your human audience.

- The title is the first glimpse of your content a search user will see. Giving your pages concise, compelling and informative titles will entice more users to click through to your page when it appears in search results.

Give each page a unique meta description

Another HTML tag that used to be very important for SEO, but is now pretty much obsolete, is the meta tag. Meta tags contain information that is accessible to browsers, search engine spiders and other programs but doesn't appear on the rendered (visible) page for the user. This meta data was once used extensively by search engines to gauge what a page was about – especially the once-obsessed-over meta-keywords tag.

These days, however, the tag that was once the staple of SEO has become more or less redundant in terms of influencing a page's ranking in the major search engines. Engines rely principally on their increasingly comprehensive ability to analyse the *actual content* of the page – the words the user sees – and on incoming and outgoing links to help them determine a page's relevance to the submitted search query.

There is, however, one HTML meta tag that is still worth including as part of your SEO, and that's the meta-description tag. As with most things in search, the opinion of leading experts in the SEO community is divided as to just how valuable the meta-description tag is in terms of search engine optimization. While it is widely acknowledged that the tag does little, if anything, to improve your page ranking, it can help to boost your click-through rate (CTR) when your page does appear in the SERPs.

Depending on the query and the page content, leading search engines will often use the contents of your meta-description tag as the descriptive 'snippet' of text that appears below your page title in the SERPs. A well-written description for each page can, in theory at least, entice more users to click through to your page when it's returned in search results.

Use of the meta-description text by search engines is inconsistent. The rules applied vary from engine to engine, and even between different types of query on the same engine. However, having compelling, informative meta-description tags is something that search engines encourage, certainly won't hurt your rankings, is beneficial to users and may well boost traffic to your site.

Content – the most important thing on your site

Content is the single most important thing on your website: period.

Unique, relevant, informative content is what sets your site apart from the competition. It's the reason users want to visit you, why other sites will want to link to you and, of course, why search engines will want to suggest your site to their users in search results.

The term 'content', if you take it literally, encompasses everything on your website. It includes all the visual elements on the site – the flashy graphics, animations, videos, banners, etc – that the search engine spiders can't see, and of course all of the text, which they can. In the context of SEO, though, when we talk about content, we're really talking about the text on each of your web pages.

When writing content for your site the key thing to remember is that you're writing it, first and foremost, for a *human audience*, not for search engine spiders. Yes, your pages need to be search engine friendly, but the spiders should *always* be a secondary consideration: put your human audience first.

Frankly, if your copy doesn't engage real, live people when they arrive – address their needs right from the start – then investing time and resources to attract more search engine traffic is pointless. If your content doesn't deliver, visitors will leave as soon as they arrive. Remember, on the web you don't have a captive audience. The user is in control… one click and they're gone.

Your copy needs to be relevant, it has to be interesting, and above all it has to provide the answers the user is looking for. It needs to do all of this quickly, in a concise, easily scannable way (see the section on content in Chapter 3 for more on creating good web copy).

Content and the search engines

Search engines have evolved rapidly, and are now in what's considered to be their third generation. Each generation has become much 'smarter' than the last at interpreting the actual visible content on a page, and judging its relevance to the user. Today's generation of search engines, unlike their predecessors, don't rely on meta data to judge the content of a page; they analyse and interpret the actual content presented to the user. And they're getting better all the time at doing it.

Ultimately, all of the mysterious voodoo behind search engine ranking algorithms is about analysing and prioritizing your content. There are all sorts of criteria that contribute to the process – some known, many guessed at, and no doubt some that we'll never know. At the end of the day, though, they all combine to measure just two things: the relevance and authority of your page content in the context of what the user typed into the search box.

Search engine optimization for sustainable high ranking, therefore, hinges on the production of great original content that appeals to real, live people.

Keywords in content

The subject of keywords in content is something that generates a lot of debate in SEO circles: where to place them, when and how often they need to appear on the page, and lots more besides. As with most things SEO, opinions tend to vary significantly on the subject.

Our advice: don't worry too much about it. If you're writing copy about a specific set of keyword phrases, there's a high probability you'll use those keyword phrases and related phrases organically in your writing, and will achieve a natural balance. That's exactly what search engines are looking for. Focus on writing compelling copy that addresses the needs of your target audience while keeping your target keywords for that page in mind, and the search engines will do the rest.

'Just make sure that your chosen keyword or phrase is contained in the title tag and URL, and then simply make sure your content's on topic,' advises Jason Duke. 'Don't worry about any other "on-page" SEO such as keyword density, meta tags, this trick or that trick, as it's all so 1999!

'Search engines are now more than intelligent enough to understand the semantic relationships between words and phrases, so trying to assist them with certain keyword densities is a fruitless effort. Leave them to their algorithms, and simply enjoy the rewards that their efforts can deliver to you and your website.'

Jill Whalen, CEO and founder of search marketing firm High Rankings and a regular columnist with the website Search Engine Land, emphasizes that there are no hard and fast rules to follow. 'Understand that there is no magical number of words per page or number of times to use your phrases in your copy,' she says. 'The important thing is to use your keyword phrases only when and where it makes sense to do so for the real people reading your pages. Simply sticking keyword phrases at the top of the page for no apparent reason isn't going to cut it, and it just looks silly.'

Links – second only to content

The critical importance of links in securing a high page ranking is one of the few things that have universal consensus in the world of SEO. Popular opinion maintains that nothing, but nothing, is more important than high-quality inbound links from 'authority' websites in achieving high rankings in the search engine results.

But wait a minute… if nothing is more important than links, why did we just say in the heading that links are second only to content? Simple: because creating outstanding content is the most effective way of attracting high-quality inbound links from authoritative online sources. And there's no doubt that those are the links that have the biggest impact on your search engine rankings.

Why are links so important?

Search engines need to determine two things when they attempt to fulfil a user's search request – they need to decide which pages in their index are relevant to the user's query, and then they need to rank those pages in terms of quality and importance. And therein lies one of their biggest challenges, because a search engine algorithm can't read the content and assess its quality the way a human can – at least, not yet.

Instead the engines have to rely on other criteria, and one of the main things that indicates a page's perceived importance to a search engine's ranking algorithm is the quantity and quality of references – or links – to that page from other web pages.

Each link to a page is, if you like, a vote of confidence for that page. The more links that point to an individual page (and globally to the site as a whole), the higher the collective vote of confidence for that page (and/or site) becomes, and the more important the page is deemed to be by the search engines.

But of course it's not quite that simple.

Votes from different pages carry more or less weight depending on the perceived importance/quality of the source page, the type of link, the anchor text used in the link and a host of other factors taken into account by the search engine ranking algorithms. When you consider the tangled skein of interconnecting links that make up the world wide web, you begin to appreciate the complexity inherent in assessing the relative importance/quality of all of those pages in relation to one another.

Fundamentally, though, what it boils down to is that incoming links in general are a good thing, and play a critical role in determining your search engine rankings. The more links you have pointing to your site, the higher your perceived authority – but there's a caveat. For 'votes' to be counted, the incoming links have to pass certain search engine filtering criteria. Those that fall outside the engines' criteria (generally any link that is designed to hoodwink search engines into assigning higher rankings rather than to guide site users to a relevant page – check the search engine guidelines for more information) are either ignored (ie their votes aren't counted), or more seriously, can have a negative impact on your ranking.

While all incoming links that satisfy the search engines' criteria will influence your ranking in a positive way, it makes sense to try to maximize the value of your incoming links by focusing your link-building efforts on quality links over quantity. Attracting high-quality, natural links from authority sites with subject matter that's aligned with the content on your site is the real key to high rankings. That's not easy, but the way to get those kinds of links is, of course, producing outstanding content that high-authority sites will want to point their users towards.

Links from authority sites are probably the single most significant factor in boosting your site's overall rankings in the SERPs. A single link from, say, the CNN.com or BBC.co.uk home page could be worth more to your site in terms of ranking and exposure than countless links from smaller, relatively unknown sites. Authority sites, by their very nature, also tend to be high-traffic sites, and you'll inevitably garner some direct traffic as people click through to your site via the link.

The flip side of this, of course, is that links from authority sites are notoriously difficult to secure, while links from smaller, less well-known sites generally take less effort. It's a case of swings and roundabouts, but in practice your aim should be to get as many inbound links as possible from sites with as high a perceived authority level as possible.

The role of internal and external links

Internal links and external links are both important for boosting the ranking of individual pages within your site. First let's define exactly what we mean by internal and external links:

- **External links:** these are links that reside on pages that do not belong to your domain – in other words, links from other websites.

- **Internal links:** these are the links that reside on pages that belong to your domain or subdomains – in other words, links between pages on the same website, or pages that reside in subdomains of the primary domain.

All of these links are important. Links from reputable external sources boost your site's perceived authority with the search engines, which in turn helps your more popular pages to rank higher in the SERPs. Internal links give you a way of distributing the 'authority' accrued by your more popular pages (like your home page, for example) to other important pages that you want to rank for.

Getting good links

There are a huge number of ways that you can encourage people to link to your site. But building quality natural links isn't easy, and it takes time. It depends on creating high-quality content, and building a reputation for excellence (or notoriety – which can work well for links, but might not project the right image to your customers) in your chosen field, which in turn encourages other website owners to link to you.

There are, of course, some quicker, easier ways to secure incoming links, but such links tend either to be of poor quality (hence of little SEO value) or to violate search engine guidelines. Search engines take a dim view of anybody trying to artificially manipulate search results. Remember they're trying to deliver the most relevant, highest-quality results to their users – and see any attempt to leapfrog a less relevant or lower-quality site up the rankings as 'search engine spam'.

Harvesting links purely for the purpose of boosting your site's rankings in the search engines is frowned upon, and while it may work in the short term, it's a risky strategy at best that will ultimately harm your rankings, and may even result in your entire site being blacklisted and removed from the search engines' indexes altogether. If you're trying to build a sustainable, long-term online business it simply isn't worth the risk.

For sustainable long-term rankings, focus instead on building high-quality links through ethical means, concentrate on your content, and build your site with your end user in mind. Exploiting search engine loopholes and 'clever' tricks to artificially boost your rankings isn't really search engine optimization, it's search engine manipulation, and that will ultimately back-fire. It may take a lot longer to achieve the rank you're looking for working within search engine guidelines, but in the end it's generally better that way.

Link building tips

- **Generate truly valuable content that other sites will want to link to**: these one-way unsolicited links are by far the most valuable kind. Search engines love them, and see them as a genuine endorsement of one site by another. As your site becomes more visible, the content will organically attracts more links, which in turn will improve your visibility, attracting even more links. When it works, this process is self-perpetuating, leaving you free to concentrate on quality content while the links look after themselves.

- **Let people know your site is out there**: people can only link to your site if they know it's there. Promote your site at every opportunity, especially in places where you know there are other website owners. Use the medium to your advantage. Online communities, forums, social networking sites and e-mail lists all offer great opportunities to get your site URL out in front of people who can link to it. Blogs are another source of potential links – some blogs are incredibly popular, and bloggers are noted for their affinity to linking. Try submitting a few poignant comments to high-ranking blogs in your sector. (Do this responsibly; aim to add real value to the discussion rather than simply promoting your site – see Chapter 7 for more on using blogs to promote your site.)

- **Create your own blog**: a blog can be an incredibly powerful promotional and link-building tool, if used wisely. If you have strong opinions, or a high level of knowledge in your industry, and you're happy to write regular posts, setting up a blog is easy and can be a great way to increase both visibility and incoming links.

- **Network, network, network**: use your network of contacts both online and offline to promote your site and encourage people to link to it, and pass it on to their own network of contacts in turn. If people look at your site and like what they see, they may well link to it.

- **Ask the people who link to your competitors to link to you**: use Yahoo!'s Site Explorer to find out who's linking to your main competition for your selected search keywords. Approach those sites and ask them if they'd be willing to link to your site too. After all, if they link to your competitors, why wouldn't they?

- **Encourage links within content and with descriptive anchor text**: links within content are preferable to links on a page that just lists links. Surrounding content helps to put a link in context, both for the user and for the search engines. You should also encourage descriptive anchor text, that if possible or appropriate includes one or two of your chosen keywords.

- **Submit your site to high-quality directories**: getting your site listed in high-quality, well-respected online directories like the Open Directory Project (**www.dmoz.com**, which is free) and Yahoo! Directory (dir. yahoo.com, which charges an annual fee for commercial listings) can be a great way to get your link building started. These links will help both search engine spiders and that all-important human traffic to find your site. As leading directories are also considered 'authority' sites by the major search engines, links from these sites will also help boost your ranking.

- **Use link bait**: link bait is anything that will entice incoming natural links from other websites or users. Link bait can be an interesting or controversial article, a downloadable document or report, a plug-in that improves the functionality of a piece of software, or useful widgets (small snippets of code) that other website owners can embed into the sidebars and content of their pages and which include a link back to your landing page. Link bait is really anything that could entice somebody else to link to your content. Be creative! Just stay within the search engines' published guidelines.

- **Offer to swap links with a select few relevant, high-quality sites**: these are called reciprocal links. Although they are less useful in terms of SEO value than they used to be, they can still be used effectively in moderation. While the power of reciprocal links to boost your rankings has been diluted, they do help to establish relevance and authority in your subject area – just be sure that you link to relevant, high-quality sites, and only swap links with a few of them. As a rule of thumb, you should *never* link to a site that you wouldn't genuinely recommend to your site visitors just for the sake of a reciprocal link.

Submitting your site URL and sitemap

Submitting your site URL, strictly speaking, isn't necessary any more. If you've followed the advice above, and have managed to secure some inbound links, it won't be long before the spiders find you. That said, all of the major search engines offer a free submission process, and submitting your site won't hurt. If you want to kick-start the indexing process, by all means go ahead and manually submit your home page and one or two other important pages.

The other thing you can do that will help search engines to crawl all relevant pages on your website is to submit an XML sitemap that adheres to the sitemap protocol outlined on **www.sitemaps.org**, which defines a sitemap as follows:

> Sitemaps are an easy way for webmasters to inform search engines about pages on their sites that are available for crawling. In its simplest form, a Sitemap is an XML file that lists URLs for a site along with additional metadata about each URL (when it was last updated, how often it usually changes, and how important it is, relative to other URLs in the site) so that search engines can more intelligently crawl the site.
>
> Web crawlers usually discover pages from links within the site and from other sites. Sitemaps supplement this data to allow crawlers that support Sitemaps to pick up all URLs in the Sitemap and learn about those URLs using the associated metadata. Using the Sitemap protocol does not guarantee that web pages are included in search engines, but provides hints for web crawlers to do a better job of crawling your site.

The sitemap protocol was originally introduced by Google in June 2005 to allow web developers to publish lists of URLs for search engines to crawl. Google, MSN and Yahoo! announced joint support for the new protocol in November 2006.

Submitting a sitemap won't do anything to up your pages' rankings, but it will provide additional information that helps search engines to crawl your site more effectively. It's one more thing you can do to improve the odds, so ask your webmaster, web developer or SEO to include a sitemap for your site, and to either manually submit it to the major search engines, or to add an entry in your robots.txt file (a file that sits in the root directory of your webserver that contains instructions for automated crawlers) that lets them pick it up automatically.

And start all over again...

Now you have your site optimized, it's time to sit back and start reaping the rewards, right?

Unfortunately not!

The ever-changing nature of the search environment means that there's no magic bullet in SEO. It's not a one-size-fits-all discipline, and it never ends. You have to work hard to find the right blend of targeted keywords for your particular business, operating within your particular market at the current point in time. You have to optimize your pages based on those keywords, and deliver compelling, high-impact content. You have to attract incoming links.

Then you have to measure, monitor and refine continuously, tweaking and tuning your optimization efforts based on changing conditions in the marketplace, the search engines and your customers. Take your foot off the gas, and that high ranking you've worked so hard to achieve will gradually (and sometimes not so gradually) start to slip away.

Optimization is a dynamic and iterative process – and if you want sustained results it needs to be ongoing. In this section we've barely scratched the surface of the wonderfully dynamic, often frustrating but potentially incredibly rewarding world of search engine optimization.

To learn more, check out some of the free and subscription-based SEO resources online like SEOMoz (**http://bit.ly/UDMSEOMoz**), SEO Book (**http://bit.ly/UDMSEOBook**) and many more… or just 'Google' it. After all, it's reasonable for you to expect the best people to advise you on your SEO to be up there near the top of the SERPs.

Top 10 organic SEO myths

Jill Whalen

SEO myths get crazier every year. Some are based partially in reality, and others have spread because it's often difficult to prove what particular SEO action caused a resulting search engine reaction.

For example, you might make a change to something on a page of your site, and a few days later notice that your ranking in Google for a particular keyword phrase has changed. You might naturally assume that your page change is what caused the ranking change. But that's not necessarily so. There are numerous reasons why your ranking may have changed, and in many cases they actually have nothing to do with anything that you did.

Mixing up cause and effect is one of the most common things new SEOs do. If it were affecting only their own work, it wouldn't be so bad, but unfortunately, the clueless often spread their misinformation to other unsuspecting newbies on forums and blogs, which in turn creates new myths. It's always interesting to see how people are so willing to believe anything they have read or heard without ever checking it out for themselves.

Here are 10 of the most common organic SEO myths:

- **Myth 1**: You should submit your URLs to search engines. This may have helped once upon a time, but it's been at least five or six years since that's been necessary.

- **Myth 2**: You need a Google Sitemap. If your site was built correctly, ie it's crawler friendly, you certainly don't need a Google Sitemap. It won't hurt you to have one, and you may be interested in Google's other Webmaster Control Tools, but having a Google Sitemap isn't going to get you ranked better.

- **Myth 3**: You need to update your site frequently. Frequent updates to your pages may increase the search engine crawl rate, but it won't increase your rankings. If your site doesn't need to change, don't change it just because you think the search engines will like it better. They won't. In fact, some of the highest-ranking sites in Google haven't been touched in years.

- **Myth 4**: PPC ads will help/hurt rankings. This one is funny to me because about half the people who think that running Google AdWords will affect their organic rankings believe that they will bring them down; the other half believe they will bring them up. That alone should tell you that neither is true!

- **Myth 5**: Your site will be banned if you ignore Google's guidelines. There's nothing in Google's webmaster guidelines that isn't common sense. You can read them if you'd like, but it's not mandatory in order to be an SEO. Just don't do anything strictly for search engines that you wouldn't do anyway, and you'll be fine. That said, the Google guidelines are much better than they used to be, and may even provide you with a few good tidbits of advice.

- **Myth 6**: Your site will be banned if you buy links. This one does have some roots in reality, as Google (specifically Matt Cutts) likes to scare people about this. They rightly don't want to count paid links as votes for a page if they can figure out that they are paid, but they often can't. Even if they do figure it out, they simply won't count them. It would be foolish of them to ban entire sites because they buy advertising on other sites.

- **Myth 7**: H1 (or any header tags) must be used for high rankings. There's very little (if any) evidence to suggest that keywords in H tags actually affect rankings, yet this myth continues to proliferate. My own tests don't seem to show them making a difference, although it's difficult to know for sure. Use H tags if it works with your design or content management system, and don't if it doesn't. It's doubtful you'll find it makes a difference one way or the other.

- **Myth 8**: Words in your meta-keyword tag have to be used on the page. I used to spread this silly myth myself many years ago. The truth is that the meta-keyword tag was actually designed to be used for keywords that were *not* already on the page, not the opposite! Since this tag is ignored by Google and used only for uncommon words in Yahoo!, it makes little difference at this point anyway.

- **Myth 9**: SEO copy must be 250 words in length. This one is interesting to me because I am actually the one who made up the 250 number back in the late 1990s. However, I never said that 250 was the exact number of words you should use, nor did I say it was an optimal number. It's simply a good amount to be able to write a nice page of marketing copy that can be optimized for three to five keyword phrases. Shorter copy ranks just as well, as does longer copy. Use as many or as few words as you need to use to say what you need to say.

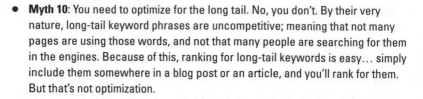

- **Myth 10**: You need to optimize for the long tail. No, you don't. By their very nature, long-tail keyword phrases are uncompetitive; meaning that not many pages are using those words, and not that many people are searching for them in the engines. Because of this, ranking for long-tail keywords is easy… simply include them somewhere in a blog post or an article, and you'll rank for them. But that's not optimization.

Before you go spreading these myths or any other SEO info that you believe is true, test it many times on many sites. Even if it appears to work, keep in mind that it may not always work, or that there could be other factors involved.

Jill Whalen, CEO and founder of High Rankings, a search marketing firm outside Boston, and co-founder of SEMNE, a New England search marketing networking organization, has been performing SEO since 1995. Jill is the host of the High Rankings Advisor *search engine marketing newsletter. This article first appeared in her '100% Organic' column for Search Engine Land.*

Advertising on the search engines

Paid search marketing, pay-per-click (PPC) advertising or search engine marketing (SEM) as it's also known, has in a very short space of time transformed search from what was essentially seen as a 'loss leader' activity into what's probably the digital world's biggest cash cow. PPC advertising is the principal way in which the search engines generate revenue… lots of revenue. According to figures released by the Interactive Advertising Bureau (IAB), PPC revenue for the United States came in at a shade over US$12 billion for 2010, a figure that accounted for 46 per cent of total online advertising spend.

What is pay-per-click (PPC) search engine advertising?

Paid search marketing refers to the paid-for advertising that usually appears alongside, above and occasionally below the organic listings on the SERPs. These are usually labelled with something like 'sponsored links' or 'sponsored results' to make it clear to users that they are, in fact, paid-for ads and not part of the search engine's organic listing.

It's no surprise that the biggest players in the pay-per-click arena are the leading search engines: Google AdWords and Microsoft Search Advertising (which also serves ads on the Yahoo! network). You'll also find a number of smaller PPC search programs out there targeting niche areas or serving particular verticals. Explore your options, because depending on your business they may offer better opportunities to reach local, industry-specific or specialized niche markets than the larger players. By and large, though, when we're talking about paid search advertising the 'big two' are where the action is for most online businesses.

How does paid search advertising work?

When a user enters a search string into the search engine, the engine returns a list of organic search results. It also shows ads relevant to the search query adjacent to the organic listings. These adds tend to be small, unobtrusive text-based ads (remember the search engines' prime directive: to serve the users with topical, relevant results).

While high ranking in the organic listing is the ideal that most webmasters are striving for (because it's 'free', and because users see organic results as impartial: they trust, and therefore click on, organic listings in preference to paid ads), optimizing a page to rank in organic search results can be difficult, and getting a consistently high and sustainable ranking takes a substantial amount of effort and a lot of time.

Time without traffic, of course, is a missed opportunity for your online business, and that's where paid search advertising comes in. By agreeing to pay the search engines a fee per click for your ads to show up as a sponsored result when a user types in your chosen keywords, you can put your site in front of your prospect in the SERPs almost immediately. When the user clicks on one of your ads, you get a new visitor, the search engine bills you for the click, and everybody's happy; at least in theory.

PPC keywords are bid on by advertisers in an auction-style system: generally the higher the bid per click, the higher the ad's placement in the SERPs. Most PPC systems also employ a 'quality' quotient into their ad placement rankings, based on the popularity of the ad (its click-through rate or CTR) and the perceived quality of both the ad content and the landing page it points to (eg Google's AdWords Quality Score).

Why use paid search marketing?

There are a lot of reasons to use PPC search marketing. Here are just a few.

It generates traffic while you're waiting for your SEO to kick in. It can take months to get your site to the top half of the first page of organic search results through SEO. PPC ads can get your site in front of your audience almost immediately.

Highly targeted ads mean a better chance of conversion. You're not broadcasting your message to the masses as you would be with a display ad or banner ad – your search marketing ad will only appear in front of users who have pre-qualified themselves by typing your chosen keywords into the search engine in the geographical regions you've selected. It can be an incredibly effective way to advertise. You only pay for your ad when a pre-qualified user clicks on it and is taken to your site. If they don't click, you don't pay. Providing your keywords are highly targeted and your landing pages convert well, it can generate a very healthy ROI. Some of the specific benefits of PPC advertising are:

- **Full financial control:** there's no minimum spend, you can set maximum monthly budgets on an account-wide basis or on individual campaigns, and you specify the maximum amount per click you're prepared to pay for each ad.
- **Full editorial control:** you're in complete control of every aspect of your campaign – from the title and ad copy to the keywords and keyword matching option to apply, to the URL of the page you want users sent to.
- **Testing, tracking and tweaking on the fly:** there are tools that allow you to run real-time comparison tests to see how differences in your ads affect your click-through rate, and a host of reporting options that let you track your campaign and tweak it to achieve better results.
- **Improve your reach:** target different keywords from those you rank for in the organic search, and broaden your reach for those more specific long-tail keywords that yield small-volume high-value traffic.
- **Transcend the boundaries of the SERPs:** for even broader reach you get to select whether you want your ads to appear only on the search engines' own sites, on their advertising affiliate sites, or even on specific affiliate sites of your choosing.

Sounds great; how do I get started?

Unsurprisingly the search engines have made setting up PPC campaigns really easy. There are automated wizards to guide you through the sign-up process, and plenty of tools to help you establish, monitor and optimize your campaign. It's all very slick, and from a standing start you can have your first ad appearing next to search results and driving traffic to your site in under 15 minutes.

But hold your horses... just because you can, doesn't necessarily mean that you should.

Rushing headlong into your first PPC advertising campaign might yield great results for you 'out of the box', and then again it might not. As always, it pays to do a bit of preparation first:

- **Choose your keywords wisely:** look for longer keyword phrases that are likely to be less competitive and send highly targeted traffic to your site. Ideally you should aim for phrases that generate a healthy amount of search engine traffic, without attracting a lot of bids from other advertisers.
- **Optimize your ads:** your ads need to entice users to click on them if you're going to get traffic. Think carefully about your title and ad

copy. Remember you want targeted copy that will appeal to people who are *ready to buy* – so be specific. Generating clicks that don't convert here *will cost you money*!

- **Converting clicks into customers**: once you get the clicks, you need to turn your new prospects into paying customers as often as you can. It's your *conversion rate* that will make or break your PPC campaign. Don't direct traffic from your ad back to your home page. Send it instead to a page directly related to the text of the ad they've just clicked on – a product page might work, but better still would be a specific *landing page* tailored to reinforce your PPC campaign. Remember, if you fail to convert your traffic into revenue, all your PPC campaign will do is haemorrhage cash.

- **Measure everything and test, test, test**: the best way to learn is to start small, track your campaign carefully and study the metrics (see Chapter 5). Try out different ad combinations, different landing pages, different keyword combinations and measure how the changes affect your CTR, your conversion rate, your cost per conversion and, ultimately, your bottom line.

Mastering the intricacies of PPC advertising could take a lifetime, but the basics are straightforward enough, and the best way to learn is to dive in and start using it. You'll also find plenty of resources to help you, both in the search engines' advertising sections and in the online marketing community. A great place to start is the free online webinars in the Google AdWords Online Classroom (**www.google.com/adwords/onlineclassroom**).

What are the downsides?

There are surprisingly few if you manage your campaign carefully and stay on top of your spending and conversion rates. The biggest one is that as bigger businesses continue to wake up to the potential of search marketing and funnel more of their advertising spend online, the cost per click of more competitive keyword phrases is being pushed ever upwards. Highly competitive keywords can soon get prohibitively expensive for smaller advertisers, but by getting clever with your use of long-tail keywords there are still plenty of opportunities to reap real rewards from PPC advertising.

The key thing to remember is that you have to pay for every click whether or not you convert – so it's important to keep track of the metrics and make sure you're getting value from your investment.

Black hat, the darker side of search

The SEO methods explored earlier in this chapter are methods that adhere to the search engines' own guidelines (or at least they did at the time of writing – but guidelines can change, so it's important to keep up to date – check the links to the webmaster resources earlier in this chapter for the latest information). Generally referred to as 'White Hat' SEO, these techniques are seen as legitimate optimization of a site to align it with the needs of the site visitor and simultaneously make the site content accessible and easy to index by the search engines.

But there is another side to SEO – an altogether darker and more sinister side, where less-ethical practitioners attempt to exploit every trick and loophole they can find to 'game' the engines, increasing their rankings and drive traffic to their sites. Dubbed 'Black Hat' SEO, search engine spamming or spamdexing (spamming the indexes), when discovered, offending sites are quickly banned from the search engine index.

But the Black Hat SEO isn't worried by bans or penalties. For a Black Hat, banishment from the search engines comes with the territory. They're not interested in building quality sites with sustainable high rankings – they're looking for short-term gains from high traffic to ad-laden sites. By the time one batch of sites has been banned they've already moved on to the next. Black Hatters typically have many sites running on many different domains across a variety of hosts, all exploiting loopholes in the system to artificially boost their rankings and generate advertising revenue.

Why should I care what colour hat these guys wear?

On one level, you shouldn't need to. The battle that's raging over artificially inflated rankings in the SERPs is between the Black Hatters and the search engines. It's up to the Yahoo!s, Googles and Microsofts of this world to wage that war.

Wherever there is a system in place you'll find people – often some of the most innovative and resourceful people out there – attempting to exploit that system for their own gain. You'll also have some equally resourceful people on the other side trying to stop them. It's human nature, and it's not going away any time soon.

Essentially, Black Hatters are simply taking the principles of SEO we discussed earlier in this chapter – creating a list of keywords, building pages, getting links – and pushing the boundaries to the extreme. Instead of a manageable selection of keywords for which they can create unique and engaging content, Black Hatters typically create lists of hundreds or thousands of keywords and stuff their pages full of keyword-rich bunkum created by automated content generation tools. Instead of building links naturally, they'll use automated 'bots' to spam posts stuffed with links into blog comments, guestbooks, forums and wikis all over the web.

Black Hats typically aren't interested in you or your site – unless it's as a possible repository for link spam in your blog, guestbook, forum or wiki (and that can generally be avoided by implementing security features on your site that require human intervention to post). What's perhaps more significant is that by pushing their spammy sites up the SERPs they're artificially pushing down more legitimate sites like yours, making them less visible to searchers and potentially affecting your traffic and revenue.

Some common Black Hat SEO techniques

- **Keyword stuffing**: repeating keywords over and over again on a given web page. This is less successful now as search engine algorithms are better at distinguishing this gobbledegook from properly written content.

- **Cloaking**: cloaking is a technique that uses code to show one search engine-friendly page to the spider, and a completely different page to a human visitor. The engines hate this as it makes it impossible for them to gauge the quality of the content a user is seeing. In early 2006 Google blacklisted car manufacturer BMW's German website **www.bmw.de**, dropping it from its index for employing a cloaking page.

- **Invisible text**: invisible text is essentially text that is the same colour as the background of the page – result, humans can't see it, search engines can. This is like keyword stuffing – but with the cloaking element of showing the search engine bot and human visitor different content.

- **Doorway page**: these are highly optimized web pages whose sole purpose is to send traffic to other pages either through an automatic redirect or by simply being full of links.

- **Spam page**: a page with no meaningful content that is full of ads that the webmaster makes money from if someone clicks on them.

- **Interlinking**: the practice of setting up multiple websites on a given topic and linking backwards and forwards between them purely in an attempt to increase their rankings in the search engines.

- **Buying and selling links to help boost search ranking**: buying and selling links purely to manipulate your search engine ranking is frowned upon by the search engines. In early 2011 leading US retailer Jcpenney hit the headlines when it was seriously penalized by Google after the *New York Times* revealed an extensive link-buying programme implemented by the company's outsourced SEO agency.

- **Buying expired domains**: buying up expired domains that contain high-ranking pages to try and garner some of the old site's inbound 'link juice'.

That's just a small selection of the techniques Black Hat SEOs use to boost their rankings and drive traffic. There are many more. As a rule of thumb for your own site, if what you're doing *adds genuine value to the end user*, you generally have nothing to worry about. If, on the other hand, you're implementing something to artificially manipulate your search engine rankings, you could be venturing into Grey or even Black Hat territory. If you value your domain's long-term reputation, be very careful.

When you come across these sites while browsing the web they can be irritating, and having to deal with spam in any medium is infuriating, but for the most part your business doesn't need to worry too much about the Black Hats who are doing their own thing to their own websites.

But there is another, more sinister aspect....

Negative SEO

Far more worrying, potentially at least, is the concept of negative SEO. Some Black Hat SEOs have started peddling commercial services not to increase their client's rankings in the SERPs but to damage the ranking of their competitors – or even to get them banned altogether.

Dubbed 'negative SEO', it is still uncommon, but is certainly something that webmasters and online marketers need to be aware of. Google maintains that there's 'almost nothing a competitor can do to harm your ranking or have your site removed from our index'. But it's that 'almost' that has people worried.

In June 2007 *Forbes* magazine brought the subject of negative SEO out of the shadows of the search community and presented it to a mainstream audience. In the *Forbes* article two SEOs admitted to journalist Andy Greenberg that they use negative SEO, and revealed some of its implications.

'I understand the rules of search,' SEO Brendon Scott said in the article. 'And once you understand the rules, you can use them not just constructively, but also destructively.' He went on to claim that he could reduce a competing site's visibility to searchers, or even make it seem to disappear from search results altogether.

Negative SEO was spawned, ironically, from the efforts of Google, Yahoo! and other search engines to filter out the spam generated by Black Hat SEO and keep their search results relevant to their users. As part of the battle against spam, the search engine algorithms identify 'spammy' tactics and penalize the offending site's rankings accordingly. If there are enough, or severe enough, transgressions to the search engine's guidelines, the site could be thrown out of the index altogether.

Some of the negative SEO tactics that could have a negative impact on a site's rankings include, but are far from limited to, the following:

- **DOS and 404 errors:** the attacker initiates a denial of service attack (DOS) to swamp the target domain. Once the target domain is down, the attacker then employs numerous methods to encourage search engine spiders to visit the site. If the spiders arrive and receive a 404 (not found) error those pages will typically be de-indexed. Once the server recovers, the website is up and running, but is no longer appearing in the search results.

- **Redirection:** the attacker redirects to the targeted pages from 'bad neighbourhood' sites like porn sites, link farms, etc. The targeted pages can end up being removed from the search engine index through association with spammy domains.

- **Link bomb**: the attacker links to the targeted pages from blatant link farms or Free For All link sites, using anchor text with irrelevant or spam-like keywords. They then submit those link-farm pages manually to the search engines, and get as many spammy sites as possible to link in to it. Search engines flag the target site as spam and remove it from their index.

- **Duplicate content**: the attacker copies content from targeted pages and duplicates that content on disposable 'bad neighbourhood' domains, embedding spammy keywords like 'porn', 'pills', 'casinos', invisible text and other spam flags; this *may* result in both sets of pages being removed from the index.

- **Black social bookmarking**: the attacker sets up multiple accounts with social bookmarking sites, and tags targeted sites excessively with irrelevant and spammy terms like 'porn', 'gambling', 'pharmaceutical', etc. As a result, the target site may be penalized heavily or even removed from the search engines' indexes once the social bookmark pages have been spidered.

Source: Fantomaster, **www.fantomaster.com**

We in no way condone any of these tactics, and list them here merely to illustrate the potential real-world threat of negative SEO for digital marketers.

Negative SEO is potentially a very real threat – but for most websites not a very probable one. It pays to be aware of the possibility, and if you're concerned that your competitors might employ such tactics it at least gives you a heads-up on the sort of things that you should be looking out for.

If you truly believe that your website is under attack through negative SEO, your best bet is to hire a specialist consultant to help you combat the threat in the short term. They will typically help you to identify the nature of the attack, where it's coming from, and to implement a security plan that will help shield your site against future attacks.

Bringing in the pros

While SEO and PPC campaigns can certainly be managed in house, if you lack specialist search talent and want to fast-track traffic to your site, then bringing in a professional search marketing consultant can pay real dividends.

If you decide to bring in an external consultancy to help with your search marketing, do your homework and choose wisely. There are many excellent SEOs out there who will do a great job of promoting your business online, but equally there are unscrupulous companies looking to exploit the uninitiated. Not all SEO companies are created equal, and it's an unfortunate fact that some of them will stray into less than ethical territory to secure high rankings quickly... making them and their services look good in the short term.

The good news is that, having read this chapter you're now armed with the knowledge you need to engage positively with your prospective search marketing partner, understand what they're telling you and discuss your SEO requirements with them in some detail.

Here are a few things to bear in mind when you engage with an SEO professional:

- Make sure you're dealing with a reputable company that has a strong track record to back up its claims.

- Ask to see case studies and get references from previous clients.

- Check their own site – has it been optimized, does it adhere to search engine guidelines?

- Look and listen for any hint of the Black Hat techniques listed above. If there's any doubt about the ethics and integrity of the company, walk away. It's your domain they'll be playing with, and it's not worth risking your reputation with the engines.

- Once you've engaged an SEO company, don't just leave them to it. You need to keep abreast of what your SEO company is doing on your behalf – after all, it's your site.

Universal search – more opportunities to rank

Universal search is a term coined by Google to describe a fundamental change in the way it presents its web search results. The company introduced universal search in mid 2007 for Google.com users, and continued rolling it out to other Google domains (.co.uk, .ca, .ie, etc) through 2008. Billed by commentators as one of the most significant and radical developments in the history of the search industry, universal search (or blended search, as it's also known) takes results from Google's specialized (or vertical) search engines (Google News, Google Books, Google Local/Maps, Google Video, Google Image, Google Groups, etc), and slots them into standard web search results in order of relevance.

Google's Vice President of Search Products & User Experience, Marissa Mayer, explained it succinctly in a post on the official Google blog (**http://googleblog.blogspot.com**) in May 2007: 'With universal search, we're attempting to break down the walls that traditionally separated our various search properties and integrate the vast amounts of information available into one simple set of search results.'

As you would expect, other major search engines weren't far behind, and both Yahoo! and Microsoft's Live Search introduced similar blended search results soon after Google. For users this development is a huge boon. Instead of having to manage and navigate multiple specialized search tools users can now enter their search query in one convenient location to find results across multiple platforms.

But what does all this mean for search marketers?

Essentially, there are two ways of looking at it. On one level it's a potential threat, in that for any given keyword phrase your pages now have to compete with results for news, video, maps, discussion groups, images and a host of other sources to get those coveted top SERP rankings. On the other hand, if you produce the right sort of content and submit it to the relevant places, universal search offers additional opportunities to rank for your chosen keyword phrases.

Universal search doesn't change any of the SEO advice we provided earlier in the chapter – but it is something to be aware of as you optimize your pages, and offers additional avenues for you to get your content in front of your target audience. As the title of Marissa Myer's blog post says, even with the roll-out of universal search, 'the best answer is still the best answer'.

FIGURE 4.2 Universal search results page on Google.com for the search term 'Darth Vader'

Shifting goalposts: search innovation and the quest for relevance

Search engines by their very nature are always innovating in their quest to deliver that optimum search experience to each and every user who types in a query. The pace of search innovation can be frustrating for search market-ers, as it keeps 'shifting the goalposts'. Just when you think you've got this search thing 'sussed', along come the leading search engines with a develop-ment that changes things again.

Here's the thing... the search engines don't care a hoot about upsetting your finely honed SEO campaign. Remember the prime directive we dis-cussed right at the start of this chapter? Search engines are striving to deliver the most relevant, valuable content to their users, improving their user ex-perience and retaining or increasing their market share.

To that end the leading search engines constantly 'tweak' their ranking algorithms, refining the way they assess relevance and authority based on content, links and other factors. This constant tinkering with the nuts and bolts of how search engines assess relevance has always been a challenge for search marketers, but more recent developments, aimed at delivering tailored search results to each individual user, have caused quite a stir in SEO circles.

Personalization: search results tailored to individual users

Back in 2007, Google started to roll out the personalization of search results for users who were signed in with a Google account. (The feature was avail-able even earlier to users opting in through the 'Google Labs' interface in their account settings.) What it meant was that Google would start taking the search history of users into account when assessing the relevance of search results.

Let's say, for example, that you searched for 'mustang' while signed in to your Google account, and you had recently been clicking on results for car-related stuff. The search engine might reasonably assume you want infor-mation relating to the Ford Mustang car rather than, say, the Wikipedia page for the mustang horse.

Then, in late 2009, Google really shook things up by extending similar search personalization to all users, whether they had a Google account or not (again users could opt out, but by default the feature was turned on). The move sent the SEO world into turmoil, and instantly rendered the coveted SEO goal of 'being number one in Google' for any given keyword phrase pretty much meaningless. Now my number-one search result could be different from your number-one search result, which could be different from everybody else's number-one search result.

Ultimately search personalization served to move the focus of SEO away from a race to the once-coveted positions at the top of the SERPs, and shifted it back to where it really should have been all along: delivering great content that adds real value for users, and making sure search engines are aware of that, and monitoring and measuring success based not on your position in the SERPs but on the actual number of targeted visitors referred to your site by the search engines.

That, after all, is what sustainable SEO is really all about: harnessing the power of search engines to help you deliver outstanding, relevant content to your target market.

Search gets social – integrating updates from online connections into search results

In late 2009 Microsoft fired the first salvo in the battle to make search more social by announcing deals with both Twitter and Facebook to include real-time status updates in its Bing search results. Google followed suit by announcing a similar deal with Twitter for its own real-time search, and by introducing a feature it called 'Social Search' into its main web-search offering.

When a web user is signed in to their Google account and conducts a web search, Google now incorporates publicly available content created or recommended by a user's online friends and connections across Google's range of products and other publicly available web services.

That means that along with regular web results, users who are signed in will see relevant content that their online 'friends' have shared publicly on YouTube, Picasa, Flickr, Twitter, on their blog, in their Google Reader and in lots of other places online.

The rationale, of course, is that old search engine mantra of relevance. The web is becoming increasingly social, and people are more willing than ever to share information, opinions and experiences. We also trust the recommendations of people we 'know' online, and by incorporating content from our extended online network into search results, search engines are betting we'll find those results more relevant, useful and personal.

What does social integration into search mean for search marketers?

On the surface, having recommendations from a search user's online social connections appear in the standard web SERPs may seem like bad news from a search marketer's perspective. It means that there's yet more content competing for those limited spaces on the first page of the SERPs for any given search term. Then again, if you're creating compelling, useful and – that word again – *relevant* content for your target audience, the stuff that's being recommended in those social search results could easily be yours.

Social search emphasizes the need to get out and engage with your customers in the social arena, to create useful, compelling content that's worth sharing, and to build enduring relationships with the people you want to do business with. The integration of a social element into search results is growing in importance, and while there are privacy concerns and other stumbling blocks that need to be overcome, ultimately the search engines' obsessive quest for relevance is turning search into a very personal experience.

CASE STUDY   Theatre breaks make search breakthrough

FIGURE 4.3 Show and Stay broadened the scope of its PPC marketing and simultaneously narrowed its focus to more specific keyword terms. The result: more effective geographical targeting, boosted conversion rates and increased ROI

The challenge

Show and Stay is part of the award-winning Holiday Extras Group, offering theatre tickets and theatre breaks for London's leading West End shows. It serves customers mainly in the UK and Europe. It needed to improve the performance of its PPC advertising campaigns, and turned to search marketing agency Go Optimization for help.

Target audience

Data shows that the target market for theatre breaks is predominantly female higher-earners, mostly over the age of 25. The majority of theatre breaks are booked for couples, but the campaign would also target larger group bookings.

Action

To achieve the objectives laid out in the brief, search marketing agency Go Optimization set about understanding how customers in the leisure market research their choices, compare prices, shop around and ultimately make their purchase. Taking Show and Stay's existing AdWords campaigns as a baseline, they employed attribution reporting and conversion funnel analysis to get the insight they needed.

Using Google's conversion funnel reporting, they analysed data on existing campaigns, and discovered that on average conversions occurred five days after customers were exposed to the first ad impression, and 16 per cent of users converted 12 days or more after seeing the first ad. The agency removed day-parting from the campaigns to ensure returning visitors were always served Show and Stay ads.

The previous agency was using a bid management tool that focused only on keywords that had converted before (such as brand terms and short-tail terms like 'theatre breaks', 'london shows', 'london theatre'). They failed to incorporate new keywords based on research of long-tail terms into the campaign mix. Go Optimization restructured the campaigns to include both keywords that had attributed to conversions, and long-tail keywords that customers were using to research their purchases (like 'london theatre breaks', 'theatre breaks by rail', 'billy elliot london theatre breaks'). The agency also examined historical data to increase keyword depth by 53 per cent.

Ads were geo-targeted for 10 of the highest-purchasing cities in the UK, and the agency created a London-only campaign to capitalize on ticket sales, as people living in the capital would be unlikely to book a break including accommodation.

Landing page and ad copy were tested using in-depth split tests to ensure that the best-performing variable was being served to customers.

Results

The campaign exceeded the following goals and is ongoing:

- Reduce cost per conversion by more than 15 per cent.

- Increase awareness of the Show and Stay brand.

- Increase brochure requests by more than 50 per cent.

- Increase e-mail newsletter sign-ups by more than 50 per cent.

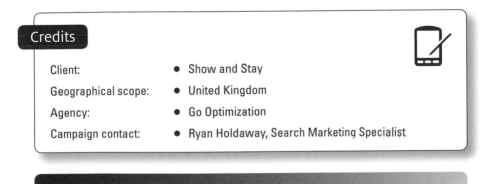

Credits

Client:	● Show and Stay
Geographical scope:	● United Kingdom
Agency:	● Go Optimization
Campaign contact:	● Ryan Holdaway, Search Marketing Specialist

05 Website intelligence and return on investment

> *Half of the money I spend on advertising is wasted; the trouble is, I don't know which half.*
> **WILLIAM HESKETH LEVER (1821–1925), THE FIRST LORD LEVERHULME (A SIMILAR QUOTE EXPRESSING IDENTICAL SENTIMENT HAS ALSO BEEN ATTRIBUTED TO JOHN WANAMAKER, THE US DEPARTMENT STORE ENTREPRENEUR AND ADVERTISING PIONEER)**

> *What we call results are beginnings.* **RALPH WALDO EMERSON**

> *I notice increasing reluctance on the part of marketing executives to use judgement; they are coming to rely too much on research, and they use it as a drunkard uses a lamp post: for support, rather than for illumination.* **DAVID OGILVY**

OUR CHAPTER PLEDGE TO YOU

When you reach the end of this chapter you'll have answers to the following questions:

- How will I know where to invest my digital marketing budget for maximum ROI?
- What information can I track on my website, how is it collected and how can I use it to inform my digital marketing investment?
- How can I track my online advertising that appears on other sites?
- What are key performance indicators (KPIs), and how can I use them to gain insight into my online marketing?
- Why is testing important, and what types of testing should I be doing?

Measuring your way to digital marketing success

So, you have your search engine-optimized website up and running. You may even have set up pay-per-click/search advertising accounts with a few providers, and tried out a few ads, just to see what happens. Now what?

Well, that depends...

I know we keep saying this, but it really does depend. It depends on your business goals, your target market, the digital marketing strategy you've defined and the budget you have available. Digital marketing isn't a prescriptive medium. There are far too many variables involved. What works for you won't necessarily work for me, and what works for me probably won't work for A N Other Inc, even though we may all be operating superficially similar businesses catering to superficially similar consumers.

The long and the short of it is that nobody can tell you categorically what will or won't work for you online, not without an intimate knowledge of your business. You (and/or the specialist you bring in to help you) have to find out for yourself what works and what doesn't in your particular circumstances. That involves a bit more work than simply applying a prescriptive formula... but it's worth the effort, because defining your own customized digital marketing equation will give you much more insight into where the real online opportunities lie for your business, and will help you to differentiate yourself from your competition.

The great news is that, in the world of digital marketing, there are all sorts of tools available to show you *exactly* what's working for you, and, just as important, what's not. The most successful marketing has always been about learning from your results: taking a finite budget and using it to do more of the stuff that is working and less of the stuff that's not. You test, you refine, you reinvest, and you test again.

Traditional marketing media threw up two major obstacles to this approach: buying advertising space to 'test' different advertising tactics was often prohibitively expensive, and measuring the results in any meaningful way was notoriously difficult. You were never quite sure which elements of your marketing mix were actually delivering the results. The internet has changed all that. With the migration towards performance-based advertising – pay-per-click and pay-per-acquisition models – you only pay for traffic, or (even better) actual conversions gained through a particular advertising channel. That makes it easy and relatively cheap for you to test different ad combinations to see what works best for you, without your costs spiralling out of control. And because you can track and measure *everything* that's channelled back through your website you can build an accurate picture of how your prospects respond to these ads at a level of granularity that's simply unheard of in traditional advertising media.

Now, for the first time ever, you can capture the results of your advertising in practically real time, and adapt your digital campaigns on the fly to maximize return on your digital marketing investment. It's a level of control that's unprecedented in the history of advertising – and with that control comes a level of accountability for results that to date has been sorely lacking.

The rise of performance-based advertising

Brandt Dainow

The web is constantly evolving, as we all know. It's a changing environment because people are in the process of migrating from traditional media to online. This migration will not be total – people will still read books and watch TV, but the emphasis is changing. Print and broadcast media are becoming alternatives to the new mainstream – online. We are passing significant markers in this migration right now.

More money has been spent in online advertising than TV since 2009. As of 2010, people under the age of 45 spend more time online than watching TV. I recently spoke to a friend whose son was starting university. He visited the student halls of residence and was surprised to see that none of the students had stereos (an essential of student life in his day) or TVs in their rooms. When he asked about this the students laughed at him – why would they need those when they had computers and internet connections? To this younger generation the idea of a device which could only handle a single medium, and wasn't connected to the web, was laughably archaic. We are evolving new ways of participating in society, new ways of communicating, and new ways of disseminating information.

A key dynamic in this process is the transition of the print and broadcast advertising community onto the web. As this occurs new models of advertising become possible.

Henry Ford once said 'I know only half of my advertising works. The problem is, I don't know which half.'

The web solves this problem. The ability to record people's behaviour online means advertising can be assessed in terms of the behaviour which people exhibit after being exposed to an ad. It then becomes possible to pay for the behaviour instead of the mere delivery of the ad. This is called performance-based advertising.

The dominating trend in the evolution of online advertising is the rise of performance-based advertising. Online advertising sales in the United States reached $26 billion in 2010, compared to $22 billion for print. Two-thirds of that involved performance-based payment. We have shifted from selling audience to selling behaviour.

The traditional form of advertising involves selling audience. In print and broadcast, advertising rates are largely determined by the number of people who will be exposed to the ad. As traditional media people moved online they took this model with them, selling 'impressions'. Banner advertising is traditionally sold this way.

Impression-based advertising simply consists of placing an ad somewhere on a reader's computer screen, in a manner similar to placing an ad somewhere on the page of a magazine. Performance-based advertising involves changing the emphasis from views to actions. Instead of paying the outlet to deliver my ad, I will pay it for delivering people.

The most common forms of performance-based advertising are PPC advertising and affiliate networks. Google's Adsense is a classic example of performance-based advertising. Advertisers pay not for exposure, but for the people Google sends to the advertiser's site.

Even where performance-based advertising is not the obvious basis upon which the advertising is being sold, it is often the way in which it is assessed. Mark Read is Director of Strategy at WPP UK (wpp.com), one of the world's leading marketing communication organizations. According to Read, many of WPP's clients, especially in finance and automotive, convert the metrics from their ad outlets back into performance metrics.

'It doesn't matter how people sell the ad space, it's bought on a performance basis whether they realize it or not,' says Read.

Read is very much in favour of this shift to performance-based advertising.

'The advantage of performance-based advertising is that it converts ad spend from a line expense to a cost of goods sold. As such the expenditure is potentially infinite... The secret of Google's success was to convert ad spend from line of business to cost of sale,' Read says.

In other words, the potential income from an ad outlet is much greater than is possible with impression-based advertising. Performance-based advertising obviously represents better value for the advertiser, but it can also represent better value for the seller.

Ben Regensburger, President of Doubleclick Germany (doubleclick.com), agrees.

'If you know your audience and your inventory well you can make more money from performance-based ads than simple impressions, especially in finance,' he says.

Christoph Schuh is CMO of Tomorrow Focus AG (tomorrowfocus.de), one of Germany's leading digital content providers. Tomorrow Focus is the largest supplier of German-language content on the web. As a media owner, someone whose income is based on selling advertising, Schuh can see issues with performance-based advertising.

'The danger in buying performance is that it ignores the value of repeated exposure and of time-delayed responses,' he says. 'I think performance buying to a single response dimension will become insufficient; we need to develop behavioural targeting.'

Notice that Schuh is not opposed to performance-based advertising. He simply wants to see performance assessment become more sophisticated.

One of the most common problems encountered when dealing with performance-based advertising is arguments between the advertiser and the publisher over the numbers. Web metrics systems are still fairly primitive, and the web analytics community has yet to establish clear procedures for measurement. As a result advertiser and publisher systems can often disagree about exactly how many people have been delivered.

'Currently ad people don't understand the metrics,' says Schuh. 'This makes resolving disputes extremely difficult.'

Addressing this issue requires training advertising sales people in web analytics so they have a language in which to communicate and so that they understand what it is their web analytics systems are telling them. In addition, resolving discrepancies between the advertiser's and the publisher's numbers usually involves a technical conversation about how the data is processed on both systems.

The field of web analytics lacks standards, and the few standards which do exist are rarely implemented consistently within analytics software. If both systems are measuring the same thing in the same way, the numbers will match to within a few percentage points. Discrepancies occur because the two systems are measuring things differently or using the same terms for different things. The integration and reconciliation of conflicting measurement systems are now the major stumbling block in performance-based ad systems. However, if the respective technicians explain to each other what their systems are measuring, and how, it is usually possible to adjust the numbers to match. This requires that advertising and marketing people have access to their web analytics technicians, and have the training to be able to communicate with them.

Much of this can be avoided if the methodology for performance assessment is agreed before the deal is signed. Once again, this requires that sales staff have sufficient training to participate in such conversations, and that, where necessary, they can call on their technicians for assistance.

For a publisher, performance-based advertising represents both an opportunity and a threat. As Christoph Schuh says: 'You have to understand your website better than your client... you have to understand the behaviour of your readers in the conversion funnel... you need an e-commerce unit within your editorial team.'

Once the editorial focus was purely on producing content which would appeal to a particular demographic. Appeal to enough readers and the advertisers would follow. In the early days of the internet we thought this was all we needed to do. Jim Barksdale, president and CEO of Netscape until the company merged with AOL, said in 1995: 'Don't worry about how to earn money online. Simply get a big enough audience and the money will come to you.'

This was true for a while, but advertisers are wising up. They're not interested in mere numbers; they want behaviour. This presents publishers with a dilemma. Mr Murdoch's attempts notwithstanding, the rest of us know you can't make money selling content to readers – they won't pay for it. The presence of huge quantities of free information on the web has devalued the perceived value of all information in the eyes of the online community. The main way to make money as a content publisher at present is via advertising.

If advertisers become completely focused on performance, editors become confronted with the need to design content in order to get the acquisitions their advertisers want. This presents these editors with a dilemma – do they write to make sales or do they write to gather audience and hope the sales just happen because they got the right audience?

> In the long term the future surely belongs to those who can develop content which attracts an audience and at the same time frame that content in a manner which encourages the behaviour advertisers want.
>
> *Brandt Dainow is CEO of ThinkMetrics, an independent web analytics and marketing consultant operating in the UK and Ireland. He works with client organizations to design, manage and tune their online marketing and sales process. For more details see Brandt's website **www.thinkmetrics.com**.*

Getting started

The ability to track, measure and refine your online marketing campaigns as they unfold is a huge boon, but it can't help to guide your investment decisions *before* you have anything to measure. So where do you start? Should you channel your budget into search engine pay-per-click advertising or would you be better off focusing more on long-term optimization for organic search results, coupled with a sprinkling of display ads on prominent, high-traffic industry websites? What about the explosion in vertical online advertising networks, or perhaps you should choose a more general ad network with broader scope?

Questions, questions, questions... when all you want is answers

While some of these questions may seem baffling, the truth is that you already have the answers you need. Remember all that research you did to define your strategy, create your website and optimize it for the search engines? At this point you know your target market, you know where they congregate online, what they're searching for, and the sort of things they like to find when they get there. You also know what your business is trying to achieve online, and have a strategy for how you're going to go about it.

Take all of that information, apply a little business acumen and that stalwart of marketers everywhere – intuition – and you'll find you have a pretty good idea of where to focus your initial investment in order to reach your objectives. Don't worry about getting things perfect from the beginning; the most important thing is to *get started*. As long as you're aiming in roughly the right direction, get your initial campaign up and running and start collecting some real data. Bias your early investment towards the area(s) you instinctively feel will yield the best return for your business... then measure, refine and reinvest.

Online marketing is an iterative process of continuous improvement. You make a change, you try something new, you test, you refine and you track your results. Invest most of your budget in what you know to be working well at any given time, but never stop experimenting with new and different approaches. You could hit on something that works even better. As you accumulate real data about how your target market is responding to your campaigns you can start making really informed decisions that will have a positive and often dramatic impact on your ROI.

How information is measured

Imagine if you could tell not just how many people were visiting your website (your traffic) but for each individual visitor you could tell where they came from (both on the internet and geographically), what browser and operating system they were using at the time, what keywords they used to find your site and on which search engine, the page they arrived at, how long they stayed for, what pages they visited while they were there, which page they ultimately left from and whether or not they came back again.

That would be really useful information, right? It would let you analyse how your users were finding your site, whether you were giving them what they wanted when they arrived, where they were leaving from, whether your site was optimized for the right search keywords, how effective your different forms of advertising were at driving traffic to your site and what proportion of that traffic was ultimately being converted into sales, leads or whatever other conversion goals you'd defined. In other words, marketing gold dust.

Well, the good news is that with modern website analytics software you can track all of that information and more. Like everything else on the internet, web analytics has gone all '2.0', so you can get all of the data you want, presented to you when you want, and in the way that you want.

Website analytics use information your visitors volunteer

It's important to note here that there's nothing underhanded about tracking and analysing website statistics. All we're doing is looking at the information that's readily volunteered by the user or the user's browser. There's no magic voodoo or (as a rule, at least) underhanded cyber espionage going on here. We're simply collecting the information that's routinely recorded when a visitor comes to our website, then using analytics software to aggregate it and present it in a format that lets us view trends and make informed decisions.

There are two main ways of collecting information about your website visitors. You can analyse the web access logs created by your own web server, or you can embed some code (called a page tag) in every page on your website that sends similar information to your chosen analytics service provider.

Webserver logs

Every time your web server receives a request for a resource (a file) on your website it stores details of that request in its server access logs. What exactly is recorded depends on a variety of factors, including the way the server itself is set up, the format of the log files it produces and the settings of the user's browser.

That said, a server log file will typically contain the following kind of information for every browser request it receives:

- the unique IP address of the computer making the request;
- a timestamp showing the date and time the request was made;
- the URI of the requested resource;
- a status code confirming the result of the request;
- the file size of the returned resource;
- the URL of the page the request came from;
- other information supplied by the 'user agent' (typically browser type/version, language and operating system).

From this information website analytics software can derive a host of useful information. For example, from the IP address it can determine where in the world the user is browsing from; the referring URL can tell it whether the user entered the site directly, was referred from a link on another site or came from a search engine, and if so what search query string they entered to reach your site. The IP address *may* also help track an individual user's path through the site during their visit (although using the IP address to track this can be unreliable and is typically augmented by the use of cookies; see later).

Log file analysis software comes in all shapes, sizes and flavours. Some merely read raw log file data, aggregate it and spit out the results as crude tables for you to trawl through manually. Others format the data to make it more readable and present it in easy-to-comprehend graphs and tables. The most sophisticated let you define your own summary reports, segment your audience, define and track conversion goals and analyse conversion 'funnels' (the navigation steps a user follows to complete a 'conversion' goal), and will integrate data from other sources to give you a complete picture of your website's overall performance.

Most web hosts provide some form of basic log file analysis software as part of their hosting package, so it's worth looking at these first to get a basic idea of the kind of information that's available in your log files. There is a wide range of software options available, ranging from free open-source offerings (like Webalizer, AWStats and Analog), to costly enterprise-level solutions from leading industry players like WebTrends and Omniture, and a host of other options in between.

Page tagging and hosted solutions

The second method is a process known as page tagging. This involves putting a small piece of code on every page of your site that you want to track. Whenever a visitor requests the page, the code sends information (gleaned in much the same way as that recorded in the server log file) and sends it to your chosen provider. This form of tracking has become very much in vogue with the rising popularity of the 'software as a service' (SaaS) concept, and has been fuelled by the introduction of free, powerful and highly configurable analytics services like Statcounter (**www.statcounter.com**) and the very popular Google Analytics (**www.google.com/analytics**).

Once the code is installed on your pages, these services will start collecting data and can provide you with a wealth of easily accessible and highly configurable information. You just have to make sure the tracking code is included on every page on your site that you want to track (including new pages you may add over time) and your service provider will look after the rest. For most sites on the web today the code simply needs to be inserted once into the main template file.

Augmenting information using cookies

Using a user's IP address to uniquely identify visitors is inconsistent and inaccurate for a variety of reasons, no matter which of the tracking methods above you choose to use. For instance, a large number of internet users (AOL users being the primary example) may share a single IP address assigned by their Internet Service Provider (ISP). That means that if your analytics solution relies solely on IP address to identify unique visitors, it will count these multiple users as the same visitor, skewing your data. On the other hand, users with mobile devices (mobiles, laptops and tablets) will be assigned a different IP address whenever they connect to a new WiFi network, so a person returning to your site would be identified as a new visitor rather than a returning one. At home, rebooting the household broadband router will often have a similar effect, causing the ISP to assign a new dynamic IP address to the router... and thus the individual's internet connection.

To get around these limitations, and to remember site settings that help to improve the user experience, many websites and third-party tracking services employ http cookies to identify individual users. Cookies are small files that are sent to the user's browser and stored on their local hard drive.

Typically they store a unique ID that allows the site (or tracking service) to identify a returning visitor, store site preference and personalization settings that enhance the user experience, and help you to track that visitor's navigation around your web site.

Cookies get a bad press because of the potential privacy issues associated with what are called 'persistent third-party' cookies, or cookies that are set by a domain other than the one you're visiting (by content on the page pulled from another domain, like ads, widgets or embedded video, for example), and that persist beyond the scope of your existing browser session. In theory these cookies could be used to track visitor behaviour across multiple websites, building up a picture of user browsing behaviour as they surf the web. That's perceived as a bad thing, because large ad-serving and tracking companies can potentially use cookies to build up profiles of user behaviour across all the websites that they serve without explicit consent from the user.

In practice, while cookies *can* be used to surreptitiously glean user data without explicit consent, they tend to be largely harmless. The plus side of cookies is that they allow websites to deliver a better user experience to their customers (storing preferences, etc), and allow more accurate tracking of website statistics, which in turn allows website owners to optimize content and improve the visitor experience.

The vast majority of internet users' browsers are set to accept cookies by default, but it's important to note that some choose to reject cookies out of hand, others accept them only for the duration of their current browser session and then delete them, while still others choose to accept first-party cookies (cookies originated by the domain they're visiting) but reject third-party cookies (originated by any other domain). All of these factors can affect the accuracy of your statistics – by how much will depend on the profile of your target audience and their acceptance of http cookies.

As a rule of thumb, if you use cookies it's best practice to include an entry in your site's privacy policy explicitly stating what you use cookies for, what information they contain, and who (if anyone) that information is shared with.

The new EU law on cookies

On 25 May 2011 the European Union's (EU) Privacy and Communications Directive on Electronic Privacy came into force. Essentially from that date onwards, any EU-based business (including international businesses with offices in the EU) setting any kind of cookie not deemed 'essential' to the function of a website or provision of an online service to a visitor has to have the user's explicit consent before doing so. Without obtaining that consent, the site is breaking the law and is open to prosecution.

Enforcement of the new law falls within the jurisdiction of individual member states, so there is scope for different interpretations in different countries across the EU. At the time of writing there has been considerable debate surrounding the implications of the new law and its potential impact on website analytics software (including the widely used Google Analytics, and other free and commercial alternatives), but as yet no real consensus has emerged on how to handle the requirement.

In general, experts believe that analytics software, which focuses on compiling anonymous aggregated data from information volunteered by a user's browser, isn't the intended target of this new privacy legislation. The real targets are persistent third-party cookies that track visitor behaviour across and between different websites without appropriate consent. But ambiguous wording in the directive means that it's open to various interpretations, and in its strictest form analytics cookies could certainly fall within its remit – which presents website owners with a bit of a dilemma.

The new EU privacy directive and your web analytics

Brian Clifton

Following new EU laws aimed at protecting the privacy of online users, there has been much said about the death of web tracking as we know it. At present (June 2011) the wording of the law is stating that visitors to your website must explicitly consent to having cookies stored on their computers.

The law has been put in place due to the failure of our industry to self-regulate privacy properly. The EU lawmakers are targeting the surreptitious tracking of individuals that has been going on for many years. That is:

- sharing cookie information collected on one website with another third-party website via third-party cookies;

- identifying anonymous visitors – either by using data from a third-party cookie where personal information was entered, or back-filling previous visit data when a visitor later creates an account or makes a purchase;

- tracking visitors even though they have set their browser privacy settings to block tracking cookies (using Flash Shared Objects).

As pretty much all web analytics tools rely on cookies for visitor tracking there are clearly implications for anyone using modern analytics tools on their site.

The new EU Privacy and Communications Directive on Electronic Privacy: a summary

- The new EU law came into effect on 25 May 2011 and is applicable to all EU member countries.

- It is up to the individual member states to enforce the law in their countries.

- As a website owner, you need to obey the law in the country/countries you operate from. So if you have an office in the UK and France, you need to comply with both UK and French laws – hopefully these will be very similar. Hosting your website in Barbados does not change this...

- The law is applicable to all websites – commercial and non-commercial.

- The reality is that no one (the regulatory bodies for each EU country) is ready and discussion is ongoing – so people are not going to be prosecuted just yet.

- The UK has announced a 12-month grace period to allow site owners to sort themselves out. That means time for you to understand the new privacy law, audit your website for tracking capabilities (such as cookie collection), and adjust your site accordingly. That means changing what information is collected, how it is collected and how the practice is communicated to your visitors.

- The law is there to protect visitor privacy – that means no third-party techniques (sharing information with other organizations) and no collection of personal information such as name, e-mail address, etc *unless* the explicit consent of the individual is given.

Reading the above list, you realize the difficulty for the authorities, such as the UK's ICO, who are trying to word this as a legal or even guideline document.

What you should do as a website owner

Don't panic! Get a full understanding of what information you are collecting. Ensure your privacy statement is up to date and accurate – keep it simple, not full of legal jargon.

If you are using third-party cookies and/or Flash Shared Objects, this law is very much targeting you. If you wish to perform behavioural targeting or collect personal information, then you need to get explicit consent from your visitors.

If, on the other hand, your site audit reveals you are benignly tracking visitors anonymously and in aggregate (as per Google Analytics), then you are going to be fine. (You must complete an audit in order to show this – that is the ICO guidance and I agree. Simply saying, 'We use Google Analytics, so we are fine' is not good enough.)

Essentially you will need visitors to provide explicit consent to continue doing this. This law forces perpetrators of such tracking to either stop doing so or suffer a poor user experience and declining web business by having to use pop-ups to gain visitor consent.

Either way it is a good thing for the web.

The impact on Google Analytics users

Google Analytics uses first-party cookies to anonymously and in aggregate report on visits to your website. This is very much at the opposite end of the spectrum to what this law is targeting. For Google Analytics users complying with the terms of service (and not using the other techniques described above), there is no great issue here – you already respect your visitors' privacy!

I agree that the wording of the ICO document is 'awkward' and gives rise to ambiguity. Essentially, they do not wish to name the technologies this law applies to (third-party cookies, Flash Shared Objects) as these can of course change. It is the method of invasive tracking they are quite rightly trying to stop, so I expect the wording of the document to be refined over time.

The ability to block first-party cookies is built into every web browser (10+ years for IE), so I feel this paragraph applies:

> (3A) For the purposes of paragraph (2), consent may be signified by a subscriber who amends or sets controls on the internet browser which the subscriber uses or by using another application or program to signify consent.

The ICO document requires you (as the website owner) to ask yourself whether tracking the performance of your website is strictly necessary. That's straightforward to answer – yes! – in the same way as tracking the performance of your business is strictly necessary.

The key phrases for Google Analytics users to remember are: 'anonymously', 'in aggregate', and 'via first-party cookies'.

This law is about behavioural targeting and the abuse of private information – and I am happy that it is here. The people who work at the ICO and other authorities are smart people who work in the digital world as much as we do. Benign, anonymous, aggregate reports – such as those provided by Google Analytics – are not the target of this legislation.

Brian Clifton (PhD) is an independent author, consultant and trainer who specializes in performance optimization using Google Analytics. Recognized internationally as a Google Analytics expert, his latest book, the second edition of Advanced Web Metrics with Google Analytics (**www.advanced-web-metrics.com**) *is used by students and professionals worldwide.*

In the UK the Information Commissioner's Office (ICO) is the body responsible for implementing and enforcing the regulation, and has issued guidelines on what UK-based website owners need to do to comply with the directive (**http://bit.ly/UDMCookies**). However, it has also stressed that the document is very much a work in progress, and has announced a year-long 'grace period' to allow website owners to conduct a 'cookie audit' and implement necessary changes before they begin enforcement of the directive.

While the possible disruption that this law is likely to cause has generated a lot of concern and debate among website owners, it is widely accepted that the law is intended to prevent the surreptitious tracking of visitors between websites, behavioural targeting and the unscrupulous collection of personal information without consent. Popular web analytics software is *not* its intended target.

With the advent of the directive, leading browser manufacturers have already updated their software to allow much more control over how cookies are handled – and while there is no definitive answer, authorities have indicated that certain browser settings may well establish the required consent for some cookies in some instances. But the onus remains very much on website owners to make themselves completely aware of what cookies are being set by their site, what information is being collected, and how the law applies in their particular case.

The pros and cons of log files vs page tagging

Advantages of log file analysis:

- Your server will generally already be producing logfiles, so the raw data is already available for analysis. Collecting data using page tags requires changes to the website, and tracking can only begin once the changes have been made.

- Every transaction your web server makes is recorded in the log file. Page tagging relies on settings in the visitor's browser (such as JavaScript being enabled), so a certain (small) proportion of visitors may go undetected.

- The data collected in your log files is *your data*, and it is in a standard format that makes it easy for you to migrate to analytics software from a different vendor, use more than one package to give you a broader view of your data, and analyse historical data using any log file analysis program you choose. Page tagging solutions usually mean you're locked into the relationship with your chosen provider – if you change providers you typically have to start collecting data again from scratch.

- Your log files capture visits by search engine spiders and other automated bots as well as human users. Although it's important that your analytics software can differentiate these from your human visitors, knowing which spiders have crawled your site and when can be important for search engine optimization. Page tagging solutions typically overlook non-human visitors.

- Server logs record information on failed requests, giving you insight into potential problems with your website; page tagging, on the other hand, only records an event when a page is successfully viewed.

Advantages of page tagging:

- The tagging code (typically JavaScript) is automatically run every time the page is loaded, so even viewing a cached page will generate a visit. Because viewing a page from a cache doesn't require communication with the server, log files contain no records of cached page views.

- It is easier for developers to add custom information to page tagging code to be collected by the remote server (eg information about a visitor's screen resolution, or about the goods they purchased). With log file analysis, custom information that's not routinely collected by the web server can only be recorded by appending information to the URL.

- Page tagging can collect data based on events that don't involve sending a request to the web server, such as interactions with Flash, Ajax and other rich media content.

- Cookies are assigned and handled by the page tagging service; with log file analysis your server has to be specially configured to use cookies.

- Page tagging will work even if you can't access your web server logs.

Bear in mind here that you're not restricted to using one type of analytics solution or the other – you're free to use both as necessary, extracting the best information from each to suit your particular needs.

Hybrid analytics solutions: the best of both worlds

A number of analytics solutions on the market, particularly at the enterprise level, have the ability to combine log file analysis and page tagging methods within the same analytics suite. These hybrid systems analyse all of the data, and consolidate the information to present a seamless reporting solution to the analyst. While these may offer the most comprehensive analytics solutions, with each data collection method compensating in part for the inadequacies of the other, it's important to remember that *no analytics solution is 100 per cent accurate*. Most, however, are near enough to the mark to allow you to spot trends and make informed decisions about your online investment.

Other sources of traffic

With log files and page tagging you can track pretty much everything that happens on your website; but what about the ads you place on other sites, your affiliate or ad-network campaigns, e-mail newsletters, or pay-per-click advertising? The good news is that the new generation of analytics software (even the 'free' Google Analytics) allows you to tag incoming links from all of your external advertising campaigns so that you can isolate and track visitors who are directed to your site from those campaigns.

All you have to do is add the appropriate parameters to the end of the linking URL, and the analytics software will do the rest. Some will even generate the tagged URL for you – you just fill in the parameters, then cut and paste the resulting code into your ad. Some tracking solutions, with the help of cookies and page tags, even allow you to recognize visitors who saw your ad on another site, didn't click on it, but some time later decided to visit your website anyway. Powerful stuff.

FIGURE 5.1 Google Analytics – free hosted analytics service using page tags

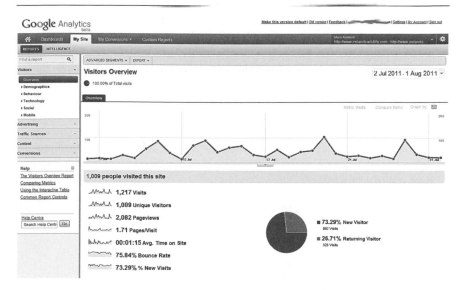

Back in the early days of the web, webmasters would get excited about how many 'hits' their sites were getting. Before long 'hit counters' – small bits of code that displayed the number of hits a site was getting – were rife on pages across the rapidly growing web, with webmasters eager to show off how popular their little corner of cyberspace had become. Their aim, of course, was to raise the profile of their sites and perhaps to attract the brave pioneers of online advertising to buy space on their site (Flashing banner ad, anyone?).

The trouble with hits as units of measuring page popularity was that they were completely unrepresentative of the number of unique visitors to a site. A hit represents a single resource request from a user's browser (or other user agent) to a web server. For a basic web page containing 10 images, the browser initiates one request for the page itself, and 10 separate requests for each of the image files on that page – or a minimum of 11 hits in all – more if there are other design elements being pulled from other files on the web server. Different pages, therefore, generate a different number of hits, depending on their make-up, which means the whole concept of using hits as a comparative measure to gauge page popularity is inherently flawed.

Thankfully, while hits are still recorded in web server log files (and you'll see the individual records if you browse through the raw text of a server log file), modern web analytics software aggregates the data into far more useful metrics. Today you're far more likely to hear about 'page views' or 'page impressions' (which mean pretty much what they say – a complete page delivered to a user's browser) or 'visits'.

With modern software you can automatically collect, collate and compile the information being volunteered by your users' browsers, then use sophisticated graphical interfaces to analyse trends, present the data in a range of different ways, and conduct comparative analysis that can help inform your digital marketing investment. Hits may well be dead as a unit of measuring website success, but take the information revealed by your web analytics solution, use it to understand your online market, and take action based on what you've learned, and your website itself is sure to be a big hit!

Measuring what's important to you

While web analytics allow you to have your finger on the pulse of your website, to monitor the beating heart of your online audience, you can easily get overwhelmed by the sheer volume of information available to you. You want to spend your time focusing on what's important to your business, not wading through reams and reams of information that may offer interesting insight but does little to further your strategic goals.

You need to determine what exactly you need to measure. What metrics are important to your business? What will help you extract maximum value from the visitor information available? If you can't answer those questions, how can you make the strategic decisions that will drive your online business forward?

The concept of key performance indicators (or KPIs) is nothing new, and has been common in the world of business analysis for many years. KPIs are used to distil key trends from complex, often disparate, pools of data, and to present them as a series of clear, unequivocal indices – a snapshot of how your organization (or website, in our case) is performing at any given time. KPIs 'do exactly what it says on the tin': they indicate progress (or lack of it) in areas that are key to your website's performance.

Why KPIs are important

The real value of KPIs is that they let you extract meaning from your website data at a glance. Without them, it's all too easy to drown in the proliferation of data your web analytics solution churns out. It's a classic case of not seeing the wood for the trees.

By defining and measuring your KPIs you're creating a regular snapshot that allows you to monitor your website's performance over time. You know that if this KPI is going up it means one thing, if that one's going down it means another, and so on. Your KPIs not only give you an immediate sense of the overall health of your website, but also help to highlight potential problems and point you in the right direction before you delve deeper into your data, looking for solutions.

Choosing effective KPIs

The main difference between the metrics you select as your KPIs and all the other metrics you can get out of your web analytics software is that the KPIs should be the ones most critical in measuring your site's success.

In 'Web analytics key metrics and KPIs' (Creese and Burby, 2005), the Web Analytics Association (WAA) defines a KPI in the context of web analytics as:

> **KPI (key performance indicator)**: while a KPI can be either a count or a ratio, it is frequently a ratio. While basic counts and ratios can be used by all Web site types, a KPI is infused with business strategy – hence the term, 'key' – and therefore the set of appropriate KPIs typically differs between site and process types.

Another thing to note is that the terms 'KPI' and 'metric' are often used interchangeably. This is misleading, because although a KPI is *always* a metric, a metric is not necessarily a KPI. So how do you tell the difference?

- **KPIs are always clearly aligned to strategic business goals.**
- **KPIs are defined by management**: decision makers have to identify, define and take ownership of the key drivers of their organization's success.
- **KPIs are tied to value drivers critical to achieving key business goals**: they should represent the 'deal breakers' in the pursuit of your organizational goals.
- **KPIs need to be based on valid data**: you only get out what you put in.
- **KPIs need to be quantifiable**: you have to be able to measure your KPIs in a consistent and meaningful way over time.
- **KPIs need to be easy to understand**: they should be a barometer of your site's performance – a quick glance at your KPIs should tell anyone in your organization, from management to intern, how well your website is performing.
- **KPIs can be influenced by, and used as triggers for, positive action**: one of the main values of KPIs is that they immediately highlight where your organization 'could do better', and highlight areas where action is required to get things back on track.

From a digital marketing perspective, choosing the right KPIs is crucial to monitoring your site's performance effectively, and allowing you to make informed decisions for continuous improvement. But with a bewildering array of different metrics to choose from, it's also notoriously difficult to pin down exactly what represents a KPI for your site.

If you find yourself struggling with this, it's an area where a session or two with a professional web analytics consultant could be money well spent. Don't let the consultant take over – you know your own business better than they ever will; rather, leverage their expertise with web metrics to help you define your own KPIs.

The important thing is that you end up with a manageable suite of KPIs (usually numbering in the single figures) that together encapsulate the performance of your website.

Some generic web-based KPIs you may find useful

- **Conversion rate**: this is the proportion of visitors to your site who go on to perform a predefined action – such as complete a purchase, subscribe to your online newsletter, register on the forum, fill in an enquiry form or any other conversion factor you've defined. Naturally, the higher your conversion rate, the more of your visitors are carrying out the actions you want them to perform on the site, and the better your site's performance. (To get an idea of some average conversion rates across a variety of online business categories, see **http://index.fireclick.com**.)

- **Page views**: simple and straightforward, this is the number of pages viewed by your visitors over a given period.

- **Absolute unique visitors**: the number of individuals who visited your site over a given period (as opposed to visitors, where each returning visitor is counted again).

- **New vs returning visitors**: the proportion of your visitors who have been to your site before, assuming the analytics package can recognize them (ie they accept and haven't deleted cookies).

- **Bounce rate**: the bounce rate is the number of people who arrive on your site and then leave again having only looked at that single landing page. This can be an important metric potentially highlighting that your traffic perhaps isn't targeted enough (your keyword choices might be too generic) or your landing page isn't delivering what visitors expect when they arrive. Bear in mind, though, that some sites will have a naturally high bounce rate (think of a dictionary site, for example: a visitor arrives at the definition page for the word they were searching for, reads the definition and leaves).

- **Abandonment rate**: abandonment rate comes in a variety of flavours – it basically highlights the proportion of your visitors who start down a predefined conversion funnel (a series of pages loading to a target action or conversion), but bail out before committing to the desired action. The classic example is visitors dumping an e-commerce shopping cart before checking out, or abandoning the checkout process.

- **Cost per conversion (CPC)**: this is basically a calculation of the total cost of advertising (or of a particular advertising campaign where you've tagged the ads so that your analytics software can differentiate resulting traffic) divided by the total number of conversions generated as a result.

A look at the 'dashboard' or overview page of your web analytics package of choice will offer plenty more, and you'll find literally hundreds of suggested KPIs online. In the end, picking the metrics that are relevant as KPIs for your website is down to you.

Thinking outside the online box

One last thing to bear in mind: you don't necessarily have to limit your KPIs to the data being churned out by your web analytics software. In fact, it might be better not to. There are plenty of tools (starting with the humble spreadsheet, right through to sophisticated customizable enterprise KPI dashboard applications) that allow you to aggregate and report on data from multiple sources. You may want to pull data from your web analytics, your back-office financial database, your call centre records, etc to build a more complete profile of your business and how your website fits into the bigger picture.

Testing, investing, tweaking, reinvesting

While collecting and analysing statistics through web analytics is an incredibly powerful approach, it's also inherently limited. It can only tell you *what's* been happening on your site; it can never tell you *why* it happened. That's where the human element comes into play: the ability to analyse the what and infer the why. There is almost always more than one explanation for why your users are behaving in a certain way on your site.

Suppose, for example, you notice that the bounce rate for visitors from a particular PPC campaign seems unusually high. That could mean there's a problem with the ad itself (copy appealing to an audience that's too generic), the choice of keyword you're bidding on (keyword choice too generic to drive targeted traffic), or that the value proposition on your landing page isn't compelling enough.

The beauty of the web is that we can try 'fixing' these things one by one, and measure the results to pinpoint exactly where the problem lies. Because we can measure everything, we can literally test each possible variation, and use real data from actual visitors to our site to identify which change delivers optimum results.

The role of testing in online marketing really can't be overstated. When you can measure, you can test; and when you can test, you can make changes based on actual visitor behaviour. You eliminate the guesswork, which in turn eliminates much of the risk.

A/B split testing

The A/B split test is a familiar tool in the marketer's arsenal. It basically means running two different versions of an ad or a page and measuring the results to identify which version produces the best results. If you conduct PPC campaigns you're probably already familiar with A/B split tests. The functionality to conduct this kind of testing is integrated into the control panel of most, if not all, of the major PPC service providers. You can also split test your online display advertising on other sites, ad networks and affiliate sites, and of course you can split test landing pages on your own website to see what works best.

The main problem with A/B split testing is that you can only use it effectively to test variances in the impact of a single page element at a time. Change more than one element, and you can't be sure which change was responsible for the change you see in the results. It's very difficult to conduct accurate tests that measure the impact of varying different components on the same landing page, and how the changes combine to impact your visitor behaviour. Or at least, it was until relatively recently.

Multivariate testing – the 'suck it and see' approach to landing page optimization

Enter multivariate testing, a process that enables website owners to test multiple components on a web page simultaneously in a live environment. Think of it as conducting tens, hundreds or even thousands of A/B split tests simultaneously, and being able to ascertain, based on real data from real visitors to your site, which combination of the variables produces the best results.

Multivariate testing is rapidly becoming the conversion optimization method of choice among digital marketers, largely because it allows for far more complex testing options than simple A/B split tests, delivers results in a short space of time and can have a dramatic impact on conversion rates.

For example, let's say you had a landing page that was underperforming, and you wanted to optimize it. To keep things simple, let's say you wanted to try out two different headlines, two different images, and whether to use a text link or a 'Buy now' button as a call to action.

That's 2×2×2 variation — or eight possible combinations to test. With multivariate testing tools you simply set up a straightforward experiment that will dynamically serve different variations of your page to your visitors and record the corresponding conversions. At the end of the experiment you're presented with data showing how each of the different combinations performed, allowing you to choose the most effective of them and implement it permanently on your site.

There are numerous commercial tools available for conducting multivariate testing, including a tool called Website Optimizer from Google, which like Google's other products is absolutely free, making it an ideal place to start. You'll find it at **www.google.com/websiteoptimizer**, where you'll also find a wealth of tutorials, articles, online seminars and documentation to help you get to grips with testing. If you'd prefer to recruit professional help for your foray into multivariate testing, a quick search should turn up web professionals in your area offering the service.

Action stations

Action! It's a relatively small word that can have a huge impact. Without action all of that theorizing, data collection and testing will yield insight… but not results.

Pretty graphs, trends, spreadsheets and experimentation are all very well, but unless you translate what you learn into tangible, measurable (that word again) action that will make a real difference to your online ROI, then it's all just theory.

Putting theory into practice means taking decisive action. That means getting real commitment from all the stakeholders in your website: commitment to take the intelligence gleaned through your analytics and testing, and use it to implement real changes to your website, to your online and offline advertising creative, to when and where you buy your online advertising… everything.

Change your site

When your tests reveal that something is working well, implement changes to echo that success in other areas. Likewise, if your data points to problems with your site, use that information to analyse and inform your refinement of the user experience. Your data offers insight into what your users want – give it to them, and you'll see your site's performance soar.

Change your advertising

Your analytics can give you powerful insight into what advertising is working best for you online (and offline, if you use unique landing page URLs in your offline ad campaigns). Use that information to inform your investment decisions: the advertising creative you develop and where you choose to place your online advertising media. Build tags into your online creative so that your analytics can track individual ad performance – and use that data to inform future online marketing investment.

Harness the power of online data and watch your ROI take off

Time spent getting to grips with your web analytics, learning to use the data to hone your understanding of your online consumers, is always time well spent. Use the insight you gain to take decisive action, implement a process of continuous improvement, and test before you invest, and you can be confident your ROI is only going to head in one direction.

Measuring the internet: evaluating data and processes to monetize online channels

Richard Foan, Group Executive Director, Communication and Innovation, ABC

In order to measure something it is a good start to understand what you are looking at. However, the nature of the internet is far from a tangible, predictable entity. It has rapidly developed into an endless, living, breathing organism that constantly extends under new guises.

Gone are the days of the internet being a collection of static or dynamic web pages. Now the internet extends across almost every platform and is intertwined with nearly every medium. People are increasingly using the internet to view TV, listen to the radio and access content while on the move. Devices are changing too; mobile technology means we can now be directly connected with the internet at any time of day from any location. Such is the change that the terms 'TV' and 'radio' are fast becoming redundant in exchange for the terms 'video' and 'audio' as the English language evolves to keep up.

This convergence towards the internet to access content sits alongside a fragmentation of audiences. The explosion of content and access options has created more niche audiences than ever before. And they are constantly dividing and subdividing and regrouping in many different forms at different levels on a national, even global, scale. Citizen publishers have created a new source of content. Publishers and broadcasters are remodelling and repositioning themselves as media companies with a mixed-content offering across multiple platforms.

The effects of the fragmentation of media and audience interests have made it increasingly challenging for sample-based research to accurately measure these fragmented audiences. For instance, there might be 1,000 people a month who are regularly using an app on share prices. These people have distinct interests and needs, access content via different devices and may well be a very valuable audience. However, in a population of approximately 70 million, these people may simply not be picked up by a panel. Measurement techniques are evolving in order to be able to keep pace with the changing face of technology and consumer behaviour. They need to take account of more variables: audience, content, channel, device and time, which can all be tracked and measured to provide valuable insight.

Over the past few years significant progress has been made to ensure measurement techniques and metrics match innovations in content delivery. The consumer move to online has opened up a new range of possibilities for tracking reach, engagement and brand loyalty. And these measures are available from a range of competing sources, often using different methodology and tracking alternative measures. There are an increasing number of digital service providers across the industry competing with their offerings. Finding a way through the range of options is becoming an art in itself and means there is a greater need for clarity on which measures and methods can be trusted to deliver reliable results. Services, however, can differ vastly, which is why ABC was asked to set up an accreditation system to confirm providers' ability to meet industry-agreed standards. This includes web analytics providers, hosting companies and other third-party providers, and providing time-stretched decision makers with confidence in the results generated by the systems they choose. ABC and JICWEBS (the Joint Industry Committee for Web Standards in the UK and Ireland) work with UKOM (who focus on panel data).

All the national newspaper brands have a thriving online presence and are offering access to content via tablet technology. National newspaper brands are leading the field with the frequency of reporting their online properties with ABC and are also taking up the option to report consumer engagement and brand loyalty. In the spirit of the new brand-led model, many are choosing to report their overall brand performance across a range of delivery channels, now including apps, of course.

The magazine publishing sector is another one keen to demonstrate digital reach with more publishers reporting digital editions alongside print circulation. Clearly multi-platform extensions for magazine brands are tapping into new audiences, offering advertisers exciting cross-platform options and opening up new revenue streams. Other sectors tapping into the benefits from regular web traffic reporting include the recruitment, business publishing, sport, automotive, lifestyle, travel, consumer publishing, property, gaming sectors and 108 government sites.

There might not be agreement as yet as to what will become the dominant publishing model in the future. What there is consensus about is that industry-agreed standards are a vital part of evaluating online performance. What is important is trusted data which can be tracked, measured and, most importantly, used to demonstrate ROI.

As the internet has matured to come of age it has brought a host of new opportunities and challenges for measuring the internet in the shape of blogs, video, audio, RSS feeds, podcasts – and the list goes on. The introduction of mobile devices adds another layer of analysis, allowing us to track across more dimensions.

For many years JICWEBS has worked to ensure independent development and ownership of standards for measuring site-centric, transactional web data. This body, whose members include the IAB, IPA, IPA digital ISBA, the NPA, NS and AOP, has moved fast to agree and evolve measurement standards for developing media against which ABC can audit. Common standards mean greater transparency and trust, which give advertisers and media agencies greater confidence in their decisions when allocating advertising budgets.

The use of industry standards is spreading across the online sectors. Right now the TV and mobile industry sectors are making positive steps to establish industry-backed measurement standards to help quantify online audiences. Broadcasters have come together to make moves to measure video delivered over the internet. The BMWG (Broadband Measurement Working Group) is working to progress the development and delivery of an industry-agreed standard for the measurement and reporting of IPTV and VOD. The aim is to take a common approach for measuring online video content viewing to deliver accountability to rights holders.

The group is made up with BBC, BSkyB, BT Vision, Channel 4, FIVE, ITV, Virgin Media and industry body the IPA, as well as ABC. The UK TV audience measurement body BARB and the PRS (Performing Rights Society) join the meetings as observers. Industry-agreed standards for measuring simulcast, streams and downloads over the internet have added the vital element of trust in the medium, enabling advertisers, broadcasters and rights holders to choose to use them with the professionalism and confidence of traditional TV advertising.

Another sector keen to measure its online presence to industry-agreed standards is the mobile sector. The GSMA, the global mobile operators' association, has worked with JICWEBS to develop and deliver a set of industry-agreed standards for the reporting of web traffic over mobile networks. This provides mobile network traffic reporting for websites from UK mobile operators O2, Orange, Three, T-Mobile and Virgin. The move to establish industry-backed mobile metrics was initiated by the demand from operators and advertisers for effective reporting and accountability in order to secure investment and to justify driving media budgets to mobile.

Advertisers and providers alike recognize both the tremendous capacity of mobile to deliver as a marketing channel and also that this is dependent on the mobile industry's ability to provide reliable usage data to justify the interest. Industry-agreed metrics underpinned by an effective verification process are helping deliver the missing link which should see this market grow.

Whilst the project focuses on the UK market, the GSMA is a global association and has ambitions to deliver standards in other countries, so the scale of the project is potentially very large indeed. ABC champions the phrase 'global standards for local markets' as a mantra for internet measurement with localized reporting rules.

Obviously the internet is a global medium and so the international implications can't be ignored. In fact, global measurement structures are helpful. The International Federation of Audit Bureaux of Circulation (IFABC) draws together ABC's sister organizations across the globe to implement constructive international measurement initiatives.

However, advertising budgets for which internet measurement is largely required are still determined in local markets and so require measurement for individual territories. Furthermore, different countries often have dissimilar methods of measuring traditional media, a factor that has shaped the practices for measurement of digital media to allow a level of comparison. Whilst an international focus is essential, localized standards are paramount and have been built on those global principles since 1997.

The UK market, however, is considerably trickier to ring-fence. The sheer number of media and their international focus present a number of challenges. With English the common language in business, online and across most of the Western world, traffic on English-language websites can have a considerable international following.

With audience and channel fragmentation rife, the one thing that can shed light on users, wherever their geographical location, is IP (Internet Protocol) addresses for a single visit. Whether someone is using Instant Messenger, looking at a blog or website, receiving an RSS feed, or watching streaming video content (to name a few of the multiple options) the one thing that identifies a machine and tracks activity is IP addresses when combined with user agent data.

Tracking online behaviour based on IP or GSM (mobile network traffic) gives new opportunities to review the consumer journey at many points and is likely to come to the fore as the best measurement medium.

The current industry-agreed approach of using IP and user agent data to underpin the unique browser metric helps get closer to the number of devices used. The important principle is to be transparent in the definitions used and encourage compatibility through standards. Using IP has the added advantage of separating the measurement of online activity from cookies and ensuring companies stay on the right side of the new EU directive on privacy which is currently being adopted into UK law. The new regulations have the potential to challenge the use of cookies as a measurement tool but this is neatly sidestepped by using the very first JICWEBS metric, the unique browser. This has been in use by ABC since 1996 and does not rely on cookies to measure online traffic. In a fast-moving industry there is still a place for this long-established simple metric.

In truth, measurement of media has always had to evolve and adapt, and it probably always will. This applies to online measurement as well as offline, as well as to the methodology used. The hybrid approach which fuses together panel and census data is coming along in leaps and bounds. It does raise questions, including which data is 'right' but fortunately there are industry bodies in place to set about achieving industry consensus as the model develops. This cross-sector consensus is a key building block, alongside effective systems to ensure compliance with industry standards, which will help push hybrid technology forward in the coming months and years.

The immediate challenge is for ABC and the media industry to continue to build a critical mass of online media reporting its traffic data to industry-agreed standards. In recent years a host of new and traditional media owners have opened up to reporting their digital audience data to industry-agreed standards through ABC and the momentum continues to build.

The more media owners that report their industry-standard online audience data, the better the result will be for everyone. Improved standards of online measurement will result in better insight and an increase in confidence in the medium.

With considerable budgets being invested online from advertisers and media owners, the commercial interest around the internet has never been so great. The best agencies have grasped the digital opportunities for brands, and media owners are increasingly relying on online as a central business pillar. Online is no longer an add-on or a testing ground. Instead it has become a central part of business.

The traditional media industry has long recognized the value of trusted industry-approved data as part of the process of trading advertising. The new media industry is discovering that this is the key to monetizing online through their industry stamp of trust.

CASE STUDY   RAC drives performance with VoucherCodes.co.uk

FIGURE 5.2   RAC decided on strategic partnership with VoucherCodes.co.uk as a smart way to add an online voucher incentive to its comprehensive digital portfolio

We've been overwhelmed with the performance of our M&S promotion via eConversion's site, VoucherCodes.co.uk. It's been refreshing to work with a publisher who is flexible and willing to find an alternative solution to fulfil the RAC Breakdown promotion. Their enthusiasm to work collaboratively with RAC and the consequent increase in ROI have benefited both parties considerably and we look forward to growing performance even further in 2011.

Elizabeth Woods, Affiliate Manager, RAC

The challenge

The RAC is one of the UK's most recognizable motoring brands. With over 114 years of motoring experience, the organization knows and understands drivers' needs intimately. It offers a comprehensive range of motoring services to both consumers and business across the UK, including breakdown cover, insurance, legal services and automotive checks and examinations.

In 2008 the RAC launched its own affiliate programme and saw a healthy 156 per cent channel growth from 2008 to 2010. The organization recognized the potential to harness online vouchers (coupons) to drive affiliate engagement and provide a compelling incentive for conversion. Its existing web platform simply wasn't geared up to deliver.

Target audience

Existing RAC customers and new prospects looking to purchase products in the motor insurance and finance space.

Action

After some deliberation, the RAC decided that a strategic partnership with a leading voucher code vendor would be the smart choice. VoucherCodes.co.uk was selected as that partner.

In late June 2010, VoucherCodes.co.uk offered a co-branded RAC–M&S voucher for £15 to its then 3 million-plus members via a number of digital channels including an e-mail newsletter and on-site banner creative. In order to promote the sales of higher-end products, the voucher was only available to customers who bought one of the RAC products above their standard roadside-assist package.

Because it was based on a CPA model, the campaign offered a low-risk, cost-effective platform to drive sales and attract new customers.

Results

The RAC's initial foray into online voucher marketing generated some impressive results. The campaign yielded an astonishing 3,000 per cent uplift in sales volume during the first month, and delivered an overall ROI of 182 per cent. Numbers continued in this dramatic vein, with a campaign in late 2010 delivering 1,800 per cent boost to sales, and another in early 2011 resulting in a record-breaking 5,431 per cent sales increase.

As a result of this success, the RAC is now exploring voucher code incentives across its portfolio of products, including car and home insurance, and hopes to achieve similarly dramatic results.

Link to campaign creative

- http://bit.ly/UDMRAC

Credits

Client:	• RAC
Geographical scope:	• United Kingdom
Strategic partner:	• VoucherCodes.co.uk
Campaign contact:	• Liz Woods, Affiliate Manager, RAC

E-mail marketing

06

> *The new information technology, internet and e-mail have practically eliminated the physical costs of communications.* PETER DRUCKER

> *E-mail marketing has been called the original social networking tool and I could not agree more. If you think about social networks in general, e-mail plays a large role in them.*
> SIMS JENKINS, AUTHOR OF *THE TRUTH ABOUT E-MAIL MARKETING*

> *We forget that the RSS-centric world we live in isn't the one many (and probably most) of our customers live in. That's why the old-fashioned occasional e-mail update – which gives people the juiciest bits and leaves out the rest – still has so much power.* MATT LINDERMANN, SIGNAL VS NOISE

OUR CHAPTER PLEDGE TO YOU

When you reach the end of this chapter you'll have answers to the following questions:

- What is e-mail marketing and how can it benefit my business?
- How can I make sure my e-mail marketing campaign won't be seen as spam?
- How can e-mail marketing tools help me?
- How can I use technology to manage my customers?
- How can I write effective copy for my e-mail marketing campaign?
- What are the main design considerations when crafting an e-mail?
- How can I test a campaign's success?

The new direct mail

E-mail marketing is one of the most powerful elements in your digital marketing toolbox. It lets you communicate easily with your customers on a personal level through a universally accepted digital medium. Choosing the right approach for your e-mail marketing communications is, of course, key. Unsophisticated mass-marketing techniques, or anything that smacks of e-mail spam, is likely to be ignored, that's if it makes it to your prospect's inbox at all.

Think of the junk mail that arrives through your letterbox every day. Most of that gets thrown out, unread, and in many cases unopened. A scene in the 1991 Steve Martin comedy *LA Story* depicts the main character, Harris Telemacher, watching a never-ending barrage of junk mail pouring through his letterbox. He nonchalantly kicks a waste-paper basket under the unwanted stream of promotional bunkum and continues eating his breakfast. While exaggerated, it's a scenario many of us can empathize with – and an apt analogy for what's happening with electronic mail today.

Naturally, as e-mail started to become integrated into our business and personal lives, so the mass marketers turned their attention to the new medium. Junk paper mail became junk virtual mail. But whether it's online or in the 'real world', if your business becomes associated with streams of junk mail (or spam) it will destroy your credibility. People will either ignore your electronic missives, or will filter them out before they even arrive.

Despite the proliferation of spam, and the fact that most people's inboxes today are bursting with irrelevant and unsolicited messages, e-mail can still be used as a beneficial and effective marketing tool that delivers real value, both to your customers and to your business.

Customers will still open your e-mail

The truth is, many customers will welcome regular e-mail communications from your business, in the same way as they may welcome the occasional traditional or 'snail' mail offering a money-off voucher for their favourite store. They'll open an e-mail containing a newsletter or promotion from you, as long as they recognize your brand, they're expecting to receive communication from you, and are confident it will contain something of value to them. The key is to make these messages relevant and interesting for your chosen audience; fail in that, and unfortunately your message is destined for the virtual recycling bin.

E-mail marketing can be a tricky field to navigate effectively. You have to simultaneously respect your customers' right to privacy, protect your brand, and ultimately maintain your value proposition over time. It's very easy for your carefully cultivated e-mail prospects to unsubscribe from your mailing list, and once you've lost them, they're probably gone for good.

What exactly is e-mail marketing?

E-mail marketing is a fusion of marketing savvy and imaginative copy. In its simplest form, it's an e-mail sent to a customer list that usually contains a sales pitch and a 'call to action'. This could be as simple as encouraging the customer to click on a web link embedded in the e-mail. Some examples of e-mail marketing campaigns could include:

- a hotel promoting a special summer discount;
- a recruitment company informing business clients about a free seminar;
- a gadget store offering a money-off code to be used at its online checkout;
- a fitness centre offering members a special printout voucher that entitles the bearer to bring a friend along for free;
- a beverage company encouraging people to download a game that integrates into the user's Facebook profile.

You can also use e-mail when you don't have anything specific to market, as a mechanism to maintain consumer engagement, strengthen brand perception and add credibility to your business. In fact, even in the Web 2.0 world of blogs, social networks and RSS feeds, e-mail newsletters are still incredibly popular, and offer a very effective way to get your brand out in front of your list of prospects on a regular basis. Examples might include:

- an accountancy firm keeping in touch with its clients by informing them about changes in tax legislation;
- a weekly newsletter from a public relations company that contains interesting snippets of industry news and web links to longer articles;
- a daily digest or breaking news alert from an online newspaper;
- a publisher of young adult books using e-mail marketing to promote free and exclusive screen savers, ring tones and wallpapers to its young readers.

Because e-mail is an incredibly cost-efficient communications medium, when used effectively it can deliver an excellent return on investment (ROI).

E-mail marketing tools

When it comes to managing and sending your marketing e-mail, you probably won't want to rely on your standard desktop e-mail client to do the job. While it's a perfectly feasible approach for very small lists, as more people subscribe to your e-mail offering it will quickly become cumbersome and unmanageable.

FIGURE 6.1 E-mail marketing specialists like Benchmark E-mail (**http://bit.ly/UDMBenchmark**) offer scalable hosted e-mail solutions to help you manage every aspect of your e-mail marketing campaigns

What you need instead is one of the many custom e-mail marketing systems out there. These can either be software you install on your local machine, software you run on your own server, or a software-as-a-service (SaaS) offering hosted by an online service provider. These systems let you manage your e-mail list, craft your design templates for your messages and, most importantly, they help you to track your e-mail campaigns.

Some of the functions e-mail marketing tools can provide (and this is not an exhaustive list) include:

- easy-to-use tools that let you create and work from e-mail templates without having to be a technical expert;
- testing tools that allow you to check that your message will make it past major spam filters;
- tracking tools that show how many people have ignored, opened or responded to your e-mail (more detail about this towards the end of the chapter);
- personalization tools that let you modify the content dynamically to individuals or specific target profiles on your list.

Customer relationship management

It's no good using e-mail marketing tools if you don't know who you're sending your e-mails to. Customer relationship management (CRM) is a business concept that has been around for about 25 years. It's the art, if you will, of keeping your customers happy and maintaining an ongoing personal relationship with them. Let's say you run a small grocery shop in a small neighbourhood. Over time you'll get to know your regular customers, their likes and dislikes, and what other products they might be interested in trying. Larger businesses struggle to maintain that sort of personal connection with consumers, and that's where CRM comes in.

For instance, if you keep a record of the products or services a customer has bought from you in the past, what they've looked at on your website, how often they've contacted you, you can merge that data with the relevant demographic details, then, using CRM technology, you can track and anticipate what those customers are likely to be interested in. The result? Relevant, targeted marketing that is much more likely to convert.

When it comes to e-mail marketing, CRM can help you segment your list, allowing you to focus highly targeted campaigns to the customers most likely to respond. You can fine-tune your e-mail offering and align it with your customers' purchase history. The possibilities are virtually endless.

If your business already uses CRM systems for more traditional marketing, then you should be able to incorporate that data into your e-mail marketing strategy. Some CRM systems cater for e-mail campaigns as part of their feature set, while others integrate with your chosen e-mail marketing solution.

We'll talk about technology where appropriate as we progress through the chapter but ultimately, e-mail marketing tools will only prove effective if you, as a digital marketer, spend time developing the right e-mail strategy for your business, and execute it in the right way.

Before you start

Before you begin planning your e-mail marketing campaign, there are a number of things you need to consider from practical and legal perspectives.

Building your e-mail list

As we mentioned earlier, people won't respond to seemingly random e-mail communications; they won't even open them. So before you can do any e-mail marketing, you're going to need to build up a list of customers who *want* to receive e-mail communications from your business. The best way to do that is to encourage them to opt in to receiving your e-mails whenever you get the chance.

Your website is the hub of your digital marketing world (see Chapter 3), and is a natural place to ask people to sign up for your opt-in mailing list. All you need to do is place a simple, prominent form on your site encouraging visitors to sign up for the latest updates, direct to their inbox. If they like your site and value your content, many will welcome the opportunity to hear from you with regular news, special offers and occasional one-off promotions by e-mail.

Use your extended web presence to encourage sign-ups too. Embed a newsletter sign-up form on your brand's Facebook page, for example, and encourage sign-ups by linking to your sign-up page from the occasional Twitter update. You could also use your e-mails to encourage readers to introduce your newsletter to their friends, and perhaps even offer an incentive for them to do so. There are lots of ways you can harness broader digital marketing principles to help you build your list organically – get imaginative!

If you're in a hurry to build a list and send out a campaign quickly, another option is to rent an e-mail list from a specialist marketing company. But be careful. You need to make sure that the organization providing you with the list is a member of your country's direct marketing association or similar, and that they tick all of the boxes in terms of their anti-spam and privacy policies. People on these lists should have opted in to receive e-mail offers from third-party companies or 'partners'. If they haven't done so, any mail you send them is essentially spam, regardless of your impeccable intentions. You'll also need to check that nobody on your rented list has already unsubscribed from your own mailing lists. If they have, you'll need to remove them before you send out your campaign.

Another way to attract opt-in is when a customer completes some kind of transaction on your website, like purchasing a product, downloading a White Paper or requesting additional information. By making an e-mail address a mandatory component of the transaction you can add to your e-mail list. Legalities vary here, but in many countries, including in the UK, it's fine to send marketing e-mails to people once they've completed a transaction with you – as long as you've given them the option to decline. This is referred to as a 'soft opt-in'. And remember, every marketing e-mail you send out must provide the recipient with a straightforward way to unsubscribe from your list – an opt-out, if you like.

Legal requirements

Another crucial factor is, of course, to be familiar with the law in your jurisdiction. Sending unsolicited e-mail to random consumers will breach spam legislation in most Western countries. Anti-spam laws are there to enforce ethical e-mail marketing practices that respect customer data and privacy. Legitimate businesses will follow the laws, but spammers are hard to trace. They will typically use underhanded techniques to harvest e-mail addresses and send large volumes of unsolicited e-mails.

Back in late 2007 spam accounted for an astonishing 95 per cent of all e-mail traffic (CNet.com article, December 2007, **http://cnet.co/UDMSpam97**). Things have improved slightly since then, and today (July 2011) M86

Security Labs Spam Statistics report that the figure is only 75 per cent (**http://bit.ly/UDMSpam11**). But that's still a ludicrously high volume of spammy e-mail.

The practice continues because it costs very little to send a marketing e-mail to millions of people on a list and even the tiniest conversion rate turns a profit for the spammer; most spam can't be traced and originates outside the relevant jurisdictions.

Just in case you hadn't picked up the vibe, we'll spell it out: SPAM IS BAD. It's almost certainly against the law in the country you're operating from, and what's more it annoys the very people you're hoping to connect with: your future customers. When you're just starting out, and don't have much of an opt-in list, it can be tempting. Don't do it!

Anti-spam legislation in the United States and Europe

US law

In the United States, the CAN-SPAM Act (Controlling the Assault of Non-Solicited Pornography and Marketing Act) came into effect on 1 January 2004. The Federal Trade Commission has a fact sheet, accessible at **www.ftc.gov/spam**, outlining legal requirements for businesses sending e-mails. The main points include:

- Recipients must be able to opt out of receiving future e-mails, and such actions must be processed within 10 business days.
- The source of the e-mail must be traceable.
- Subject lines must not be deceptive.
- The sender's full postal address must be included.

Apart from being fined up to $11,000 for violating any of these terms, there are additional fines for using spammers' techniques, including automatically generating e-mail addresses or harvesting them from the web.

European law

The Privacy and Electronic Communications (EC Directive) Regulations 2003 is the overriding anti-spam legislation. You'll find that individual countries will interpret the law in their own ways, and you'll need to take data protection legislation into account, too.

In the UK, you can download a fact sheet for marketers from the Information Commissioner's Office website at **www.ico.gov.uk**. This clearly outlines, in Q&A form, what digital marketers can and can't do with e-mail. As we've mentioned, having the recipient opt in to marketing messages is crucial. (But don't forget the soft opt-in, which means that once you've collected contact details from someone who's bought a product or service from you, or expressed an interest, then you can go ahead and market to them as long as they've been given an easy way to opt out.)

Logistical problems

Sometimes the mail just doesn't get through.

There are a variety of reasons why your e-mails may not arrive in your customers' inboxes. They may have been inadvertently/incorrectly categorized as spam by the ISP (Internet Service Provider), or filtered into a junk-mail folder by a web-based or desktop e-mail client. Spam filters are so aggressive these days that people may not see much spam in their inbox, but an over-zealous spam filter can sometimes intercept legitimate mail too.

For the customer this seems great, but it does mean that they're missing out on potentially useful and informative e-mails – like your latest newsletter!

In e-mail marketers' jargon, when a legitimate e-mail is blocked by a spam filter it's called a 'false positive'. These false positives can be a real setback to your e-mail marketing endeavours. Even discovering that your opt-in marketing e-mail is being blocked can be a tricky proposition, and resolving the problem can be difficult, especially when you feel you've followed the rules to the letter.

Your best bet is to try and avoid the spam trap problem from the beginning by making sure your e-mails don't look and read like spam. If your e-mail software has an option to test how well your message will fare with spam filters, use it, and change anything that it flags as potentially suspect. You should also make sure that all of your e-mail can be traced back to a valid IP address from a reputable host. If you do that, there's no real reason for your e-mails to be blocked.

An organization called the Spamhaus Project (**www.spamhaus.org**) works to track and block spammers. You'll find more information on why legitimate e-mails can sometimes be blacklisted, and what you can do to resolve the problem, on their website.

E-mail formats

Another reason your e-mails may not be seen is that you're sending them out in a format that your recipients' e-mail clients – the software or website used to read and reply to e-mails – doesn't recognize. This isn't as much of a problem as it used to be, because the adoption of internet standards has improved significantly, and pretty much all of the e-mail clients today will handle rich text or HTML e-mail seamlessly unless the user has specified otherwise.

When you send out your marketing e-mail, you can normally choose to send it in its most basic plain-text form (with no formatting). You can be pretty certain that all of your prospects will be able to read it, but it's hardly the most aesthetically pleasing experience. One step up from plain text is rich text format, which allows you to format the text with font sizes, colours, bold and italics, and allows recipients to click on web links. This looks better than plain text, and can be very effective for simple informational newsletters.

The most sophisticated e-mails are built using HTML (the same code that developers use to build web pages). This essentially means that your e-mail can look exactly like a regular web page, complete with images, web links and all the rest. Images aren't usually sent with the e-mail, but are usually pulled in from a web server when the e-mail is viewed. HTML e-mails can tie in with the look and feel of your website, providing a consistent look and great brand continuity when your prospects click through to your landing page.

For most e-mail marketers, HTML is now the standard format for sending mail, but it's important to remember that many e-mail clients (and web-based e-mail like Hotmail and Gmail fall into this category) automatically block external images for security reasons until recipients override the setting either for an individual message or for all messages from a particular sender. It makes sense, therefore, to do two things: make sure that your e-mail message works even without the images (ie ensure your value proposition and call to action are clearly outlined in the text) and encourage your readers to automatically allow images from your address for future e-mails.

Generally you won't need to worry about sending different versions of your e-mails to different customers. An internet standard called MIME (Multipurpose Internet Mail Extensions) means that messages today go out in 'multipart' format. This means your recipient's e-mail client will be able to view the message in the best way it can, and if a recipient has set their client to receive text-only e-mails, then that's what they'll see.

Planning your campaign

As with any part of your digital marketing strategy, to get the most out of your e-mail you'll need to define who you are targeting, why, and what you want out of it. Do you want to generate more sales? Or are you looking to maintain a relationship with your customers by keeping them up to date with the business? It's important to be specific here, and to make sure that your e-mail marketing strategy feeds into your overall business goals.

Digital Customer Relationship Management (CRM) can help you to segment your customers, and to target specific groups with tailored e-mail offerings if that makes sense. You can also deliver personalized content to them, and wherever possible you should endeavour to personalize all of your e-mail marketing as much as you can. At its most basic, this involves using your prospect's real name in your e-mail messages, but more sophisticated software will allow you to pull in specific dynamic content based on a particular customer profile. For example, an e-mail from an airline could highlight the number of frequent flyer points a customer has left to spend before the points expire, or an online bookshop could recommend new books based on a customer's purchase history.

Focus on great content

Good e-mail design is important, and it makes a lot of sense to establish some brand continuity between your e-mail templates and your website design. Every aspect of your digital marketing campaign should, of course, work seamlessly together. But *always* remember that your e-mail content is paramount. Your template design should complement, rather than compete with, your e-mail content for your readers' attention.

In general you aim to make your e-mail copy punchy, scannable and engaging – much like effective web copy. Long, sales letter-style e-mails tend to be less effective, but remember that it very much depends on your business and your audience. Use your judgement, your knowledge of your business and your customers, and craft your message to suit. Test your content regularly, and tweak it to yield optimum results.

Above all, remember that crucial call to action.

When and how often?

You should think carefully about the frequency of the e-mails you send out to your list. Send mail too infrequently and you drop off your customers' radar, but send them too often and you start to irritate them. People don't want to be bombarded with marketing e-mails – even the ones they've opted in for.

Sometimes it can be hard to predict how often you should send out marketing e-mails, and when, in fact, is the best day or time to send them. That's another reason why it's so vital to track and analyse every aspect of your e-mail campaign. If you notice people suddenly starting to unsubscribe from your lists, ask yourself why. Perhaps you're sending e-mails out too often; or has a change in format prompted the exodus? Whatever it is, keep a close eye on your campaigns and the data they generate, and when things do go awry, try to rectify the problem as soon as you can. If you don't, you risk your e-mails being perceived as spam, and that can do more than just damage your e-mail campaign; it can have a serious impact on the broader online reputation of your business.

Lessons from your own inbox

You can learn a lot about what works and what doesn't in e-mail marketing by taking a closer look at your own inbox. Examine the array of newsletters and marketing e-mails you've signed up to receive. Do any of them jump out at you and scream 'Read me'? Why? What is it about a particular message that makes you want to open it? Are there any e-mails you've signed up for that you actively look forward to receiving? Are there some that you never open?

Analyse the marketing e-mails in your own inbox, deconstruct them, and apply what you learn to your own e-mail marketing campaigns. As your e-mail campaigns evolve, you'll naturally start to find what works best for you... after all, nobody knows your business or your customers like you do.

E-mail marketing dos and don'ts

Sean Duffy shares his dos and don'ts for the six key areas of successful e-mail marketing.

There are six core areas that represent the essential stages of e-mail marketing at its best. They are delivery, content, timing, testing, legal and measurement.

Delivery

There is no point in looking at e-mail marketing until we address how to miss the junk folder and land in the inbox. The messages you are sending are, of course, going to be legitimate and opted-in but unfortunately they share many characteristics of spam e-mail such as large volume being sent in a short period of time, and the sales-focused copy with words like 'Free' or 'Offer'.

Over the years ISPs and spam filters have tried many ways of trying to distinguish between spam and legitimate e-mail. First they looked at the content of the e-mail and in particular keywords used. However, spammers quickly learned to get around this by changing 'viagra' to 'v1agra' or hiding their text within an image.

Therefore there has been a shift to looking at the reputation of the sender instead. If the server sending the e-mail has a history of a high number of complaints or invalid addresses, then the ISP is more likely to block the e-mail. However, even this was not enough as spammers moved on to switching servers very quickly. Therefore ISPs looked to change the emphasis so new servers found it harder to get e-mail campaigns delivered than an established server with a good reputation.

All of this has made e-mail delivery a complex area and helped create further growth in the E-mail Service Provider (ESP) industry. ESPs help take the majority of the burden off you for only a few pounds a month, allowing you to concentrate your time on creating quality e-mail campaigns.

Do:

- Keep your lists clean. ISPs will look at the amount of bad addresses you are sending to, and complaints your e-mails are generating from their customers as to whether you deserve your e-mail to be delivered.

- Be relevant with your e-mails. Just blasting your database with non-targeted offers will lead to higher complaints, as well as having other detrimental effects on the success of your e-mails anyway.

- Use an E-mail Service Provider – even if you have limited budget there are providers who will manage the send from their white-listed servers for a few pounds a month, taking the burden of looking after all the technical aspects required to get good delivery rates.

Don't:

- Just think that using an ESP will guarantee good inbox placement. An ESP will help out with providing the technical infrastructure to achieve good delivery rates but only you are in control of your sending reputation.

- Add any e-mail addresses to your list that you can get hold of. Sending unsolicited e-mails or to old lists will cause delivery issues.

Developing content for e-mail

When thinking about developing content for an e-mail it is useful to think about the context of your customer checking their e-mail account. Increasingly the inbox is becoming overcrowded with a high number of messages received per day. This allows for less time per message, which means you need to stand out among the clutter and grab their attention when they do open your e-mail.

In addition, there is the longer-term impact of getting your content right or wrong. Those brands which are trusted by the customer and have provided relevant e-mail content previously are more likely to be opened than those sent by brands whose messages have failed to send anything that inspired or was relevant. Your customers will learn to know which brands' e-mails aren't worth their precious time to open.

Do:

- Write punchy short copy. E-mail users tend to scan an e-mail to see if there is anything of interest, so you need to grab their attention. Writing long copy may work in a direct mail letter but the way people read e-mail is different.

- Focus your effort on the top of the e-mail, which is visible when opening. This is known as 'above the fold'. If you don't engage them here they won't scroll to find something else in the e-mail.

- Be relevant. This is common sense but if there is nothing of interest in the e-mail they don't need to respond. Worse still, if the customer develops a perception that there is never anything relevant to them in your e-mails, even when there is, the chances are they will ignore the e-mail. Either send different versions to different segments, or utilize dynamic content where whole areas of the e-mail are tailored to the customer's preferences or past purchases.

- Craft your design so your key messages still jump out even when the e-mail client does not download images without the recipient first clicking.

Don't:

- Worry about certain keywords or content getting your e-mail blocked. The days of the word 'Free' causing your e-mail to land in junk are over. What is important is your reputation as a sender with ISPs.

- Include any attachments, JavaScript, Flash or video. They won't work and will cause many of your e-mails to be blocked as ISPs consider these to be a security concern.

Timing and frequency

When is the best time to send an e-mail? How often should you e-mail your customers? These are probably the two most-asked questions in e-mail marketing.

Of course, the answers to either are not simple. The best time to send an e-mail is not as important as the quality and relevance of the message. There are plenty of examples of e-mail campaigns which perform extremely well no matter what time of day.

Second, how often to send to your database should really be geared around how often you have something valuable and relevant to say. This will not be the same for each segment of your database. New customers should get a welcome programme, defected customers might get an incentive to come back and make a purchase or you might want to follow up on those that requested a brochure to convert them to a purchaser. E-mail marketing is not just e-mail newsletters.

Do:

- Only send when you have something of value. Don't get fixated by needing to maintain a certain frequency.

- Time e-mails around the customer life cycle, not just when you have an offer. Instead of treating everyone the same, think how you can improve conversion rates, encourage loyalty and reduce defection through 'triggering' special e-mails at key times in your relationship with the customer.

- Send an e-mail before they forget who you are. After putting all the effort in getting website visitors to part with their e-mail address, don't leave it a few weeks till they get your first e-mail. By then the relationship between you and the customer is likely to be colder, and therefore it is more difficult to engage with them through e-mail.

Don't:

- Presume that additional e-mails will always generate more revenue. A long-term effect of too many e-mails will lead to your subscribers switching off and ignoring your messages, reducing the revenue generated from e-mail.

Testing

One of e-mails' greatest strengths is the ability to get a message out to your customers in minutes. This presents a danger and an opportunity when it comes to testing.

First, the danger is to skip necessary but tedious pre-flight checks through the desire for speed of delivering the e-mail. E-mail has a certain complexity which means your e-mail may not display as you intend or may get caught in spam filters.

Then the opportunity. Due to the speed to create a campaign and collate the results, marketers can test different versions to samples of their database. This takes the guesswork out of what type of subject line or call to action creates the most opens and clicks.

Do:

- Try different A/B split tests to prove what works best. Ensure that you send to a minimum of 1,500 per test, otherwise the results are unlikely to be reliable.

- Test in different e-mail clients and webmail providers to make sure the e-mail arrives in the inbox looking exactly how you intended. Alternatively, use an application like Litmus.com which does all of this for you.

Don't:

- Test more than one thing at a time when split testing, otherwise you won't know what caused the change in results.

- Send your e-mail without having sent yourself a test as an e-mail. E-mail clients can mangle text and break links as they are not as strong as your browser at handling HTML.

Legal and ethics

The law around who you can send marketing e-mails to does vary from region to region. In Europe the privacy legislation is also implemented differently in each member state. In the UK marketers are required to get consumers to opt in to receive e-mails; however, they can operate on an opt-out basis with corporate customers. This means you can send e-mails until the receiver tells you to stop. With all types of e-mail marketing an option to easily unsubscribe through a link or e-mail address must be included in each message, and actioned promptly.

While it is important to understand the law, just ensuring you don't end up in court is not enough. There are many examples of brands pushing the law – whether by making it difficult not to opt in, or indeed difficult to opt out. This is self-defeating. If someone does not want to be on your list there is no point in keeping them. It can cause deliverability issues as more recipients use the 'Report as Spam' button. Damage to your brand can also occur.

Do:

- Make it clear on your data-capture forms what customers are opting into, what they will receive and how often.

- Make it easy to unsubscribe, and honour those unsubscribes.

Don't:

- Think that just because you are within the law your data capture policy is ethical. In reality, spam is defined by what the recipient thinks is spam, not what the courts say.

Measurement

E-mail marketing campaigns can be fully tracked to enable you to see who got the e-mail, who opened the message, clicked or purchased an item. This presents marketers with a wealth of data in which actionable decisions can be made to improve their e-mail marketing.

Do:

- Track opens, clicks and conversion activity. Every ESP enables you to do this and even Google Analytics will allow you to track how many sales can be attributed to a specific e-mail campaign.

- Report trends, not just specific e-mail campaigns. This enables you to identify if you have declining performance and to project what would happen if that trend continues.

- Analyse per segment of your database. The more you break the reporting information down, the more insight it will give into where your e-mail marketing is and is not working. For example, how do new customers perform compare to existing customers? Is there a difference between genders? What content does each segment prefer? All of this will then lead on to ideas about how you can improve underperforming segments.

Don't:

- Just measure short-term metrics of what happened in that campaign. You need to take a long-term view. Here is an example. If you average 15 per cent open rate, is it the same 15 per cent each time? If so, why are the remaining 85 per cent so inactive? Now you have identified those people it provides a huge untapped opportunity.

- Be happy with industry benchmarks. Just because your competition may average 12 per cent open rates and 3 per cent click rates does not mean you should settle for these. Those brands which put the time and effort into making their e-mail marketing programme relevant and timely usually improve on the benchmarks by at least 50 per cent.

Sean Duffy, an e-mail marketing expert, is Principal E-mail Marketing Consultant at Emailcenter, a leading E-mail Service Provider based in the UK.

E-mail design

Many of the same usability principles that apply in website design apply equally to the design of an effective HTML e-mail template. You will want your message to display consistently and effectively across as many platforms as possible. People will be viewing their e-mails using different screen widths and formats, and will be using all manner of different e-mail clients to display your messages. Make sure your template degrades gracefully (works well without images, and is viewable and makes sense using the lowest common denominator in e-mail formats: plain text), and test your templates thoroughly on as many different platforms as possible to make sure they work (or use a service like Litmus.com to take some of the pain out of cross-platform e-mail testing).

When working on your e-mail design think in terms of 'above the fold': just as with a newspaper folded in half, the top of your e-mail should capture the recipient's attention immediately and encourage them to read on. Don't force them to scroll through pages of text before they reach your once-in-a-lifetime, never-to-be-missed offer. Get to the good stuff early, and leave less important stuff and supporting information for lower on the page. Also remember that e-mail clients often show a short 'preview' of the message body below the subject line in the inbox. Use this: engage prospects with those first couple of lines and entice them to open your message.

Your design should reflect your corporate identity and branding, and should extend through to the landing page the e-mail links back to. Consistency and continuity are key here, and a seamless experience between your e-mail and your website promotes trust and, crucially, improves conversion.

Use rich media judiciously

By and large you should avoid rich media (Flash, video, audio, interactive banners, etc) in your e-mail marketing. Rich media can be really useful in augmenting the content on a web page, but it rarely adds value to e-mail communications, and often has the opposite effect.

While it is possible to embed all sorts of interactive content into HTML e-mail templates today, you need to think very carefully about why you're doing it. Does it really add value and enhance your message? Will your e-mail still degrade gracefully and work for people who have rich media content disabled or whose e-mail software can't handle it? Would your rich media content be better employed on the landing page your message sends people to, rather than in the body of the message itself?

Apart from the inherent distraction risk of rich media content, there's also the issue of your message being routinely blocked by corporate firewalls and e-mail security systems that view active content in incoming e-mail as a potential security risk. That means if people are signing up to your mailing lists from a work account, or your target market consists of business users, there's a good chance they'll never see your all-singing, all-dancing, multi-media-infused masterpiece.

Attachments are another thing that tend to be a bad idea in e-mail marketing. Avoid sending out PDFs or (worse) MS Word documents with your marketing e-mails. By all means tell your subscribers about your new brochure or latest White Paper, but don't include it. Instead, link to a landing page on your website with more information and the option to download the file if they choose to. It's a simple, effective and much more user-friendly alternative than sending unsolicited file attachments to thousands of e-mail addresses – and has the added bonus of potentially encouraging incoming links to your landing page, delivering SEO benefits and the prospect of new e-mail signups. How's that for a win–win?

Remember: mobile users read e-mail too

More and more people are accessing their e-mail – including your e-mail marketing missive – on their smartphones and mobile tablets while on the move. That presents a challenge for the e-mail marketer. Think about small display sizes; users may not see your entire subject line, for example, and small display size may affect the way your carefully crafted e-mail looks. Think about mobile users when you're designing your message, try to ensure it will work on a smaller display, keep your key content to the top left of the e-mail, and make sure it works in text-only form too.

With a small display you have less room to manoeuvre, so be sure to 'hook' the reader in early with killer content.

Writing killer e-mail copy

While the design and look of your e-mail are important, it's the copy that's going to galvanize people into action. Beneath the gloss and the sheen, you'll need to write compelling, engaging copy to get results.

First, it should be instantly obvious that the e-mail is from you. Use your company or brand name in the 'E-mail from' field – and make sure it matches the brand the user signed up for. It's important that people recognize instantly that this is an e-mail they've opted in to – or they may inadvertently flag your legitimate message as spam (using the 'Report as spam' button that's integrated into many e-mail clients today). That not only means future messages from you will be relegated to that particular user's spam folder, but if it happens too often, may ultimately have repercussions for the deliverability of all your e-mail.

Crafting the e-mail subject line is one of the most important steps in writing your e-mail. The subject is the one piece of creative copy you know your prospect is going to see *before* clicking through to open your message. It's your one chance to engage and enthral them – to entice that click.

Great subject lines should be catchy, but they also need to instantly communicate the value proposition of your message. Why should the prospect open your e-mail from a list of tens or potentially hundreds of messages landing in their inbox every day? Your subject line should answer that question.

Don't try to be too clever with your subject line – clever subjects can be ambiguous, and ambiguous e-mails rarely get read. Your subject needs to be descriptive, yet compelling, which can be a tricky combination to pull off; but if you manage it, you'll see your e-mail open rates soar.

For the main body of your content you need to ensure you're talking your customers' language. Always remember to keep your target audience in mind, and write accordingly. Remember that people are busy, and e-mails need to get to the point relatively quickly to hold attention and interest. Make sure your value proposition and call to action are crystal clear, and that key elements of your message (including links back to your website) are easily scannable and stand out from the body of your copy.

Keep text short and punchy, and avoid lengthy paragraphs (unless you're a particularly skilled and engaging writer, and you know longer copy works for your particular audience… *there are always caveats*). Long paragraphs can be unwieldy unless they're exceptionally well written. They are difficult to write well, and when written poorly are even more difficult to read. The result: people don't read them. Short copy is easier to get right, will lend your content life and energy, and will help zip readers through your e-mail quickly.

Keep the tone of your copy friendly and approachable, and tailor the language to your audience. Yes, this is a business-communication medium, but formal corporate prose is the last thing people want landing in their inbox. Keep things light and conversational, engage with the reader on a personal level (address the individual, not the crowd). You may be sending to a list of thousands, but to the reader it's one to one.

Proofread everything at least twice… and then get somebody else to read through it too. Read it in plain text and in its final, HTML form. Make sure your content is accurate not only in terms of spelling and punctuation, but also in terms of the detail. Double-check things like prices, dates, contact details, etc. Then, when you're ready to click Send, check them again!

E-mail delivery

Making sure your e-mails are delivered to the people on your list is another crucial element in your e-mail marketing. It's good practice to send your e-mail out to a few 'test' or 'seed' e-mail addresses of your own to make sure everything's arriving in the inbox as you expect it to before you send it out to your entire list.

Keeping your mailing list 'clean' is vital, and you should endeavour to honour unsubscribe requests as soon as they arrive. Many of these will be handled automatically by your e-mail service provider or e-mail software, but you should also monitor for unsubscribe requests through other channels (think other company e-mail addresses, social media, etc) and remove them manually where necessary.

If you find mail to certain addresses on your list is bouncing regularly (ie messages are undeliverable), investigate why. If the address is dead, purge it from your list (but don't remove addresses immediately; e-mail downtime is a fact of life, and occurs more often than you might think). Most e-mail service providers allow you to specify a bounce limit beyond which they will automatically purge addresses from your active lists and move them to a separate bounce list. You can then view them and either delete them or reinstate them as part of your routine list housekeeping.

If a lot of your mail starts to bounce, it's worth checking to see if a particular ISP or webmail provider is blocking your e-mail. If it looks like that's happening, it's important to contact your e-mail service provider immediately to try and get the situation resolved.

When you send out your messages you should be prepared for a rush of incoming replies. 'Out of office' autoresponders and 'unsubscribe' requests will start to arrive as soon as your e-mail message hits people's inboxes, so don't be surprised to see them. This is probably the main reason you want to choose a dedicated (but monitored) e-mail address as the 'From' address for your campaigns.

One other thing worth noting here is that if you're starting with a small list, and want to use your desktop e-mail software to send out a few exploratory marketing e-mails to get your toes wet, *please* make sure you use the 'BCC' (blind carbon copy) field rather than the regular 'To' field for your list of e-mail addresses. If you don't, everyone on the list will see everyone else's e-mail address… and we're betting that's not covered in your privacy policy!

Measuring your success

Analysing the success of your first campaign can provide you with valuable data that can shed light on how you progress and evolve future campaigns.

You can use e-mail marketing tools to analyse:

- approximately how many people opened the e-mail (called the open rate);
- when people typically opened your e-mail;
- what links people tended to click on (the click-through rate);
- the percentage of people who opened the e-mail who then went to click through to the website (the click-to-open rate);
- who never opens their e-mails;
- the types of e-mails with the best conversion rates;
- tracking of e-mails that regularly bounce;
- how many people unsubscribed from your lists;
- which e-mail clients/providers (if any) blocked your messages;
- how frequently a series of e-mails is opened by a particular subscriber.

Target your campaigns

The more data you have on your subscribers, the more you can split and segment them into niche groups that you can target with more specific campaigns, as long as your set-up can support it.

If you have a complex business with a wide array of different customers, investing in a sophisticated CRM system will let you build an even more detailed profile of your customer base and their purchasing behaviour. By linking their customer account (if they have registered on your website) to other databases within your business, and 'mining' customer data from a variety of sources, you can get an increasingly granular view, and can target ever more relevant messages to particular segments of your e-mail lists.

Test your techniques

To gauge the success of a potential e-mail campaign, you can also run A/B split tests with groups of subscribers. This simply means sending two (or more) versions of an e-mail that communicates the same message in different ways (using a different subject line, for example), and monitoring to see which one is more effective. Based on the results, you then send the most effective version of the message out to your entire list.

Here we asked Simon Bowker, eCircle's Managing Director for the UK and a leading practitioner of e-mail marketing to provide a point of view and some advice for digital marketers.

Measuring e-mail success

Simon Bowker, Managing Director of eCircle UK, shares some invaluable insight and advice for e-mail marketers.

The 'MarketingSherpa 2011' benchmarking report showed that consumer campaigns record an average ROI of 256 per cent. However, digital marketing is no longer about e-mail vs SEO or website design vs social media; serious brands understand there is no such thing as a single solution. Integration between e-mail, social, SEO and analytics has never been more important.

Recent research eCircle conducted with Nielsen shows that the combination of display and e-mail marketing campaigns significantly increases ad recall and the propensity to buy.

It is vital that businesses understand exactly what the aims and objectives are for their e-mail marketing. There are a number of important questions marketers should ask before starting a new e-mail campaign. For example, is there an existing database or do you need to purchase data from another source or create a mechanism to get your customers signed up to e-mails? Will your e-mails target customers effectively at different times in their life cycle?

It is possible to analyse e-mails in a number of different ways. Marketers need to ensure that the best possible ROI measurement tools are linked to the aims of the campaign. One of the most basic figures that every e-mail marketing campaign is assessed on is open rates. Different e-mails will generate very different responses; however, your first contact with a new customer or the welcome e-mail to a new subscriber to your newsletter tend to be some of the best read. This means that your subject line and starter offers are extremely important and should not be neglected.

To begin an effective e-mail campaign you need to do more than just capture e-mail addresses. The more information you collect at the sign-in process, the better the opportunity to personalize and target the e-mail content – which ultimately increases the chances of your e-mails being read. Segmentation is fundamental to ensuring that your e-mail campaign is targeting the most appropriate audience. Dividing your database allows you to send more thorough, focused, targeted and personalized e-mail communication, leading to a higher positive response rate. In making the choice about which way to segment your data, it is helpful to consider the different types of segmentation models that can be applied – these include profile-based segmentation (age, gender, geographic location, key dates) and behavioural-based segmentation (analyse click behaviours and browsing or purchase history).

Leading on from segmenting your database, the best approach to target your different segments needs to be determined. On a basic level, segmentation can be implemented in order to test different subject lines depending on who the e-mail is being sent to. Although simple, it is still an effective way to use segmentation due to the high level of impact a subject line can have on opening of an e-mail and helps to gain further insight into visitor behaviour and to increase conversion rate. A/B split testing is when you have two versions of an element (A and B) and a metric that determines the most successful. To establish which version is better, both versions are tested simultaneously to measure which version was more successful and which performs the best.

The number of customers clicking through from your e-mails to your website is another important metric. Last year the average click-through rate was below 5 per cent. To increase this you have to keep two things in mind: segment your database into appropriate target groups and ensure that you are sending your subscribers targeted and relevant content.

To really gain insight from both the click-through and open rates you should look to find a ratio between these two figures. If you divide the click-through rate by the opening rate, you will gain insight into the success of your campaign from the addressees who opened the e-mail. This indicates whether readers considered the content interesting or whether you need to look at ways to optimize it further. The key metric for all e-mail campaigns is the conversion rate, which analyses the number of recipients who have carried out a specific action – eg purchase, download or registration – in relation to the broadcasted volume of e-mails.

Analytics

The process of integrating the different strands of marketing analytics can be daunting. However, the good news is that the best e-mail service providers (ESPs) will be able to provide you with a 'plug-and-play' solution that will join your e-mail and web analytics packages seamlessly.

Before making significant changes to your digital marketing strategy, it is often worth considering an e-mail audit to assess exactly what stage you are at now, and gain a better understanding of which parts need improving. Broadly speaking, this should cover six core areas; strategy, segmentation and personalization, layout and content, list growth, automation and efficiency, and analysis.

E-mail Service Providers' technology should give you direct access to critical information such as impressions, clicks, open rates and bounces. With the additional support of specialist web analytics companies you can also drill down much deeper into your customers' behaviour to see click-through rates from specific sections of the e-mail, revenue and orders from a campaign and conversation rates.

Information gathered from the analytics packages can then be fed back into your database and used to enhance future campaigns. For example, if you can identify customers that have clicked through from the campaign but have not purchased, you can then target these people with an automatic abandoned basket campaign – reminding them to return to their purchase or offering them suitable alternatives. Results from abandoned basket campaigns are typically very high, with 25 per cent open rates and clicks of 15 per cent.

Case studies

Argos user-generated content

Background: Argos is a unique multi-channel retailer selling general merchandise and products for the home from over 700 stores throughout the UK and the Republic of Ireland, online and over the telephone.

Challenge: Argos wanted to introduce a product review section on their website to help drive sales of reviewed products online and to engage customers further with the Argos brand.

Campaign: eCircle devised an automated e-mail programme, whereby customers who purchased products on the Argos.co.uk website were sent an automated e-mail two weeks after a purchase was made, thanking them for their custom and giving the opportunity to review the product they had purchased. Ultimately this would help drive sales of reviewed products online, and would help Argos to understand what customers feel about the products they purchase.

Results: An initial target was set by Argos to generate 209,000 product reviews in six months. In the space of just four months, they had already generated 203,095 reviews. The highly personalized e-mail campaign, due largely to its dynamic content, also boasted open rates of almost 25 per cent and click-through rates of over 34 per cent.

Center Parcs trigger messages

Background: Center Parcs revolutionized the holiday market when it launched in the UK in July 1987, offering short-break holidays on a year-round basis. As the leader in the UK short-break holiday market, Center Parcs occupies a unique position, enjoying enviable annual occupancy rates in excess of 90 per cent.

Challenge: Center Parcs wanted to get more of its customers to pre-book their holiday activities online, making the process easier for both guests and staff, and ensuring guests didn't miss out on popular activities that can book up quickly. Center Parcs wanted to increase loyalty and generate stronger relationships with their guests.

Campaign: Center Parcs set up a series of triggered e-mails to send to their guests over a specified period, providing information on different offers and activities specific to the resort and the holiday booked. As the holiday draws nearer, content changes to promote different activities. The activity bookings e-mail campaign was designed to be highly personalized and segmented to ensure customers received the most appropriate information.

Results: The campaign has seen consistently high open and click rates and significant revenue thanks to the more sophisticated targeting and personalization, with around 80 per cent of activities pre-booked on the web. In addition, the revenues generated from pre-booked activities have dramatically increased, on-site staff time has reduced and consequently productivity has increased, with happier guests.

The future of e-mail marketing

Everybody is always talking about the next big thing and the future of e-mail, but marketers should really be concentrating on what's happening *now* and how their customers are interacting with them *today*. How many marketers are actually taking advantage of all the marketing tools at their fingertips (advanced e-mail applications, web analytics, social media, social commerce, recommendation engines, mobile applications and so on) to work towards a common goal right now? Not many. The process of understanding our customers 'in the moment' and tailoring our relationships to support that interaction will evolve our tools and techniques for communicating with them so that our transition into the future will be a natural event.

However, we have begun to see a number of trends emerging since early 2010 that are affecting the way we communicate. The rise of the mobile has seen consumers increasingly access their e-mails on the go and have technology on them at all times to create a link between the online and offline worlds. The increase of mobile access to e-mail has had a serious impact on the content and format of e-mails as different devices vary the way e-mails appear.

As new forms of social media and online networks emerge we are likely to see a raft of new ways to integrate campaigns seamlessly. Consumers do not necessarily differentiate between how the brand communicates on e-mail or Twitter, so brands must maintain a high level of consistency between the channels. Early research is already indicating that brands need to do a lot more to integrate their social media and e-mail marketing campaigns.

Data is the oil of digital marketing and it is likely to continue to grow in importance. Understanding your database and being able to pull out very specific segments to target, whether these are new customers or lapsed customers who appear to have lost interest, will need to become increasingly more sophisticated to make sure that you continue to send relevant, targeted e-mails that ensure the success of your e-mail campaign.

User-generated content and true e-mail dialogue between customers and businesses are also more focused than ever. With the increasingly available and affordable technology that can be easily integrated with existing systems we expect to see adoption of user-generated content across the board, from SMEs up to multinational companies.

E-mail: a vital component of digital marketing

The real beauty of e-mail marketing is that it lets you deliver your message directly to an individual who actually wants to hear from you. Compare this to your website, which is necessarily more generic (to appeal to a broader audience) and needs to work harder to attract and retain a visitor's attention.

While e-mail marketing is just one of the many ways of connecting to and maintaining a relationship with your customers, and is perhaps getting a bit long in the tooth compared to the young and dynamic social media channels that are emerging, it nevertheless remains a stalwart of the integrated internet marketing strategy, and when executed properly can be incredibly effective.

CASE STUDY E-mail CRM boosts booking engine's bottom line

FIGURE 6.2 Personalised e-mail with targeted promotions helped boost repeat business for Toptable

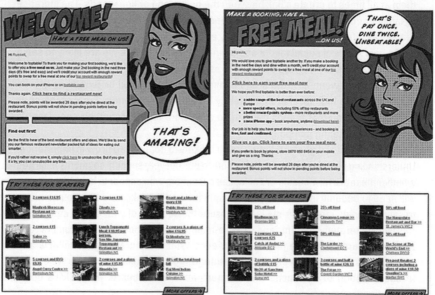

The challenge

Toptable is a leading online restaurant-booking service based in the UK and featuring top restaurants in over 15 countries. It is a wholly owned subsidiary of OpenTable – a provider of free, real-time online restaurant reservations for diners, and reservation and guest management solutions for restaurants.

A large percentage of Toptable diners had only ever used the service once. With Toptable earning a commission on every booking, the key to improving revenues was to encourage these users to use the service repeatedly, developing a habit for using Toptable to make all of their dining reservations.

Target audience

Toptable customers who had only used the service to make a single reservation.

Action

To engage effectively with users, encourage repeat use of the site, build advocates and retain customers, Toptable decided to enhance their e-mail-based CRM programme.

Before implementing the new system, Toptable's e-mail stream consisted of two e-mails a week sent to their entire user base, with little segmentation, personalization or testing. The first step in refining relevance and engagement was to include targeted content based on proximity to the recipient's home or work location. That way customers would receive details for venues where they were actually likely to go and eat. A personalized reward points message based on the customer's status in Toptable's loyalty scheme was also added to the message, encouraging them to make more bookings to move up to the next level.

The next step was to set up automated e-mails that went out at various stages during the typical customer life cycle. These included a welcome message sent out to new users letting them know about the key features and benefits of the service and how to make the most of them. There was also a 'winback' e-mail that would go out automatically to anyone who hadn't used the service for a few weeks, offering the incentive of a free meal if they made another booking.

Extensive split testing was employed across all of the new e-mails to ensure that each part of the new campaign resulted in improved performance.

Results

Although this was an e-mail programme, Toptable knew it was important to look beyond open and click rates to measure campaign success. Open and click rates can look good on paper, but the bottom line is directly dependent on the number of bookings generated – so bookings were the only real metric that mattered.

The life cycle e-mails resulted in an immediate uplift in winning back defected customers. Booking rates for defected diners jumped by 1,600 per cent compared to the generic newsletter control. There was also a 400 per cent increase in defected customers becoming loyal regular users. Booking rates for new customers receiving the educational welcome e-mails increased by 10 per cent within the first three months of using Toptable. The improved personalization of the newsletter led to an increase of 50 per cent in bookings compared to the generic version.

The overall impact of all of the changes led to a 76 per cent increase in bookings within the first year.

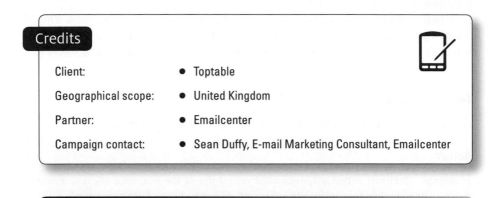

Credits

Client:	• Toptable
Geographical scope:	• United Kingdom
Partner:	• Emailcenter
Campaign contact:	• Sean Duffy, E-mail Marketing Consultant, Emailcenter

Social media and online consumer engagement

07

> *Informal conversation is probably the oldest mechanism by which opinions on products and brands are developed, expressed, and spread.*
> **JOHAN ARNDT**

> *Why does listening to your customers sound like a Web 2.0 idea? It should be a business 1.0 necessity.* **JEFF JARVIS**

> *We have technology, finally, that for the first time in human history allows people to really maintain rich connections with much larger numbers of people.* **PIERRE OMIDYAR, FOUNDER OF eBAY**

OUR CHAPTER PLEDGE TO YOU

When you reach the end of this chapter you'll have answers to the following questions:

- What does the term 'social media' really mean?
- How are these media changing the digital marketing landscape?
- Why should I get involved?
- How can I harness the power of social media to reach and engage with my target audience?
- How can consumer input help me do business more effectively and refine my products and services?
- What are the social media rules of engagement?

Join the conversation

Do you listen to your customers... really listen to them? Do you take their opinions, ideas and criticisms on board, and allow them to inform your business decisions? If you do, you're ahead of the game. Historically marketers have focused on delivering a particular message, to a predefined target audience, with the aim of eliciting a specific response. Consumers were sometimes consulted in the process, of course – through market research, consumer surveys, focus groups and the like – but by and large the marketing tended to be 'show and tell' in nature, the consumer's role that of a passive recipient of information peddled by the marketer.

Now, thanks to the increasingly interactive nature of the internet, and a shift in the way people are consuming media, all of that is changing. Consumers are talking, just as they always have, only now they're talking online to more extensive groups of their peers. The conversations they're having seamlessly transcend geographical, temporal and cultural boundaries. The web is abuzz with a billion conversations, and that presents exciting opportunities for marketers who are brave enough to engage.

Marketing too is evolving rapidly to become more of a conversation than a lecture. Progressive marketers realize that to be heard in today's interactive world, they need to participate in that conversation... and, of course, if you want to get the most out of any conversation, you have to spend part of your time *listening*.

Listening isn't a trait marketers are traditionally renowned for, but to truly embrace the opportunity presented by Web 2.0 and beyond, we need to sit up and take notice of what our online customers and prospects are telling us about our brand, our industry and the world in general.

Through blogs, wikis, social bookmarking, online discussions, social networks, peer review sites and other online media, we have the potential to foster a much more productive and meaningful relationship with our customers, to gain powerful insight into their perceptions of our products, services and brands, and allow them to contribute and collaborate in our businesses in ways that were never possible before.

Understanding social media demands a paradigm shift for the marketer. We have to realize that our target audience is, in fact, no longer an audience at all. They are now active participants in a constantly evolving debate; it's a debate in which we as online marketers can't afford to sit on the sidelines.

What is social media?

'Social media' is the umbrella term for web-based software and services that allow users to come together online and exchange, discuss, communicate and participate in any form of social interaction. That interaction can encompass text, audio, images, video and other media, individually or in any combination. It can involve the generation of new content; the recommendation of and sharing of existing content; reviewing and rating products, services and brands; discussing the hot topics of the day; pursuing hobbies, interests and passions; sharing experience and expertise... in fact, almost anything that can be distributed and shared through digital channels is fair game.

In a webcast for Search Marketing Now (**www.searchmarketingnow.com**), Xoogler (ex-Googler or former Google employee) and leading social media commentator Vanessa Fox described it as follows: 'There are all kinds of ways that people talk online, and social networking really is anywhere people are talking online. From a corporate perspective what you're most interested in is where people are talking about you, talking about your products, and talking about the topics that you care about.'

A huge range of websites now leverage elements of social media to engage with their audience, and some, including a number of the highest-profile sites to emerge in recent years (the Facebooks, YouTubes and Twitters of this world), base their entire business model around the burgeoning popularity of online social media, user participation and user-generated content (UGC).

Social media is nothing new

One of the biggest misconceptions about social media is that they're a new phenomenon. Online social interaction has been around since the very beginning. In their crudest form social media predate the web by some two decades. Primitive dial-in bulletin board services (BBSs) and online communities like Compuserve and Prodigy allowed users to post messages online for other members to read and respond to, UseNet newsgroups (early internet discussion groups) allowed like-minded participants to exchange views about all sorts of topics ranging from brain surgery to budgerigars. E-mail discussion lists did the same, Internet Relay Chat (IRC) introduced real-time chat into the mix, and browser-based forums and chat rooms brought the discussion onto the web. Social media, one and all.

What have changed over recent years are the reach and penetration of these social media technologies, their adoption into the everyday lives of a mainstream audience, and the proliferation of user-generated content and peer-to-peer interaction that result from them. In the past, online discussion was generally restricted to early adopters: technologists who felt comfortable interacting over the net, and who had the technical skills to fathom clunky, often unwieldy user interfaces to accomplish their goals. Today, though, anyone can participate through slick, well-designed browser-based user interfaces that adopt conventions that everyone is comfortable with.

It's easy, it's convenient and it's incredibly powerful; not because of the technology, but because of how that technology nurtures the connections between people.

FIGURE 7.1 The proliferation of social media sites on the internet today is making it incredibly easy for like-minded consumers to connect with each other. They're talking about everything... things that are important to you and your business. It's time to join the conversation!

Social media is naturally compelling

The proliferation of social media is a natural extension of increasing levels of internet usage and the penetration of always-on broadband access. As more people head online and start weaving the internet seamlessly into the fabric of their daily lives, it's only natural that they bring the very human need to interact and belong with them. We're biologically programmed to be social and gregarious creatures. The need to interact with other people is hard-coded into our DNA; it's part of who and what we are, and that's as true online as it is offline. That's one of the main reasons so many of us find social media incredibly compelling.

Social media is nothing to be afraid of

Compelling it may be, but for many marketers the thought of venturing into this openly interactive, anything goes, consumer-championed world can be daunting, even scary. The rules here aren't dictated by marketers, but by consumers – media-savvy consumers who can spot marketing hype a mile away, and want nothing to do with it. It's a dynamic, unpredictable world, and if you get things wrong you risk the very real prospect of a backlash that will travel throughout the network in the blink of an eye.

Worrying? Possibly, but at the end of the day you have to remember that social media is just about people talking, connecting and sharing with other people. Marketing as an industry is (or at least should be) also all about people: understanding them and communicating with them. As a marketer, is the prospect of talking with the very people you want to connect with really such a frightening prospect?

With or without you – why it's good to get involved

But, we hear you cry, how can you hope to control this open conversation? You can't – so don't even try. What you can do, however, is choose to participate in that conversation, and strive to have a positive influence on its direction. That's fundamentally what social media marketing (SMM) is all about.

One thing is certain: your customers are already talking to each other online; they're talking about your industry, your competition, your company, your brand and other topics that are relevant to what you do. The conversation is happening, regardless of whether you choose to get involved or not. Surely it's better to be aware of what's being said, to listen, engage and foster relationships with these communities, rather than wondering from the periphery.

Effective social media marketing is about leaving the sledgehammer approach to product promotion at home. Stop beating your prospects over the head with the cudgel of marketing hyperbole, and instead work to develop your skills in the subtler art of consumer engagement. Find out what people are interested in, what they're talking about, and then provide useful information, advice and content for them. Talk to them, not at them, and above all, *listen to them*. If you manage to do that effectively, then social media can have an incredibly positive impact on your organization's online profile.

FIGURE 7.2 Why it's important for your business to get involved in social media (slide courtesy of Vanessa Fox: **www.ninebyblue.com**)

- Deeper engagement with customers
- Get insights not available any other way
- Your customers are online already

Just how deep you choose to steep yourself in the social media marketing game will depend a lot on your business, your customers, your goals and your overall digital marketing strategy. But there really is something out there for everyone. Here are just some of the potential benefits of engaging with your customers through online social channels:

- **Stay informed**: find out what your customers really think. Get invaluable insight into their perception of your products, services, brands, industry and more general topics of interest. Knowing your customers is the key to effective digital marketing – and engaging with them on a social platform can be incredibly revealing, without being intrusive.

- **Raise your profile**: by engaging proactively through social media you appear responsive, and can build your reputation as an authoritative and helpful player in your field of expertise.

- **Level the playing field**: focus groups, market research surveys and other offline methods of gauging consumer sentiment are expensive and can be well beyond the means of smaller businesses. Now, any organization can immerse itself in the social web to discover what consumers are talking about and how they feel, with little or no financial outlay.

- **Influence the influencers**: often the people who are most active in social media circles will be the element of your target market who can be classified as *influencers*. While small in number compared to the market as a whole, these influential individuals have already gained the trust and respect of their online peers, and fostering their good opinion can have a disproportionate impact on your broader online reputation.

- **Nurture brand advocacy**: by engaging positively with people who already have a positive attitude to your brand, you can nurture passionate brand evangelists who will voluntarily advocate your organization through online social media.

- **Pass it on**: one of the most powerful aspects of social media is its capacity for viral propagation. It's the online equivalent of word-of-mouth marketing, except that online the word can travel further, faster. Whether it's a video on YouTube, a high-profile news story about your company, a post on your blog that's picked up and distributed by your readers – if it hits the right note, suddenly it's everywhere, and your profile soars. If you get it right, there's no more effective way to promote your business.

- **The wisdom of the crowd**: you know what they say: two heads are better than one. Well, hundreds, or even thousands, of heads are better still. Smart companies realize that by harnessing the collective intelligence of online communities they can find answers to some of their most challenging business problems. Getting input from online communities using social media is affordable and effective. As well as helping to solve real business dilemmas it can also help you to make more informed research, design and development decisions based on what customers actually want. Now there's a radical concept!

Different forms of social media

Social media websites come in a wide variety of 'flavours', which are all broadly based around the premise of personal interaction; creating, exchanging and sharing content; rating it and as a community discussing its relative merits. The content can be links to other websites, news articles or blog posts, photographs, audio, video, questions posed by other users... anything, in fact, that can be distributed in digital form.

Most social media websites don't sit neatly into a single category; they tend to mix a range of social components that transcend the discrete boundaries people try to define for them. Still, given our human propensity for filing things into nice, neat boxes, there are several generally accepted groupings into which most social media sites sit with relative comfort, based on their primary function. The following list is a taster, and is far from exhaustive. Start looking, and you'll find plenty of social media sites or components out there that don't fall neatly into any of the categories we outline below, some that span multiple categories and others that defy categorization altogether. All of which demonstrates the dynamic, constantly evolving nature of the space. As the saying goes, we live in interesting times.

Social bookmarking

Social bookmarking sites, like delicious (**www.delicious.com**), ma.gnolia (**www.ma.gnolia.com**) and others allow users to 'save' bookmarks to their favourite web resources (pages, audio, video – whatever), categorize them using tags (labels that help you to identify and filter the content you want later) and share them with their online friends. The concept is much the same as adding a page to your browser favourites, just taken to the next level.

Now, instead of having your bookmarks stuck on the hard drive of a single computer, they're up in 'the cloud' (the fashionable umbrella term for the amorphous mass of software and services that run in the ether of cyberspace), which means you can access them from anywhere. That also makes them easy to share with friends, colleagues or the world at large, and the tag-based organization means no more cumbersome hierarchical folder systems to remember. Just choose a tag and you'll be presented with a list of all the bookmarks labelled with that tag. Simple.

Behind the scenes these sites anonymously aggregate the data submitted by all of their users, allowing them to sort and rank sites according to their user-defined tags and popularity.

What's in it for marketers

- **Amplify your exposure and traffic**: by creating compelling, useful content and making it easy for visitors to bookmark your pages (by providing 'Share this' links/icons encouraging them to do just that), you can harness the social element of these sites to improve your reach and get valuable, targeted traffic in return.

- **Increase your perceived relevance and authority**: the tags applied to your pages by people who add them to social bookmarking sites can help search engines and visitors to gauge what your site is about more effectively. This can boost its perceived relevance and authority for particular keywords, which can in turn help your search visibility.

Social media submission sites

Social media submission sites, like Digg (**www.digg.com**), Reddit (**www.reddit.com**) and StumbleUpon (**www.stumbleupon.com**) are rather like social bookmarking sites (see above) only instead of saving personal bookmarks for your own future reference, you actively submit links to content you 'like' for the online community to rate and rank. The more people who 'vote' for a particular content item, the higher up the rankings it rises. Submissions that get enough votes end up on the site's home page, which can drive significant traffic spikes to the site in question.

As well as the votes, of course, there also tends to be a lot of discussion and debate on these sites, which means they can offer tremendous insight into the way people think and react.

What's in it for marketers

- **Find out what people are interested in**: you can use social media submission sites to gauge what type of content in your particular field people find compelling. Look at the content that's floating to the top. Ask yourself why it's so popular. What's appealing about it, and how can you draw on that to make your own content more compelling?

- **What's the buzz?**: As well as what's 'hot' on the sites, there's a lot of discussion going on around popular content items. The more popular an entry gets, the more people see it and the more debate there is. Examine what people are saying – look at reviews, comments and discussions; find out what people like, what they don't like, and use that insight to inject that elusive 'buzz' quotient into your own content.

- **Amplify your exposure, traffic and online reputation**: as with social bookmarking, having articles and other content ranking highly on these sites can give you a tremendous boost in traffic. However, they also give you the opportunity to raise your profile and perceived authority within your online community. By contributing constructively, submitting relevant and interesting content, and joining the debate surrounding on-topic content you can boost the community's overall perception of your brand – and by extension your power to influence others.

Forums and discussion sites

Online forums and discussion sites have been around since the early days of the internet. Broad, general discussion groups like Yahoo Groups (**http:// groups.yahoo.com**) and Google Groups (**http://groups.google.com**), where anyone can sign up and start their own online or e-mail discussion community on any topic under the sun, are still popular, and you'll find a tonne of other discussion sites focusing on general, industry-specific (vertical) and niche communities covering every topic imaginable.

What's in it for marketers

- **Get closer to your customers**: checking out what consumers are talking about in forums is a great way to find out what makes them tick. The more you can learn about your customers, the better prepared you will be to engage with them in a meaningful way.

- **Raise your profile**: contribute to the discussion, offer help and advice, demonstrate your expertise. Pretty soon people will start to respect and trust your contribution to the community – and that can do wonders for your online reputation and profile.

- **Nip bad things in the bud**: by participating in forums you will be able to spot potentially negative comments or conversations relating to your business or brand, and be proactive in resolving them before they escalate (more about this in the next chapter). What's more, if you're already participating as a valued member of the community, you may well find others jumping to your defence.

- **Targeted traffic**: traffic shouldn't be your main reason for joining a discussion forum – blatant off-topic promotion and linking to your own site for the sake of it are frowned upon, but most forums allow (even encourage) one or two links in your signature (a short snippet, usually a few lines, that is appended to the bottom of every post you submit to a forum). Make sure you follow the forum rules on this, but by including links in your signature you give other people on the forum a convenient way to find your site(s), and to discover more about you and your company. Many will click through for a closer look, particularly if you make regular, valuable and relevant contributions to the forum.

Media sharing sites

Media sharing sites are incredibly popular. Sites like Flickr (**www.flickr.com**) and Picasa Web Albums (**www.picasaweb.google.com**) allow communities of members to upload, share, comment on and discuss their photographs. YouTube (**www.youtube.com**), Blip.tv (**www.blip.tv**), Vimeo (**www.vimeo.com**) et al do the same for video content, and a host of other social media sites support alternative media types: Slideshare (**www.slideshare.com**), for example, is a site that allows people to upload, share and discuss their presentation slides with the world.

The sites typically allow you to make content publicly available, or restrict access to the people you specify, to send content to your 'friends' and even to 'embed' (seamlessly integrate) the content in your blog post or website for others to find it, distribute it and discuss it.

What's in it for marketers

- **Find out what turns your target market on**: by analysing the popularity of items on content submission sites, and reading the user comments, you can gain insight into your target market's likes and dislikes, and can incorporate that into your own content creation.

- **A ready-made vehicle for content distribution**: these sites are the ideal vehicle for rapid distribution of your own digital media content. In fact, a whole micro-discipline of digital marketing has evolved around YouTube and viral video content. Hit the right buttons with your audience, and who knows, maybe your video clip could become the next 'The man your man could smell like' (from Old Spice: **http://bit.ly/UDMOldSpice**), with 33,437,143 views... and counting.

Reviews and ratings sites

Reviews and ratings sites do exactly what the name says: they allow users to review and rate companies, products, services, books, music, hotels, restaurants... anything they like. They can be stand-alone review sites, like Epinions.com (**www.epinions.com**) or Reviewcentre.com (**www.reviewcentre. com**), or a review component added to a broader site, such as the product rating and review facilities on e-commerce sites like Amazon (**www.amazon.com**).

You'll also find specialist industry-specific review sites covering many vertical markets, like TripAdvisor (**www.tripadvisor.com**), which focuses on travel, or RateMyTeachers (**www.ratemyteachers.com**), which allows pupils and parents to rate and comment on their educators.

What's in it for marketers

- **Advertising**: most review sites rely on advertising to generate revenue, and therefore offer advertising opportunities for businesses either directly or through advertising and affiliate networks.

FIGURE 7.3 Epinions.com allows consumers to submit and share independent reviews of the products they use every day

- **Insight into what's good and what's bad**: even if people aren't rating your business directly, you can still get valuable information on these sites on what's working and what's not working for consumers within your particular industry. If you run a hotel, for example, you can see what people's main gripes are, and what they particularly appreciate – then apply that knowledge to your own business.

- **Find out what people really think**: if consumers are posting reviews about your business, that sort of feedback is pure gold – reinforcing what you're doing well, and pointing out areas where you can improve. It's market research… for free.

Social network sites

These are your archetypal social media sites – the FaceBooks, MySpaces, LinkedIns and Google's new G+. These are the sites people automatically think about when you mention the words 'social networking'. They are, to paraphrase Facebook's opening gambit, 'social utilities that connect you with the people around you'. They basically let users build up a group (or several discrete groups in the case of G+ Circles) of 'friends' with whom they can share things in all sorts of ways – from videos to articles, to games, to groups and causes, to… well, if you haven't got one already, sign up for a profile of your own, and you'll soon get the idea.

Huge numbers of people use social networking sites, and numbers are growing all the time as those people invite all of their friends and contacts to join them. Today Facebook heads the social networking pack with more than half a billion active monthly users. The numbers are staggering when you consider that Facebook was only created in 2004, and that it wasn't opened up to the general public until April 2006. At the time of writing (July 2011), Facebook is the second most popular site on the internet, nipping at Google's heels, according to its Alexa Traffic Rank (**www.alexa.com**).

Social network sites are popular because they offer users the ability to find and connect with people they already know in novel, convenient ways, rekindle old acquaintances and reinforce new ones. They make the process of communicating with a large network of people easy and painless. You post information to your profile and it's instantly available to those of your friends who are interested. You can broadcast information to all of your friends simultaneously, or choose who you want to share specific content with.

Talking to a room full of software developers in San Francisco in 2007, Mark Zuckerberg, Facebook's youthful founder, summarized the company's mission thus: 'At Facebook we're pushing to make the world a more open place, and we do this by building things that help people use their real connections to share information more effectively.' Which pretty much encapsulates the social networking phenomenon that's gripping the online world today.

What's in it for marketers

- **Advertising**: social networks offer flexible advertising options, usually based on the PPC model, for businesses looking to target their ads based on the profile information of users and/or particular actions. While the targeting angle is a compelling one, and social network audiences are large, it's important to remember that most users visit social network sites to *socialize*. They're not really in 'buying' mode, and many experts question how effectively social network advertising converts. It's something to consider, certainly, if it's a good fit for your business and you have a clearly defined audience that's interested in your product or brand, but be cautious, and track your results carefully.

- **Improve your online exposure/reputation**: social network sites usually allow organizations to set up their own profile or page. Members of the network can then become 'fans' or 'like' these pages. Your page is essentially a business hub within the network, and it can be a great way to build a community around your brand and monitor what consumers think about you, find out more about them, and offer valuable content. Having a presence on these networks, keeping your content up to date, relevant and valuable to your audience, and responding positively to the feedback you receive are further great ways to boost your online reputation.

- **Nurture social evangelists:** your social network can be a great place to attract brand advocates and to recruit and nurture brand evangelists. People on social networks love to share. Find the people who are passionate about your industry, your brand, your products, reward them with valuable information and content... then watch as they put all of their passion, zeal, and social media acumen to work promoting your brand to the rest of their social network.

Blogs

In the space of a very few years the widespread popularity and adoption of the blog (derived from 'weB LOG') as a medium of self expression and communication have caused one of the most fundamental shifts in the history of modern media. Suddenly, anyone can be a publisher.

Barriers to entry have come crashing down, and free, easy-to-use blogging platforms have liberated millions of individuals, giving them access to a global audience. Setting up a blog can take as little as five minutes of your time on a free hosted service like Blogger (**www.blogger.com**) or WordPress (**www.wordpress.com**), and setting up a blog on your own domain and hosting service is only marginally more complicated.

People all over the world are using blogs to report local news, vent their frustrations, offer their opinions, share their visions and experiences, unleash their creativity and generally wax lyrical about their passions. And the world is listening and answering.

The blogosphere (the collective name applied to the global blogging community) is *the* home of internet buzz. If something is worth talking about online (and often even if it's not) it will be written about, commented upon and propagated through the blogosphere. There are, of course, millions of blogs out there that simply don't make the grade – but they don't get an audience. The best blogs float to the top (largely through online word of mouth, effective search engine ranking and the effect of the social media submission and social bookmarking sites we've already mentioned).

It's not just private individuals who are blogging, of course – the blog is becoming an important tool in the business marketing arsenal too, adding a personal element to the bland corporate façade, helping companies to reach out and make human connections in an increasingly human online world.

Bloggers read each others' posts, they comment on them, they link to each other prolifically, and the best of them have massive followings of avid and loyal readers. These readers go on to elaborate on what they've read in their own blogs, and spread the word through their own online social networks.

If you choose to do only one thing in the social media space, then get to know the popular blogs in your industry. Who are the people behind them, what are they writing about, what turns them on (and off), which topics generate the most comments? Prominent bloggers tend to be the biggest online influencers of them all – you need to be aware of them, build a relationship with them, and leverage that position where possible to help spread the word.

Never underestimate blogs. Their simplicity belies an unprecedented power to mould and influence online opinion. For a digital marketer, blogs and bloggers can be your salvation... or your damnation. Treat them with the respect they deserve.

What's in it for marketers

- **Potentially massive exposure**: traditional press releases to your local media outlets are all very well, but get your story picked up and propagated by prominent bloggers and you'll get more online exposure, traffic and inbound links (think SEO) than any traditional press release could ever hope to achieve. (For more tips on getting online press releases picked up by bloggers, see the Online PR section in the next chapter.)

- **Consumer engagement**: use your own corporate or business blog to add your voice to the blogosphere. Show your customers a personal side to your business, give them valuable information they can use, provide answers and improve their overall experience of dealing with your company. Try not to use your blog as a vehicle for blatant product and brand promotion, but rather as a platform to offer your readers a personal insight into your company and brand. Sure, product announcements, and press release-like posts are fine, but look to add value with genuinely useful content too. You could offer your opinions and insight into industry news and events, comment on and link to other blogs that are discussing relevant issues, or get your resident experts to post how-tos on getting the most out of your products. Engage with the online community, and they'll engage with you in turn. The more you give of yourself, the more you'll get back.

Podcasts

Podcasts are, in many ways, just the rich media extension of the blogging concept. A podcast is simply a series of digital media files (audio or video) distributed over the internet. These can be accessed directly via a website or, more usually, downloaded to a computer or synchronized to a digital media device for playback at the user's leisure. They tend to be organized as chronological 'shows', with new episodes released at regular intervals, much like the radio and television show formats many of them emulate. Users can usually offer their feedback on particular episodes on the accompanying website or blog.

Whatever your area of interest, you'll find podcasts out there covering it... and podcast portals like Podcast.com (**www.podcast.com**), Podomatic (**www.podomatic.com**), and Apple's iTunes (**www.apple.com/itunes**) offer convenient hubs to find, sample and subscribe to podcasts of interest.

What's in it for marketers

- **Listen and learn**: leading podcasters in your industry will very probably be talking about things that are relevant to you as a business and to your customers. Podcasters also tend to be social media enthusiasts – influencers who have their finger on the digital pulse of their audience. You can harness their understanding of the online community in your particular space by analysing their podcasts, and the comments and feedback from their audience, to feed into your own digital marketing efforts.

- **Do it yourself**: podcasting is easy to do – but can be difficult to do well. At its most basic, all you really need are a digital audio recorder (your computer and an attached headset will work fine), some editing software and a place to post your files once they're ready. Depending on your business, your audience and your goals (back to strategy again), podcasting may well offer you a valuable additional channel to reach your market. It could also help position you as a progressive digital player in your industry.

Micro blogging

Micro blogging is a relatively new craze that has become popular with a mainstream audience (and hence with businesses, brands and the mainstream media) in a very short space of time. Its rapid rise in popularity is thanks in no small part to widespread adoption of the best-known microblogging platform, Twitter, by well-known celebrities, and the voyeuristic compulsion of millions of fans to check out what their idols are doing 24/7.

In May 2007 there were approximately 111 micro-blogging services online around the world. Today (June 2011), while there are still other services out there (like Google-owned Jaiku: **www.jaiku.com**, and identi.ca: **www.identi.ca**), by and large when we talk about micro blogging from a marketer's perspective Twitter (**www.twitter.com**) really is the only show in town.

Twitter is essentially a short-message broadcast service that lets people keep people up to date via short, public text posts of up to 140 characters. Leading social networks, like Facebook and LinkedIn, also offer similar micro-blogging functionality within their 'walled garden' networks through the 'Status updates' feature.

At first glance, micro blogging may seem a bit pointless. After all, what can you really say in the Twitter-imposed limit of 140 characters? Well, think about SMS text messages on your phone – for a long time there was a 160-character maximum limit, and billions of people managed to communicate effectively with them every day.

The true value of micro blogging isn't necessarily in the individual posts; it's in the collective aggregation of those mini posts into more than the sum of their parts. When you receive frequent, short updates from the people you're connected to you begin to get a *feel* for them, to develop a better understanding of what they're all about, and to feel a stronger connection with them. Twitter can offer an immediate and surprisingly accurate barometer of public opinion on the web.

What's in it for marketers

- **Your finger on the digital pulse**: micro-blogging platforms give the marketer access to high-profile thought leaders in your industry. The most progressive among them are likely to use micro-blogging services to post snippets about what they're doing, how they're doing it, links to new online resources and thoughts on developments at the bleeding edge of the industry. By 'following' these thought leaders you can harness that valuable intelligence and use it to inform your own marketing decisions.

- **Understand the influencers**: follow the influencers in your industry, and influence them in return. Identifying influencers is easy – they'll be the most active participants talking about topics relevant to your business, with the most followers. You'll be amazed how much insight following the micro-blogging streams of a group of industry influencers can provide.

- **Communicate with your customers**: why would you want to micro blog to your customers? Well, some very high-profile companies do (including Dell, the *New York Times*, ITN News, the BBC, South West Airlines and British Airways, to name but a few), not to mention prominent politicians (Barack Obama and Hillary Clinton, for example, were both prominent on Twitter during the 2008 presidential campaign), and other high-profile public figures. In a world where e-mail has become increasingly noisy, offering a micro-blog feed provides beleaguered consumers with a convenient alternative way to subscribe to your updates without adding yet another newsletter to their cluttered inbox.

- **Raise your online profile**: micro blogging offers you yet another opportunity to get in front of your online audience and establish your expertise. Be forthcoming, answer questions, provide interesting snippets of news and advice, direct people to useful blog posts, articles and other resources – yours and other people's. Help people, learn about them, listen to them, and give your online reputation another boost.

- Generate traffic: while not the primary goal, links on your micro-blogging profiles, and in your posts, can have the residual benefit of directing traffic to your website.

Wikis

Wikis are online collections of web pages that are literally open for anyone to create, edit, discuss, comment on and generally contribute to. They are perhaps the ultimate vehicle for mass collaboration, the most famous example, of course, being Wikipedia (**www.wikipedia.org**), the free online encyclopedia.

At the time of writing (June 2011), Wikipedia reports that it has a staggering 3,668,000 English-language articles in its database. To put that number into context, the most recent edition of *Encyclopedia Britannica* (**www.britannica.com**), a leading commercial encyclopedia, contains 100,000 articles. Despite criticisms from some quarters over the accuracy of some of its articles and the perceived authority of the information it contains, according to independent web-tracking company Alexa (**www.alexa.com**), in the first quarter of 2007 Wikipedia received roughly 450 times the online traffic of its commercial rival Britannica Online (**www.britannica.com**).

The name 'wiki' originates from the Hawaiian word for quick – although it's sometimes also used as what's been dubbed a 'backronym' (a sort of reverse-engineered acronym) of 'what I know is'. And essentially, that's what wikis do – they let large communities of people collaborate to share their knowledge, experience and expertise online. Wikis are created and policed by the community. Because of their open nature, inaccurate or misleading information can find its way on to a wiki, but if the wiki is active and vibrant, inaccuracies are usually picked up quickly and eradicated by other community members. So wiki articles are constantly evolving, and tend to become increasingly accurate and authoritative over time as the community grows, and tend to be updated with new information as it becomes available.

What's in it for marketers

The concept of using wikis as a marketing tool is still a new phenomenon, and their value may not be as readily apparent as some other forms of social media. However, they are a powerful collaborative tool, and with collaboration between companies and their customers in the ascendancy, look out for increasing use of wikis by innovative organizations in the not too distant future.

- Build a strong collaborative community of advocates around your brand: wikis can be a great way to encourage constructive interaction and collaboration between people inside your organization and people outside it (your customers). Consumers begin to feel ownership and connection with a brand that encourages, facilitates and values their contribution. That ownership evolves into loyalty, then advocacy: powerful stuff from a marketing perspective, especially when you consider these contributors will often be online *influencers* who will go on to sing your praises on other social media sites.

- **Harness the wisdom of the crowd:** how much talent, knowledge and experience do you have inside your organization? Probably quite a lot – but it pales into insignificance when compared to the massive pool of talent, experience and expertise you can access online. Retired experts, up-and-coming whiz kids, talented amateurs, undiscovered geniuses... they're all out there. Wikis give you a simple, powerful and compelling way to draw on and capture some of that collective intelligence. Why not harness a wiki, for example, to help refine the design of your products, come up with your next great marketing campaign, define a more efficient business process, produce and/or augment product documentation, develop a comprehensive knowledge base... or anything else that might benefit from a collaborative approach?

Social media dashboards – all your updates in one place

The proliferation of social media platforms today can make keeping track of what's going on between all of your different social media accounts pretty daunting. Luckily it's easy to consolidate your various social media streams and updates in one convenient location using tools dubbed 'Social media dashboards'.

Dashboard software takes a variety of forms, from desktop-based applications to web-based services and mobile applications that let you keep track of and update your accounts on the move. Tools like HootSuite (**www.hootsuite.com**), Seesmic (**www.seesmic.com**) and Tweetdeck (**www.tweetdeck.com**) have evolved quickly from straightforward Twitter clients into fully integrated social media dashboards that incorporate multiple social media accounts spanning different platforms. You'll also find 'enterprise'-class social CRM software, which essentially does the same thing.

Ultimately these dashboards give you a convenient place to monitor all of your social media activity in one place, and the best of them offer built-in statistics and measurements, scheduled updates, keyword monitoring and more. If you're new to social media you'll probably start off on the website of the service you want to use. Over time, though, most marketers will find an integrated social media dashboard invaluable.

The rules of engagement

Social media, then, offer a wealth of opportunity for consumer engagement and building brand awareness, but in such an open and dynamic space it's critical to consider what you're doing carefully. Social media is consumer driven, and the very characteristics that make them such an enticing proposition for marketers – the interconnected nature of online consumers, and the staggering speed at which information traverses the network – can just as easily backfire.

The 'rules' of social media are really about applying a bit of common sense to what are essentially human relationships. The key thing to remember is that these are *social* media – people are going online to interact and exchange information and content with similar, like-minded people. They're unlikely to be interested in your latest sales pitch, and they're certainly not interested in promotional hype. They want interesting, fun, informative, quirky, addictive... whatever turns them on.

When it comes to social media, you're not just sending out a message, you're inviting a response, and what you get might not be quite what you're expecting. You need a plan to engage in social media marketing, but you also need to be flexible and respond to the community:

- **Draw on what you already know**: you already have a wealth of knowledge about your customers – who they are, what they like to do, where they hang out online. Okay, so one of the main reasons you're getting involved in social media is to get to know them a little better – but the point is that you're not going into this blind. Use that knowledge: apply what you already know about your customers, your business and your brand to your social media strategy. As you learn more, refine what you're doing accordingly.

- **Don't jump in unprepared**: have a clear plan before you start – know who you're trying to engage with and what you want to achieve. Define ways to gauge and measure your success, with frequent milestones to help keep you on track. But remember to be flexible, and modify your plan as necessary in response to community feedback.

- **Look, listen and learn**: before you engage in social media marketing, spend some time 'lurking' (hanging around without contributing). Familiarize yourself with the different types of social media sites that you plan to target. Go and use the sites, read the blogs – immerse yourself in the media. Look, listen and learn. Just like in real life, every online community is different. Familiarize yourself with the various nuances before you dive in.

- **Be open, honest and authentic**: nowhere is the term 'full disclosure' more appropriate than in social media. Don't go online pretending to be an independent punter extolling the virtues of your brand. You will get found out, and when you do your company will go 'viral' for all the wrong reasons. There are some high-profile examples of companies getting this spectacularly wrong, with disastrous results. Never pretend to be someone or something you're not.

- **Be relevant, interesting and entertaining**: everything you do should add value to the community, as well as moving you towards your business goals. Be helpful, be constructive, be interesting and entertaining – join the conversation, offer valuable, authoritative and considered advice. Make a real effort to engage with the community on their terms, and you'll usually find them more than happy to engage with you in return.

- **Don't push out a 'spammy' message**: don't join social media sites just to submit a tonne of links and push information about your own products, or flood the community with posts on why your company is the best thing since sliced bread. It smacks of spam, and adds nothing to the conversation. At best the community will ignore you; at worst, well, we're back to the negative viral effect again.

- **Respect 'rules'**: if the site you're frequenting has policies, guidelines and rules, read them and abide by them.

- **Respect people**: always be respectful to your fellow community members. That doesn't mean you always have to agree with them; healthy debate is good in any community. When you do disagree, though, always be polite and respectful of other people. They have as much right to their opinion as you do to yours. Don't make it personal.

- **Respond to feedback**: if users give you feedback, that's invaluable. Let them know that you appreciate it, that you're interested in what they have to say. Be responsive, and show them how you've used that feedback constructively.

Adding social media to your own site

Remember, social media isn't the exclusive province of specialist social and community websites. You can integrate social media components into your own website and begin to harness the collective talent and intelligence of a vibrant community of users. Perhaps the most obvious example is Amazon's reviews and ratings system – emulated around the web – which allows consumers to review the books and other products the site sells.

Another area where social media really come into their own is in allowing your consumers to collaborate with you – such as in forums like Dell's IdeaStorm (**www.ideastorm.com**), which allows customers to suggest and vote on features they'd like to see implemented in the computer manufacturer's product line-up. It's like a next-generation business suggestion box and focus group rolled into one. The ideas that get the most votes from the IdeaStorm community rise to the top of the heap, much as items on social media submission sites like Digg do. The top ideas are then evaluated by the company and selected to go into production.

Through IdeaStorm, Dell's customers are having a direct, positive and tangible influence on the design and development of Dell products. The consumer feels more involvement and connection with the brand, while the company enjoys an improved reputation in the community and ultimately delivers a better end product to its customers. It's a classic win–win scenario.

Then, of course, there are customer support forums – where the community can answer each other's queries about your products and services. People get quick answers to their questions, and over time you build an invaluable, search-enabled knowledge base of solutions to common problems.

Because consumers are responding to each other's queries you improve the overall customer support experience, while reducing the burden on your own support resources – again a win–win. There are literally hundreds of

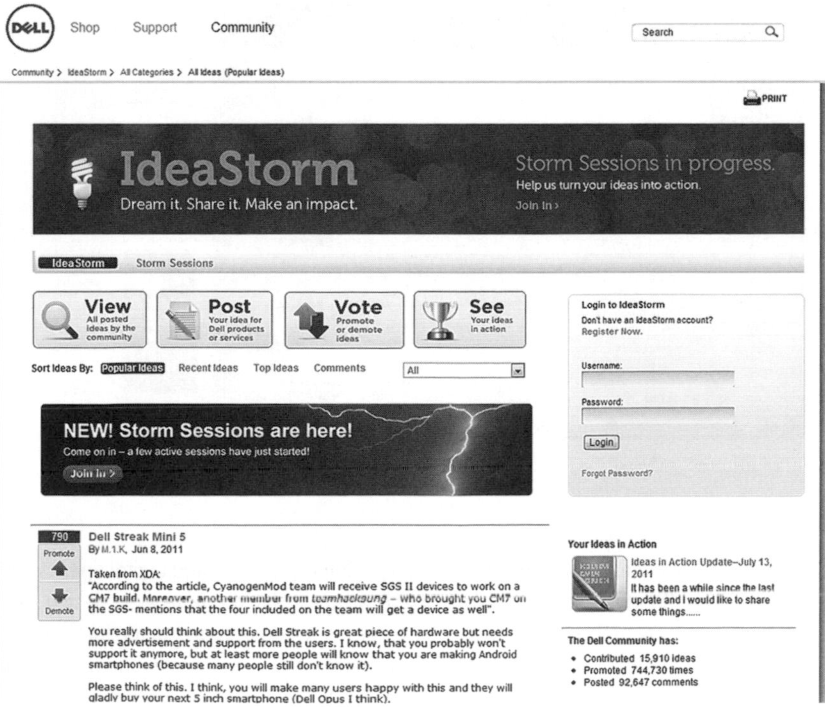

FIGURE 7.4 Dell IdeaStorm is a great example of a company harnessing the collective intelligence and creativity of consumers to inform real business decisions. This ultimately fosters consumer buy-in and delivers what customers want

ways to use social media to harness the collective intelligence, experience and latent talent of your customers and the broader online community. Imagination, openness and a willingness to engage with and learn from others are all that it takes.

Whatever social media strategy you choose to implement, remember that even when you host social media components on your own sites, the same rules of engagement apply: be open, be honest, be considerate... and most of all *listen* to your customers, hear what they have to say and *respond* in a proactive and positive way.

Welcome to the conversation; welcome to the future of marketing!

CASE STUDY   Online games help give Kellogg's customers a new krave-ing

FIGURE 7.5 Driving engagement with a new product through online social gaming and mobile – Kellogg's Krave Krusader

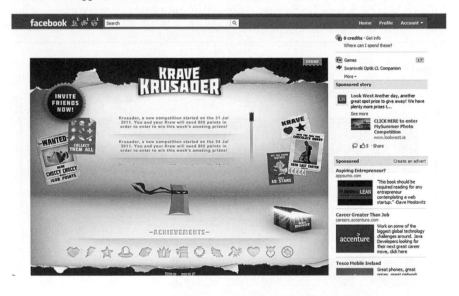

The challenge

In 2010, leading multinational cereal manufacturer Kellogg's appointed digital agency CMW to develop a social media and extended digital strategy for the launch of a new cereal brand: Krave. The agency was tasked to bring the new brand property to life through social media platforms and deliver a deep level of engagement with the core audience of young adults.

Krave represents Kellogg's first foray into the young adult market and this was the first time a Kellogg's brand had embraced social media as the key driver in its marketing.

Target audience

Young adults aged 16–25.

Action

As part of their remit, CMW created Krave Krusader, a 2D side-scrolling platform game available as a Facebook app and as a mobile app for iPhone and Android platforms. The game serves to recruit new Krave Facebook fans to the existing Facebook community, and to provide current fans with engaging new content around the brand.

This 'social' game was designed to engage and involve Krave's core audience with the brand and to bring the core ad concept underpinning Krave to life: the character's relentless pursuit of chocolate. The game reflects the personality, behaviour and movement of the Krave character, who will stop at nothing to satisfy his appetite, including sneaking up and pouncing, or adopting devilish disguises such as a sinister cloak to lure the chocolate pieces in.

The mobile apps incorporated additional features, including a real-world chocolate hunt. This virtual treasure hunt offered the reward of finding real chocolate chunks hidden near to the player's current location. By checking in at these locations using their device, players could 'capture' the chocolate and add it to their virtual Facebook tally, earning achievement bonuses and rewards to progress to more advanced levels of the online game.

Initially the game incorporated leading multiple chains, with the prospect of adding independent retailers as the campaign evolved. The mobile game was promoted on packs of Krave, and via a QR code that would allow iPhone and Android users to download the game directly to their phones with a single click.

Kellogg's also promoted the Krave brand at a series of summer festivals across the UK. Festival-goers who visited the Kellogg's 'Tunes and Spoons' area could get a discount on their breakfast when they checked in using their mobile phone.

Results

At the time of writing, this is an ongoing campaign, and results are still being collated based on factors that include number of game plays, number of referrals, average time spent playing the game, level of character customization, social media sentiment and other metrics.

To date the average time spent playing the Krave Krusader online game is five minutes.

Link to campaign creative

- www.facebook.com/kravekrusader

Credits

Client:	● Kellogg's
Geographical scope:	● United Kingdom
Agency:	● CMW
Campaign contact:	● Matt Smith, Account Director, CMW

Online PR and reputation management

08

> *People don't really care how much you know until they know how much you care.* **MIKE MCNIGHT**

> *It is not the strongest of the species that survives, nor the most intelligent that survives. It is the one that is the most adaptable to change.* **CHARLES DARWIN**

> *It isn't what they say about you, it's what they whisper.* **ERROL FLYNN**

OUR CHAPTER PLEDGE TO YOU

When you reach the end of this chapter you'll have answers to the following questions:

- What is online PR, and why is it pivotal to your online success?
- What channels can you use to get your message out there and raise your profile online?
- Why is looking after your online reputation so critical?
- How can you get the right people talking about your brand online?
- How can you find out where people are talking about you and your brand online?
- What should you do to manage negative online conversations and repair your online reputation?

Fostering a positive online image

Spin and hype, those old stalwarts of marketing and public relations professionals around the globe, are falling by the wayside; 'open, honest and engaging' is the new mantra of communications in the connected and interactive online world.

There are a number of reasons why online PR is and will remain a crucial component of your digital marketing success. For a start, there's the undeniable fact that traditional media channels are constricting – while digital channels are expanding at a phenomenal rate. Digital channels, as we discovered in the last chapter, are also two way. In a world where you're judged not just by your own words and actions, but by the reactions and influences of others, a world where information traverses the network in a heartbeat and online conversations blossom and flourish in a thousand different places simultaneously, a world where social influencers can make or break your online reputation with a single online post to a blog or forum, promoting, monitoring and *managing* your online image are more important than ever.

First impressions matter; lasting impressions matter more

Making a good first impression is just as important online as it is when dealing with your customers face to face. But online PR is about taking a broader view: first impressions matter, but lasting impressions are what you really want to cultivate online. You want your relationship with your customers to flourish, grow and endure: you want a positive image of your brand at the forefront of their minds whenever they consider your products or services. And more than that… you want them to tell their friends.

Online PR and reputation management is about sowing seeds in fertile ground, tending them carefully as they grow, creating the conditions for them to thrive, pulling the occasional weed and ultimately reaping a bountiful harvest.

Defining online PR

In 2007 the Chartered Institute of Public Relations in the UK defined online PR as: 'communicating over the web and using new technology to effectively communicate with stakeholders'.

That's a broad statement that encompasses a huge array of different disciplines. From a digital marketing perspective some of the things it would typically include are:

- raising the profile of your business or brand using online channels;
- monitoring conversations and managing your online reputation;

- developing online word of mouth and creating 'buzz';
- identifying online advocates and detractors (fostering the former, minimizing the impact of the latter);
- identifying online trends and issues in your industry;
- managing information flow;
- seamless integrations with the other elements of your digital marketing campaign.

Essentially it distils down to two key things: raising the online profile of your business, products and services by contributing positively to the online community; and managing your reputation by monitoring, assessing, responding to and influencing online conversations about you.

Promoting your business through online channels

When it comes to getting your business and brand out in front of online consumers, there are a number of tools you can use. First and foremost, of course, you can and should use your own website as a vehicle to make your PR-related content available to both media professionals and consumers. It's perhaps the only place online where you have direct control over every aspect of your content: how it looks, how it's presented and how people interact with it. Your site is also the ideal place to host added-value content that supports your broader off-site PR campaign, enticing people to click back to your own online real estate, where you can track and measure their engagement.

But having compelling content on your own site is only a very small part of the online PR story. The whole point of online PR is to raise awareness of your business and brand among the broader online community and to generate interest that exploits the viral potential of online social media. When word-of-mouth marketing meets online social networking the result is massive latent potential – a groundswell that savvy online marketers can tap into.

To do that effectively, of course, you need to know who your customers are, where they congregate online, what turns them on... all the strategic stuff we covered earlier in the book. Use your knowledge of your customers to find them online, then join them. Engage with them on as many different platforms as you can effectively manage. Your ultimate goal may be to guide visitors to your site, but rather than relying on them coming to you, go out to them. Seed your best creative content, put it to work for you in the places where your customers are already engaged.

By adding genuine value to the conversation on sites that your customers frequent regularly, you not only raise your online profile, you also establish a willingness to enter into a productive two-way relationship with them. That in turn builds trust, and makes them far more likely to engage with you. As your network of contacts grows, and your relationship with the community develops, you can begin to generate a bit of buzz around your brand, build advocacy and develop that groundswell of positive influence we mentioned earlier.

Getting the word out with online press releases

Just like their offline equivalent, online press releases are a way of getting prominent, *newsworthy* stories about your product, brand or company out in front of as many eyeballs as possible. In many ways they are similar to the standard press releases you'd submit to offline media contacts to announce significant developments and/or news in your business.

When writing your online press releases, bear the following points in mind:

- **A story worth reading**: if you're going to pique the interest of online publishers and make them want to pick up and run with your story, you'll need to do more than simply announce a new product, website or special once-in-a-lifetime offer. Your press release needs to be compelling, interesting and relevant. Tell a story – this is no place for a sales pitch; that can come later when the reader clicks through to your website. Your press release is designed to inform publishers about your story and encourage them to write or comment about it online. Think beyond your immediate readership and write your press release to appeal to the publishers' readers.

- **You need a strong hook**: your headline and first paragraph should capture the reader's attention and draw them in. As with any other form of online content, you literally have seconds to catch them before they click on something else.

- **Story first, detail later**: use an 'inverted pyramid', journalistic style of writing. Distil the main elements of your story into the first few sentences, then use the rest of your press release to elaborate on specific and relevant details. As a guide, your readers should be able to break off at any point and still get the gist of your story.

- **Keep it concise, objective and to the point**: keep your press release short and to the point. Don't over-elaborate, and avoid excessive use of adjectives, descriptive prose and flowery language. Keep it balanced and objective, and steer clear of promotional spin. Be ruthless. If a sentence doesn't add to the substance of your story, strip it out.

- **Use active, compelling language**: your press release should zip along at a healthy pace. Use short, snappy sentences to keep it moving. Make use of the active voice in your PR writing – instead of statements like 'The ground-breaking report was commissioned by Company X', try active voice equivalents like 'Company X commissioned the ground-breaking report' (for more examples of active/passive voice take a look at Purdue University Online Writers Lab page here: **http://bit.ly/UDMOwl**).

- **Accessible and jargon free**: remember, you don't know where your press releases are going to be picked up. Your story should be instantly accessible to a broad and general audience. Write your press releases in plain language, steer clear of industry jargon wherever possible, and when it is necessary, give a brief explanation.

- **Contact details**: your press release should *always* provide details of how to contact a real person in the organization, who is ready to provide any additional information or direct input required. This information should include your web address, contact telephone number and an e-mail address.

- **Be keyword optimized**: your press release is going to end up on the web – so you should treat it as a piece of web content. Write your copy to maximize its search visibility (see Chapter 4). Target specific, search-relevant keyword phrases in your writing – but not at the expense of human readability: think people first, then search engines. Wherever it ends up, your press release will serve as an additional opportunity to rank for your chosen keywords and phrases in the SERPs.

- **Link back to your site**: some online press release distribution services may restrict the use of links, limit their number, or only allow them in the company boilerplate text ('About us' stuff) at the end of the piece. Where possible, aim to have at least one, and possibly two or three, active back links to your website (but no more: too many and your carefully crafted press release will start to look like link spam). Links will direct traffic to your site and can potentially help with your SEO link-building efforts. If you want to track the responses to a particular press release, make sure you tag your links so you can identify click-throughs from that particular piece in your web analytics solution (see Chapter 6).

- **Stick to the guidelines**: whatever distribution service you choose to use, make sure that your press release adheres to their published guidelines for formatting, links, length, content, etc. Doing so will ensure it passes their editorial requirements and will maximize your chances of being picked up by content publishers.

Getting it out there

Once you've written your press release you'll need to distribute it. You will naturally want to add it to the 'Press' or 'PR' section of your own website, and may have your own list of local, national and international media contacts you regularly send news items out to. However, to maximize the potential penetration and exposure from your press release you're going to want to spread it a bit further afield. You can do that by submitting it to one or more online press release or news distribution services like PR Web (**www.prweb.com**), Business Wire (**www.businesswire.com**), MarketWire (**www.marketwire.com**), PR.com (**www.PR.com**) or Click Press (**www.clickpress.com**). You'll find plenty more by searching for 'press release distribution' in your favourite search engine.

Some of these services offer free basic distribution, with paid upgrades, while others require payment on either a subscription or per-item basis. Which option best suits your business will depend on your particular needs.

As well as making your press release available on their own sites, these services also tend to distribute releases via news feeds to online and offline journalists, media websites and news aggregation services like Yahoo! News and Google News, which could result in a phenomenal amount of exposure for a newsworthy story.

Blogger outreach

Blogger outreach is the rather grand moniker that PR professionals apply to the process of reaching out into the blogosphere and persuading popular bloggers to write about your brand. It can be an incredibly effective way of raising your online profile, generating online traffic and improving your reputation. We've already seen that high-profile bloggers can have a disproportionate amount of influence and reach within their online community. What better way, then, to reach your prospective audience than to make advocates of these influential and vociferous commentators?

So, once you've submitted your finely honed press release to your distribution service of choice, you might be tempted to simply fire that same release to the top 10 bloggers in your industry. After all, you've done all the hard work, and sending out a group e-mail would be quick, easy and convenient, right?

It would also be doomed to failure.

Why? Because bloggers are typically dismissive of generic, often highly irrelevant press releases pitching for free online exposure. Unless you're lucky, and your generic release just happens to dovetail nicely with the blogger's specific interests, it will be painfully obvious that the pitch has come from someone who doesn't read the blog, and hasn't taken the time to do their homework.

A 2007 study by APCO Worldwide and the Council of Public Relations Firms found that 42 per cent of bloggers receive an e-mail pitch from a PR professional at least once a day, 27 per cent reported getting more than one a day and 63 per cent were contacted by a PR professional at least once a week. That's a lot of press releases – most of which end up in the junk mail folder!

So how can you entice bloggers to give you some valuable exposure on their oh-so-popular web sites? Well, it's important to remember that blogs are a form of social media, and the usual rules of engagement apply (see Chapter 7). Also, generally speaking, bloggers tend to be writing voluntarily about subjects that they're very passionate about. That's one of the things that makes bloggers so valuable when it comes to promoting your brand... but to harness that passion, you need to show them that you understand and respect it:

- **Get to know the blogs you want to target**: it's important to get a feel for things before you jump in with both feet. Spend a bit of time familiarizing yourself with the top blogs in your industry, subscribe to their RSS feeds and *actually read* the posts (or, if you're in a hurry, you could skip to the archives and read up on some recent posts there): look, listen and learn. Before long you'll start to get a feel for the writer's style, their personality, their likes and dislikes, what turns them on and what turns them off.

- **Engage through comments, or by a link from your own blog**: make sure your pitch isn't the first thing the blogger sees from you. If you spot a post that sparks your interest, or that makes a relevant point about your industry, engage by submitting a thoughtful, considered comment or two – or, if you have a company blog, why not write your own post that links to the post in question? Your link will normally appear as a special kind of comment known as a 'Trackback' in the comment section of the destination blog. Make it a blogger–blogger interaction rather than a blogger–company or blogger–PR one. Engage in the conversation in an open, responsible and constructive way, and you'll find bloggers much more receptive to your pitch when it does arrive.

- **Build a relationship**: if you attend trade shows in your industry, make a point of finding out if prominent bloggers are attending, and get an introduction. If you can't meet them in person, leverage the power of social media to get to know them online. A blogger who feels they already have a relationship with you will be far more receptive when your proposal lands in their inbox.

- **Make it relevant**: you know what each blogger you're targeting writes about – make sure that what you're pitching matches the subject matter of the blog in question (you'd be amazed how often people get this wrong). Pitch to their passions!

- **Tailor made**: at the end of the day, bloggers write about the stuff that they care about. It's what makes blogs so compelling – and why more people in the United States today read a blog than buy a daily newspaper. Your proposal has to connect and resonate with the individual blogger. Tailor your message, and you stand a much better chance of success.

- **Transparency is crucial**: always be completely open and honest about who you are, and why you're contacting them. It's unethical to do otherwise, and besides, things don't stay hidden for long online, and the last thing you want is a potentially nasty backlash.

Ogilvy PR's blogger outreach code of ethics

In September 2007, after rumblings in the blogger community about the way they were being approached by PR and marketing companies, Ogilvy PR drafted a code of ethics for marketers and PR professionals reaching out to bloggers. They posted it on their 360° Digital Influence blog. They then opened it up to the online community for discussion and feedback. The results of this ongoing discussion, as of 6 June 2008, are outlined below.

Our approach

- We reach out to bloggers because we respect your influence and feel that we might have something that is 'remarkable' which could be of interest to you and/or your audience.

- We will only propose blogger outreach as a tactic if it complements our overall strategy. We will not recommend it as a panacea for every social media campaign.

Outreach

- Before we e-mail you, we will check out your blog's About, Contact and Advertising page in an effort to see if you have blatantly said you would not like to be contacted by PR/marketing companies. If so, we'll leave you alone.

- We will always be transparent and clearly disclose who we are and whom we work for in our outreach e-mail.

- If you tell us there is a specific way you want to be reached, we'll adhere to those guidelines.

- We won't pretend to have read your blog if we haven't, and we'll make a best effort to spend time reading the blogs we plan on contacting.

- In our e-mail we will convey why we think you, in particular, might be interested in our client's product, issue, event or message.

- As available, we will provide you with links to third-party information/blog coverage of the campaign we are pitching to you (via Web Strategy with Jeremiah and MC Milker).

- Our initial outreach e-mail will always include a link to Ogilvy PR's Blog Outreach Code of Ethics.

Building a relationship

- Whenever possible, we will articulate how blogger outreach, and your blog in particular, fits in with our overall campaign strategy (via Neville Hobson).

- We will seek to present you with a range of opportunities to work together around a campaign, so that you can create the best experience possible for your audience. We acknowledge that, when it comes to knowing your audience, you are the expert.

- NEW! We'll let you know who we are by providing you with a link to some background or bio information on the individual contacting you (via 93 Colors).

- We won't leave you hanging. If your contact at Ogilvy PR is going out of town or will be unreachable, we will provide you with an alternative point of contact.

- We encourage you to disclose our relationship with you to your readers, and will never ask you to do otherwise.

- You are entitled to blog on information or products we give you in any way you see fit. (Yes, you can even say you hate it.)

- We understand that when you agree to blog about a campaign it's not going to happen overnight. We'll work with you to develop a reasonable timeline for posting that fits with your schedule – and we won't pester you to put up your post (via LA Daddy).

- If you don't want to hear from us again, we will place you on our Do Not Contact list – which we will share with the rest of Ogilvy PR.

- If you are initially interested in the campaign, but don't respond to one of our e-mails, we will follow up with you no more than once. If you don't respond to us at all, we'll leave you alone.

- Compensation and product access. If we reach out to you with news about a product, campaign or issue, we will not provide monetary compensation, because we believe it is unethical to 'buy' favourable reviews and do not want to appear as if we are.

- If you have advertising opportunities on your blog, we will counsel our clients to consider purchasing advertising as a way to reach your readers. We will make it clear, however, that paying for advertising does not mean that you will post about the campaign or that, if you do, you will do so in a way that is favourable to them.

- If we ask you to review a product and, therefore, provide you with the product to enable you to 'experience' it, we will ask that you be transparent and reveal that you have been given the product temporarily, or permanently.

- If we engage you as an advisor on a specific project, we will consider providing you with compensation (agreed upon at the start of the project). This compensation will solely be for your time as an advisor and will not include an expectation that you will write about the project – favourably or unfavourably.

*This Blogger Outreach Code of Ethics was created by the 360° Digital Influence Group at Ogilvy Public Relations Worldwide. You'll find it posted on their own blog here: **http://blog.ogilvypr.com/?p=243**.*

Article syndication

When it comes to boosting your reputation and demonstrating your expertise, writing helpful, authoritative articles has always been a very powerful marketing tool. In the past it meant pitching ideas to editors to get your articles into mass-market print publications or high-profile trade journals. Yet again, though, the internet has taken a traditional marketing avenue and turned it on its head. Now anyone can write articles and syndicate them online... for free.

We've all heard the adage that on the internet content is king; we even used it ourselves earlier in the book. But creating compelling, high-value content can be a resource-hungry, time-intensive process. For thousands of websites, webzines (web magazines) and e-zines (e-mail magazines) out there, getting fresh, cost-effective, high-quality content to fill the next issue is a constant challenge. That's where article syndication comes in.

How article syndication works

Online article syndication basically involves experts (you or somebody in your business, in this case) writing authoritative, compelling, high-value articles in their area of expertise, then making that content available free of charge for use by online publishers on their websites, newsletters and e-zines. As a condition of using your content, the publisher agrees to present the article in its entirety, carrying your byline and, crucially, retaining your unique 'Author resource box' at the foot of your article – including biographical information, contact details and a live link back to your website.

Article syndication is available to anyone, and offers a great way to increase your online exposure, build a reputation for expertise in your field and get some valuable back links that can deliver both direct traffic and indirect search optimization benefits. The best articles can be picked up by different publishers again and again, offering cumulative long-term benefit to the original author.

Writing effective articles

Writing effective articles can be tricky – but remember, the whole point here is that you're writing in your area of expertise: you already know a lot about your subject matter. As in any other discipline, practice makes perfect – so give it a try, measure your results and refine things as you go. Try writing articles in different ways, then monitor the responses to see which approach gains more traction.

Here are our top tips to help you write more effective articles for syndication:

- **Write what you know**: a bit clichéd, but unless you're an experienced writer it really is better to stick to topics you know a lot about – especially if one of your goals is to build up your online profile as an expert in your field. You'll be more confident writing about subjects you're comfortable with, and that confidence will shine through in your writing, lending your copy more authority.

- **Write for your audience:** this can be tricky when you're writing for syndication, because you never really know who your final audience might be – but you can make an educated guess. Think to yourself 'What would a typical reader of this type of content be looking for?' then write your article for them, not for yourself.

- **Write keyword-optimized articles:** use keyword research (see Chapter 4) to find out what people are searching for, then write articles optimized for those target keyword phrases to maximize your article's potential search exposure. Just make sure that your optimization doesn't compromise the article's effectiveness for human readers.

- **Focus on your niche:** more focused, specialist articles may have narrower appeal in terms of overall readership, but they are much more likely to get picked up by publishers in the area you want to gain exposure in. That means your articles will ultimately reach readers who are interested in your area of business.

- **Make your articles valuable:** share your expertise, offer advice, deliver genuine value to your readers. Remember you're positioning yourself as an authority in your area of expertise.

- **Consider their longevity:** whenever possible, you want to maximize the shelf life of articles that you write. A useful 'How to' or top-tips article could be just as useful (therefore just as likely to be syndicated) in two years' time as it is the day you write it. Try and keep your articles as date neutral as possible to maximize the potential return on the time you invest in writing them.

- **Avoid the hype:** your articles aren't the place for promotional language – stick to the facts and your unique expert opinion.

- **Write with a consistent style and voice:** while it's fine to experiment with a different style and voice between articles, within a single article stay consistent. If you're writing in the first person (I, we, etc), retain that voice throughout, and keep the same tone and writing style throughout.

- **Keep them short:** articles for online syndication should typically fit comfortably on a single web page. Readers typically don't like reading very long articles online, and the longer the article, the more difficult it becomes to hold the reader's interest. Aim for a word count somewhere between 300 and 1,000 words per article, with 400–600 words as the ideal.

Where to submit your articles

Your content is an incredibly valuable commodity. There are literally thousands of online publishers whose businesses rely on sourcing high-quality, authoritative articles for their readers: articles just like yours. But how do you get your article out in front of as many prospective publishers as possible? As always seems to happen on the internet, where there's a need, websites spring up to service it, in this case article directory sites.

Article directories are basically websites that bring article authors and online publishers together. They usually consist of a searchable article repository, where authors can sign up to submit articles on a wide variety of topics. Submitted articles are normally reviewed by a human editor before being published to the site, where they then become available for syndication by online publishers and through the site's own newsletters, e-zines and RSS feeds. Web publishers can subscribe to receive alerts when new articles are submitted in their topics of interest.

There are literally hundreds of article directories out there. Top sites like EzineArticles (**www.ezinearticles.com**) or GoArticles.com (**www.goarticles. com**) are a good place to start your foray into online article syndication. These sites cover a vast range of subjects, and attract a lot of interest from online publishers, but bear in mind you'll also be competing with more authors (at the time of writing, EzineArticles reported 396,859 of them) and articles on the most popular sites. It's also worth looking at specialist sites that focus on articles in your particular vertical or subject niche, and submitting articles to them too. They may not get the same traffic as the mainstream directories, but the traffic they do get will be much more targeted.

FIGURE 8.1 Writing informative articles and submitting them to online article directories like EzineArticles (**www.ezinearticles.com**) can be a very effective way to boost your authority, demonstrate expertise, increase online exposure and drive qualified traffic to your website

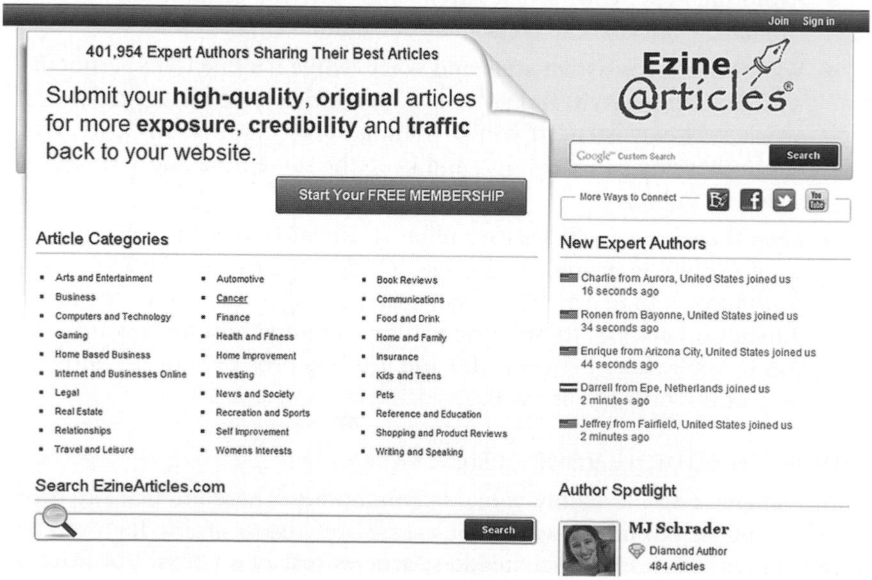

While in theory you could submit a small number of articles to a large number of article directories in the hope of increasing your exposure, in practice it's better to focus on writing a higher volume of high quality articles and submitting them to a small number of quality article directories.

Company blog

A company or corporate blog is both quick and easy to set up. It offers you a platform that you can use to communicate and interact with consumers on a much more personal level than you can on a corporate website. Company blogs are typically written by an individual or a team of people, and offer a convenient way to publish news and announcements, helpful articles relating to your products and services, comment on industry developments and to offer your customers a bit of insight into the culture of your organization and the personalities behind it.

You can also invite comments from readers on your blog – another medium where you can engage in conversation with consumers, ask their opinion and gauge their reaction to what's happening both in your company and in the marketplace.

While company blogs can be employed for a variety of different reasons, and the way you approach yours will very much depend on what it is you're trying to achieve, there are a few general guidelines that are worth bearing in mind when you embark on a company blog:

- **Blogs are social media**: this might be your site, but the social media rules of engagement from the previous chapter definitely still apply.

- **Blogs are not purely promotional platforms**: don't use your blog as a broadcast medium to push promotional messages to your audience... or before long you won't have an audience.

- **Engage**: make your blog posts topical, interesting, entertaining and genuinely valuable to your readers, and encourage them to respond.

- **Be yourself**: leave the stuffy, corporate communication for your main site – keep your blog light, fresh, conversational and personal.

- **Update regularly**: unlike your corporate site, your blog needs to stay fresh and current or it loses its value and appeal – having no blog is better than having a dead blog.

- **Encourage comments**: write posts that encourage feedback from your readers. Ask for their opinion at every opportunity – your blog is an invaluable platform for information exchange... use it.

- **Don't censor comments**: naturally you'll want to stop unsolicited link spam and obscenities from being published in your blog comments – but don't censor negative comments. They can often be among the most valuable feedback you can get, highlighting problems that you need to address, and giving you the opportunity to show your customers that you listen and respond quickly and positively to the issues they raise.

- **Empower the blogger**: it's important that whoever is writing your company blog has the authority to respond to customers directly, and to make decisions and commitments for the organization in response to comments received on the blog. Whoever is running the blog shouldn't need to ask permission from a manager or supervisor before posting a response... if they do, then perhaps the manager or supervisor should be the one writing the blog instead.

- **Optimize your blog**: your blog is a website like any other – optimize it for search engines as you would your main site (see Chapter 4). Due to their regular supply of topical content and their interactive nature, blogs tend to attract links more readily than corporate websites, and often do rather well when it comes to search rankings – improving the overall visibility of your brand.

Social media engagement

If you're looking to promote your business online today, you can't really avoid getting involved with social media. Nor would you want to. Social media offer the opportunity to get to know your customers in ways that simply weren't possible before. Engaging with consumers through social media gives you the chance to build real relationships with them.

We covered the relative merits of different types of social media in the last chapter, and won't re-explore them here. Suffice it to say that wherever your customers are congregating on social media websites, you have a priceless opportunity to get involved in the conversation, add value, build trust, improve your reputation and foster advocacy for your brand.

Monitoring the conversation – reputation management

As we discovered in the last chapter, people talk online all of the time – and as social media continue to mushroom they're talking more and more, about anything and everything, including your industry, your brand, your product. Some of these conversations may be incredibly positive, others benign and uninteresting, and a few may be damaging... but regardless of what's being discussed, you absolutely need to know when people are talking about your organization online.

Whether it's to foster and encourage positive conversation and buzz, to engage productively with the online community or to respond to negative sentiment before it gets out of hand, the first step is to discover what's being said and where.

What to track

The specific terms you'll want to track will vary depending on your business, but you'll probably want to track a list something like the following:

- your company name, brand names, any trademarks you own and product names, including variations and misspellings (which applies to all of the other points here as well);

- the names of your CEO, executives and other key employees;

- your competitors, their brands, trademarks, products and the names of their key employees;

- all of the above, prefixed or suffixed with common negative modifiers (eg '[your company name] sucks');

- terms specifically related to your industry.

How to track them

The first and most obvious option is to get involved in the online conversation wherever your customers are active. If you're an active member of an online community you'll generally be aware of who the main influencers are and what they're saying. With the best will in the world, though, you're unlikely to be able to maintain an active presence across all of the online communities where people could be discussing your brand.

There are quite a number of online services that specialize in monitoring online conversation and buzz – and as this topic gains in prominence there are more joining them all the time. Services like Nielsen Online (**www.nielsen-online.com**), BuzzLogic (**www.buzzlogic.com**), Cymfony (**www.cymfony.com**) and Trackur (**www.trackur.com**) offer different reputation and social media monitoring options ranging from costly enterprise-level solutions to more affordable basic services tailored to smaller businesses.

If you're looking for a less polished but more cost-effective monitoring solution to get started, you can set up your own basic monitoring system using freely available online tools and services:

- **Set up alerts:** the first thing to do is go to Google Alerts (**www.google.com/alerts**) and Yahoo! Alerts (alerts.yahoo.com), and set up alerts for the terms you want to monitor. These services will send you an e-mail alert with links to news articles, blog posts and web pages they index that mention your terms.

- **Set up RSS feeds:** go to the social media sites and content aggregations sites (Bloglines, Technorati, Google News, Google Blog Search, Twitter Search, BlogPulse, Icerocket, Tweetscan, FriendFeed, etc) that you want to monitor. Many will let you search for keywords and subscribe to custom RSS feeds based on your search terms. You can then aggregate and organize all of these feeds in your RSS reader of choice (Google Reader, Feedreader, Newsgator, FeedDemon, etc; for an introduction to the concept of RSS feeds, check out this video on YouTube by CommonCraft: **http://bit.ly/UDMRSS**).

- **Custom search engines:** a useful way of searching across multiple sites that you want to monitor, but which don't offer the RSS search functionality outlined above, is to create a custom search engine using a service like Google Custom Search (**www.google.com/cse**) or Rollyo (**www.rollyo.com**). You could cover all of the sites you want to monitor with an individual custom search engine, or create a different one for each type of site you want to monitor – eg one for consumer review sites, another for complaint sites relating to your industry and another for your industry-specific news sites.

Once you have your monitoring system up and running, establish a procedure for checking it regularly. Time is often of the essence – especially if there's something negative afoot – and it's important to catch things early. The key thing with reputation management is to engage as soon as possible, and try to influence the conversation in a positive way, or at least to give your side of the story to the community. Ideally you want to prevent negative comment from spreading through social networks and reaching the SERPs, where they could be presented to literally millions of people.

FIGURE 8.2 RSS readers, like the free web-based tool Google Reader (**www.google.com/reader**), allow you to subscribe to website 'feeds'. The reader aggregates and sorts all of your feeds and presents them in one convenient location for you to read at your leisure. Feed readers can also be invaluable monitoring tools to help you manage your online reputation

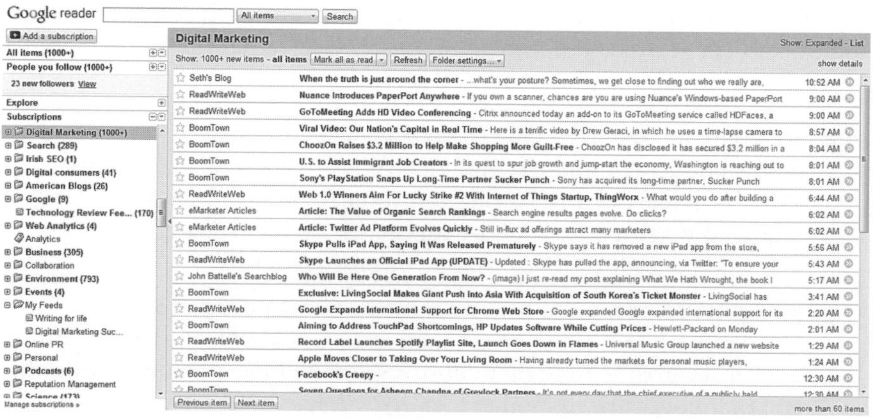

Damage limitation: turning the tide when things go wrong

Bad things happen sometimes. That's life!

When they happen, and people start talking about them online, though, word can spread quickly, and unless you do something to limit the damage it can escalate to become a groundswell of *bad* publicity. The power of social media, the ubiquity of the internet and everything that works so effectively to help you build a good online reputation can tarnish that reputation even more quickly. Whether it's a genuine grievance, a simple misunderstanding or a malicious rumour, you need to act, and act quickly to mitigate the potential damage.

Prevention is always better than cure

Do everything you can to avoid negative online publicity occurring in the first place. Minimizing bad online press is much easier than mitigating the damage in its aftermath. That sounds like obvious advice, but with so much at stake it bears a mention. Review your processes and procedures, make sure customers have a clear and straightforward way to air their grievances with the company rather than taking it into the public domain. Deal with customer correspondence quickly, professionally and effectively. Make it your goal to turn negative customer sentiment into a positive customer outcome before it becomes a bigger problem.

Another effective way to minimize negative online publicity is to actively participate in the online communities that matter most to your business. Don't just monitor them remotely, get in there at the coalface and actually become part of the community. If people know and trust you within that community they'll be much slower to lend credence to spurious negative remarks.

Do something

Once you identify a negative post that carries any significance or weight, you will need to do something about it. Don't bury your head in the sand in the hope it will all sort itself out. Quite often it's not the negative sentiments themselves that do the most damage to a company's online reputation; it's the lack of response, or an inappropriate response, that fans the flames of malcontent.

- **Analyse what has been said:** get a handle on what you're dealing with. Before you dive into the conversation, do a bit of digging. Does the grievance have merit, is it just a misunderstanding, or is it malicious gossip? Know where you stand and have a plan of action before you engage.

- **Engage positively in the conversation**: don't try to hide the truth. It won't just come back to haunt you, it could come back and bury you! Be open, honest and forthcoming. If you have made a mistake, admit it, and ask what you can do to help resolve the matter amicably. Look for a win–win.

- **Politely point out any misunderstandings**: if the problem was caused by a misunderstanding, clarify the matter publicly. Put all the facts on the table and let other community members make up their own minds. Be professional and courteous, and point out what you'll be doing to prevent such a misunderstanding arising in the future.

- **Stay calm, professional and respectful**: aggrieved people can be touchy and our immediate human instinct is to protect what's ours – in this case our reputation. Don't overreact. Keep calm – far better to fight fire with water, not more fuel. You might even try thanking the poster for their valuable feedback – analysis of negative comments can often prove more valuable than positive ones, pointing to things that your business could be doing more effectively. Never, ever lose your cool and resort to vitriol… it helps nobody.

- **Post additional and supporting information on your website**: whatever response you make, action you take and resolutions you agree, post updates and additional supporting information on your website, and link to it from the original conversation and other places you frequent online. Your site is the first place people will look for clarification – make it easy for them to find.

- **Be responsive and informative**: respond to what people are saying to you online. Don't become entrenched – this is not a battle. Be open and flexible. Look, listen, learn and respond in a positive way.

- **If it's malicious, counter it**: if the negative statements are malicious (competitors posting inaccurate and damning consumer reviews of your products, for example, or an unjustified smear campaign by a disgruntled former employee), you should contact the website owner and ask them to remove the offending material. You should also ask them to publish clarifying remarks on the site, and publish a prominent and comprehensive counter-statement on your own website. As an absolute last resort you may have to resort to legal action, although it's not generally necessary, and you should avoid getting the lawyers involved if at all possible.

When negative pages hit the SERPs

Hopefully, by having an effective monitoring system in place, being active on popular sites and following the mitigation strategies outlined here and elsewhere, you'll be able to counter negative publicity before it makes its way into the SERPs and gets in front of millions of eyeballs. If negative stuff does hit the search engines, with any luck your own content around the web will be well enough optimized to outrank it for the keywords that matter to you. If not, you have two choices – live with it, or work to optimize your own content so that it outranks the offending material and pushes it down the SERPs.

Dell learns to listen: the computer maker takes to the blogosphere to repair its tarnished image

Jeff Jarvis

In the age of customers empowered by blogs and social media, Dell has leapt from worst to first.

Start with the worst. In June 2005, I unwittingly unleashed a blog storm around the computer company. Terminally frustrated with a lemony laptop and torturous service, I vented steam on my blog under the headline: 'Dell sucks'. That's not quite as juvenile as it sounds, for a Google search on any brand followed by 'sucks' reveals the true consumer reports for that company's customers. Thousands of frustrated consumers eventually commented on and linked to my blog, saying, 'I agree.' They were a leading indicator of Dell's problems, which the company – and analysts and reporters covering it – should have heeded. My story ended, I thought, that August when, after returning the Dell and buying a Mac, I blogged an open letter to Michael Dell suggesting his company read blogs, write blogs, ask customers for guidance, and 'join the conversation your customers are having without you'.

The following April, Dell did join that conversation. It dispatched technicians to reach out to complaining bloggers and solve their problems, earning pleasantly surprised buzz in return. That July, Dell started its Direct2Dell blog, where it quickly had to deal with a burning-battery issue and where chief blogger Lionel Menchaca gave the company a frank and credible human voice. Last February, Michael Dell launched IdeaStorm.com, asking customers to tell the company what to do. Dell is following their advice, selling Linux computers and reducing the promotional 'bloatware' that clogs machines. Today, Dell even enables customers to rate its products on its site.

Has Dell really gotten the blog religion? I recently visited the company's Round Rock (Texas) headquarters to find out. Founder Dell, who took back the CEO reins in January, acknowledges its problems – 'We screwed up, right?' But then he starts to sound like a blogger himself: 'These conversations are going to occur whether you like it or not, okay? Well, do you want to be part of that or not? My argument is you absolutely do. You can learn from that. You can improve your reaction time. And you can be a better company by listening and being involved in that conversation.'

New metrics for success

Dell's worst problem had been that customers were having too many of the wrong conversations with too many service technicians in too many countries. 'It was a real mess,' confesses Dick Hunter, former head of manufacturing and now head of customer service. Dell's DNA of cost cutting 'got in the way', Hunter says. 'In order to become very efficient, I think we became ineffective.'

Hunter has increased service spending 35 per cent, cut outsourcing partners from 14 to six (and is headed to three), and retrained staff to take on more problems and responsibility (higher-end techs can scrap their phone scripts; techs in other countries learn empathy). Crucially, Hunter also stopped counting the 'handle time' per call that rushed representatives and motivated them to transfer customers so they would be someone else's problem. At Dell's worst, more than 7,000 of the 400,000 customers calling each week suffered transfers more than seven times. Today, the transfer rate has fallen from 45 per cent to 18 per cent. Now Hunter tracks the minutes per resolution of a problem, which run in the 40s. His favourite acronym mantra (among many) is RI1: resolve in one call. (Apple claims it resolves 90 per cent of problems in one call.) He is also experimenting with outreach e-mails and chatty phone calls to 5,000 selected New Yorkers before problems strike, trying to replace the brother-in-law as their trusted adviser.

Has it made a difference?

The crucial word you hear at Dell is 'relationship'. Dell blogger Menchaca has led the charge in convincing bloggers that 'real people are here to listen', and so he diligently responds and links to critics, and holds up his end of the conversation. 'You can't fake it,' he says. Dell's team is staunching the flow of bad buzz. By Dell's measure, negative blog posts about it have dropped from 49 per cent to 22 per cent. And the Dell Hell posts on my blog, which used to come up high on a Google search for the company, are now relegated to second-page search engine Siberia. 'That change in perception just doesn't happen with a press release,' Menchaca says.

But reality still has to catch up to perception. To this day, I get blog comments and e-mails from disgruntled Dell customers. The University of Michigan's PC satisfaction scores show Dell dropping from 78 per cent in 2006 to 74 per cent this year. Internal Dell measurements showed satisfaction was actually much worse than that. A year ago, it was 58 per cent among core users, even lower in the high end. That, Hunter says, made the boss 'go ballistic'. Today, Hunter's measurements show satisfaction among high-end customers at more than 80 per cent and among core consumers at 74 per cent – numbers that he says must further improve. 'I think what the Web has brought is the voice of that 25 per cent,' Hunter says.

Customer collaboration

But the opportunities created by the conversation go far beyond dousing fires. The cant among executives trying to play the Web 2.0 game is that the customer is in charge. Well, if you really mean that, if you cede control to your customers, they can add tremendous value. Dell's customers not only make product suggestions and warn of problems, they help fellow customers fix them. Today, customers share their knowledge in so many ways that Dell's team says the challenge is to manage that knowledge and spread it.

To enable collaboration, the company is starting wikis that users can edit together. To encourage interaction, Dell plans to experiment with loyalty programmes, rewarding good customers with gifts, opportunities to meet Michael, service upgrades and possibly discounts. I ask whether they'd compensate helpful users, creating a marketplace of advice.

But Manish Mehta, head of e-commerce, is uncomfortable with payment, fearing it might compromise the credibility of these customers in their communities. And credible advocates are at the heart of the strategy Dell's new chief marketing officer, Mark Jarvis, is devising. 'By listening to our customers,' he says, 'that is actually the most perfect form of marketing you could have.'

I contend that this marks a fundamental shift in the relationship of customers with companies. Dell and its customers are collaborating on new forms of content and marketing, but note that they are doing this without the help of media and marketing companies.

Michael Dell predicts that customer relationships will 'continue to be more intimate'. He even speaks of 'co-creation of products and services', a radical notion from a giant manufacturer. 'I'm sure there's a lot of things that I can't even imagine, but our customers can imagine,' Dell says, still sounding very bloggish. 'A company this size is not going to be about a couple of people coming up with ideas. It's going to be about millions of people and harnessing the power of those ideas.' Once you can hear them.

Jeff Jarvis is the author of What Would Google Do?, *published by HarperCollins in 2009. He blogs about media and news on his blog at Buzzmachine.com. He is associate professor and director of the interactive journalism programme and the new business models for news project at the City University of New York's Graduate School of Journalism.*

This article was first published in 2007, but still highlights an iconic example of how brands can harness negative buzz as a catalyst for real and lasting positive change.

Online PR and reputation management, through monitoring, analysing and influencing online conversations, has become a crucial part of any digital marketer's arsenal. It serves to raise your profile, and to bolster and protect the hard-earned online reputation that is so essential to your online success.

CASE STUDY Write the future

FIGURE 8.3 Online video played a fundamental role in Nike's integrated global campaign 'Write the Future'

The World Cup has been won, and the winner is... Nike.

Telegraph

The challenge

Nike wanted to own the buzz around the 2010 FIFA World Cup, despite the fact that it was not one of the competition's official sponsors.

Target audience

Primarily football-(soccer-)obsessed teenagers around the world. Secondly the campaign was also designed to appeal to a broader audience of global football fans.

Action

Nike started talking to fans online about the consequence of both victory and defeat well before the first ball was kicked. One month before the tournament began, Nike invited fans and bloggers to take a glimpse into the future, exclusively on Facebook.

Following the social media launch, the 'Write the Future' film aired simultaneously during the Champions League Final on TV stations spanning 32 countries around the world. Concurrent global takeovers took place on Xbox LIVE, Facebook and YouTube.

Nike kept the conversation fuelled with a constant supply of content on Facebook and in print, outdoor and retail placements. It also asked fans to take a look into their own future and see it play out in a number of ways, culminating in 'The Chance', where true ball players could showcase their talent on Facebook for Nike scouts to see.

Finally, the team used social media to light up the sky in Johannesburg, with fans' headline predictions being beamed in 16 languages onto one of the biggest skyscrapers in the city.

Results

The campaign was deemed a tremendous success, generated unparalleled online buzz, and delivered tangible bottom-line results for Nike:

- Orders on Nike products grew by 7 per cent globally.

- There were over 40 million online views of the film and 1.9 billion impressions on Facebook.

- Nike Football Facebook fans were up by 336 per cent, from 1.1 million to 4.8 million in the campaign period.

- Nike became the most shared brand online in 2010.

- Nike garnered 30 per cent of brand buzz during the tournament, more than double its leading competitor, Adidas.

Link to campaign creative

- http://bit.ly/UDMNike

Credits

Client:	Nike
Geographical scope:	Global
Agency:	Wieden + Kennedy
Campaign contact:	Bella Laine, PR and Marketing Manager for W+K London

09

Affiliate marketing and strategic partnerships

> *Give me a set of golf clubs, fresh air and a beautiful partner and you can keep the clubs and the fresh air!* JACK BENNY

> *In this new wave of technology, you can't do it all yourself, you have to form alliances.* CARLOS SLIM HELÚ

OUR CHAPTER PLEDGE TO YOU

When you reach the end of this chapter you'll have answers to the following questions:

- What is a strategic partnership and how does it work?

- Would a strategic partnership suit my businesses?

- How do I go about setting up a strategic partnership?

- What is affiliate marketing and how does it work?

- What can affiliate marketing do for my business?

Recognizing opportunities for strategic partnership

In the context of digital marketing, 'strategic partnerships' are most often defined by a deal between two (or more) parties where the desired outcome is a win–win for all concerned. Ideally a strategic partnership should be about synergy: all parties should come out of the relationship with more than any of them could have achieved alone.

One way to visualize a strategic partnership is in a bricks-and-mortar retail context: suppliers rent space in high-traffic department stores in order to sell their products or services to customers who visit that store. The store brings in the traffic, the supplier sells their wares, the customer gets more choice... everybody wins.

Almost exactly the same process occurs online. A website that attracts large volumes of traffic will seek out long-term partnerships with suppliers to rent space in sections of their website; at the same time, online retailers or 'e-tailers' are looking for additional online 'venues' to pedal their wares. When they come together in the right circumstances you have all the ingredients for a mutually beneficial strategic partnership. Of course, the $64,000 question in all of this is agreeing the balance of risk.

Online strategic partnerships usually go something like this

A large portal with a million visitors per day sells inventory (space) on its site to a travel company to advertise its products and special offers. In that scenario the burden of risk is entirely with the travel company – they're paying to advertise on the portal's website in the hope of attracting new customers. But wait a minute, isn't that just a form of online advertising?

Yes, except that, in order to mitigate some of the risk, the travel company may negotiate with the portal to lower the cost of rental in exchange for certain incentives. The incentive could be exclusive products or offers for the portal's users (increasing the perceived value of the portal site, attracting and retaining more visitors).

With a tangible mutual benefit on the table, there's a good chance the portal site will be tempted to reduce the required advertising investment in return for:

- guarantees for their users in relation to a special offer – possibly around exclusivity;
- a revenue share of business accruing from the campaign, which can be tracked using page tags and analytics software;
- a long-term deal that can guarantee portal owners a healthy ROI.

Because portal owners now have a vested interest they also agree to do some editorial and PR around the advertising to build up the partnership.

Hold on, though – doesn't that smack a little of sponsorship? The burden of risk is still almost completely with the e-tailer. While there may certainly be some value in the 'exclusivity' element of the deal, it still doesn't feel balanced, because on the basis of no business being transacted, the only real loser is the merchant – in our case the travel company. And if it's a long-term deal that doesn't bode well for them.

A strategic partnership should be clearly balanced on both sides with risk being shared throughout. Just because a portal has millions of users and a premium for advertising space on its site doesn't mean it is going to be worse off by adopting a revenue-share approach rather than one which consists of guaranteed cash. That view may not be the one regularly pedalled by portal owners around the world... but nonetheless, it is true!

Surely the aim of the portal owner should be to maintain and grow traffic to their site, ensuring the content is up to date, up to scratch and that they offer users something of real value – in that respect they're like good old-fashioned media. How then does it suit users if the site offers a series of exclusive offers backed by marketers and ultimately paid for by the highest bidder? In a word, it doesn't... but it's a practice that has been rife among websites who, understandably, have been focused on using every trick in the book to maximize advertising revenue on the site, often enticing marketers with that tired old formula of advertising masquerading as editorial (or special offers) in an effort to bolster advertising opportunity.

Tips on entering into strategic partnerships

Our advice to marketers seeking strategic partnerships with high-traffic websites is as follows:

- Do not enter into long-term arrangements without fully testing the site first. This is the real beauty of digital marketing – the ability to test before you invest.

- If you do decide to go for a long-term deal, make sure this is going to be of ongoing interest to the end users. Vary the content, change your offers regularly, use seasonality or other features to mix things up. You don't want to end up with the same message, day in, day out – except, of course, when it works!

- Talk to the site's other strategic partners – find out how long deals have been in place and how they value the association. Ask them how they go about tracking performance, etc. If possible, find out which strategic partnerships they no longer run on the site, and what happened. Marketers can be quite guarded with this kind of information, so you may not get it – but if you can overcome their reticence the information can be invaluable.

- Agree how performance will be measured from day one, and ensure your advertising and promotional messages are fully tagged to track all necessary data remember: it's not about clicks; it's about actual conversions.

- Be prepared to disclose profit margins; seek to build a close, transparent relationship with the site, a relationship where both parties fully understand the commercial realities and the mutual benefit involved. A little bit of patience and commitment upfront will certainly help to establish realistic expectations.

Affiliate marketing

The most basic explanation of affiliate marketing is that it is the process whereby a brand site, such as an electronics retailer, attracts customers by rewarding a third party (the affiliate) for promoting their products and driving converting traffic to their website.

The crucial element of the definition is the 'converting' part. It's the conversion – or action – from the consumer which forms the heart of the affiliate relationship, and the beauty of that from an online brand's perspective is that you get to define exactly what that action is.

In retail terms, for example, an action could be as simple as the sale of a product. It's important to note, though, that affiliate marketing is far from just a playground for retail companies. Some of the first vendor sites to embrace affiliate marketing were about as far away from retail as you can get. Gaming and gambling sites were among the pioneers, harnessing the power of a 'virtual sales force' to attract new members... and they're still blazing a trail in the space.

As the online landscape evolves, affiliate marketing is being employed on a more widespread basis, with almost every industry now utilizing some sort of affiliate activity to drive their online business forward. In fact, we're affiliates ourselves: if you get an e-mail from either of us, click on the *Understanding Digital Marketing* link in our signature and go on to buy this book, we'll receive a small percentage of the sale as a commission for sending you to the vendor's website. Simple, isn't it?

Of course, affiliates can be rewarded for more than just sales. It all depends what the brand or vendor's marketing goal is. It's not unusual these days to see affiliates rewarded for a wide variety of consumer actions. Things like clicking on a link, 'liking' a page on Facebook or retweeting a great offer on Twitter can all trigger an affiliate transaction.

Who are the players?

In most affiliate marketing transactions, there are four parties involved, although it's not always that straightforward and there can be more.

The merchant

In our earlier example the electronics retailer was the merchant in the affiliate equation. Merchants are the companies who want their products and services advertised on the internet and are trying to attract new business. They could be from any industry, including finance, gaming, retail, mobile phones, data collection (survey companies), charities... the list is almost endless.

The affiliates

Affiliates are the virtual sales force. They typically control online real estate and advertise the goods and services offered by the merchants in return for a reward. Later we'll explore the different types of affiliates, and how they go about attracting customers to merchants' offers.

The affiliate network

To reward affiliates for an action taken by a consumer, merchants need to be able to track when the action has been completed and know which affiliate to credit for it. This is where affiliate networks come into the frame.

Networks provide the technical solutions to be able to track consumer activity online and allocate rewards to affiliates once consumers have completed the prescribed action. Affiliate networks often act as middlemen, introducing merchants to affiliates relevant to their industry, and suggesting improvements to maximize consumer interaction.

In some cases, merchants may decide to forgo the use of a network and opt instead to implement their own tracking technology. In these cases, the in-house tracking solution fulfils the same role, on a technical level, as the affiliate network. However, it does require the merchant to administer their own network of affiliates and undertake the tracking, support and payment of each individual partner.

It is for this reason that many merchants opt to use an affiliate network as not only do they benefit from the personal introductions a network can offer, but the administration resource required to effectively manage an affiliate programme is significantly reduced.

The consumers

This is the business end, not just of affiliate marketing – but of all the online marketing activities we've discussed throughout the book. Consumers are the target market we're all vying to attract and affiliates are doing everything they can to get consumers interested in merchants' offers and generate affiliate commissions.

How does affiliate marketing work?

FIGURE 9.1 How basic affiliate marketing works

For simplicity, Figure 9.1 shows a 'Do it yourself' affiliate arrangement, where the web merchant is running their own affiliate programme. Things can get a little more complicated when an affiliate network acts as an intermediary between merchant and consumer, but the basic premise remains the same.

In its simplest form affiliate marketing works like this:

- **Step 1** – a consumer visits an affiliate's website, arrives at their search-optimized landing page, receives their e-mail promotion, reads their tweet, status update or PPC ad, etc.

- **Step 2** – the consumer clicks on an affiliate link, and is taken via the affiliate network to the merchant's landing page or product page. The affiliate network tags the customer's browser, normally with a cookie, recording which link the customer clicked on, from which affiliate and when. Normally the consumer is oblivious to this process, and continues to browse the merchant's site as normal.

- **Step 3** – the consumer performs the desired action on the merchant's site, and a small piece of embedded code on the merchant's site informs the affiliate network. The network checks for the relevant cookie on the consumer's computer, and if present allocates payment to the referring affiliate.

The process is relatively simple... but what happens if a consumer visits two or three different affiliate sites before deciding to complete their action? Wouldn't the merchant end up paying multiple times for a single user action?

In this scenario the networks typically reward the latest click – so the most recent affiliate to refer the visitor is rewarded for the action. Whenever a customer visits an affiliate site and clicks on a link, the browser cookie is updated with the last referring affiliate's details, ensuring that only the last click will result in a payout.

Admittedly the last-click-wins model is a crude method of determining the influence of an affiliate's contribution to a consumer's action. After all, the initial and subsequent affiliate referrals could well have contributed significantly to the consumer's ultimate decision to act. While it's not ideal, the last-click-wins model is currently seen as the best solution available. A lot of research is currently underway to investigate the consumer journey, looking at different ways to identify where each party adds value in the sales funnel and how credit (and rewards) can be apportioned accordingly.

Many industry insiders are of the opinion that, in the not too distant future, merchants will seek to divide the reward they offer to remunerate more affiliates involved in the process.

What does an affiliate look like?

Is there such a thing as a typical affiliate? Can you identify an affiliate site or an affiliate's activity right off the bat?

Think about some of your favourite sites and try to identify how many you think are affiliates. You'll be surprised by the numbers that, behind the scenes, are being rewarded for actions you take.

Let's take a look at some of the more common affiliate types consumers may encounter as they browse the web. This list is by no means comprehensive but it will give you a flavour of the sort of affiliates you might encounter as an online merchant:

- **Cashback/loyalty sites** – consumers love getting something for nothing and this is the driving force behind the rise in popularity of cashback and loyalty sites. Consumers can choose to shop at any one of hundreds, if not thousands, of sites and will receive money back on their purchases. This cashback can be in the form of cold, hard cash or in the form of points or some other virtual 'currency'. Quidco.com and Nectar are two very good examples of this type of affiliate.

- **Comparison sites** – we've all used them when comparing products online. However, not many consumers are aware that their purchases through a comparison site earn the site a reward. MoneySupermarket.com is one of the best-known comparison sites but there are smaller sites comparing some very specific industries. A good example is compareandrecycle.com, which compares the prices consumers can receive for recycling their unwanted mobile phones.

- **Content sites** – this category of affiliate acts as an umbrella for a number of different types of sites. Most recognizable would be blogs, where the content is written by a company or individual. However, any site which carries information could be classed as a content site. These sites predominantly operate in two ways. The first is creative placements surrounding the content. Using our example of an electronics retailer again, you may find an article on the latest plasma television accompanied by a creative ad for the same, or similar, product. The second is contextual linking, where text links are inserted into the content. An article reviewing a new plasma television may link certain key phrases within the text to a retailer using an affiliate link in the hope that once a customer has read the content, they'll be compelled to buy the product and will click through their link.

- **E-mail affiliates** – as the name would suggest, these affiliates specialize in advertising to consumers via e-mail. At some point in the past, the consumers have given their consent for their e-mail addresses to be used for this purpose. E-mail affiliates generally own, or have access to, lists containing thousands of e-mail addresses. Merchants would provide e-mail creative promoting a specific action and these affiliates would e-mail the proposition to their list(s) in the hopes that sufficient consumers will complete the action required.

- **Paid search specialists** – pay per click, or PPC, is a popular method of promotion for affiliates. These affiliates bid on terms or phrases in the search engines and include ads in the sponsored listings driving traffic either directly to the retailer or to customized landing pages to help with the consumer conversion. Like normal paid search, these affiliates pay the search engines per click but only receive a reward from the merchant should the consumers complete the required actions. Therefore, paid search affiliates take a comparably higher risk as they pay for clicks out of their own pocket on the assumption consumers will be enticed to interact with merchants.

- **Retargeting specialists** – while surfing the internet you may have seen an ad for a product you've just reviewed on a merchant site. It may seem like these ads are following you, promoting products you've already seen. This is the basis of retargeting, where affiliates serve dynamic ads including products you've already seen, from sites you've already visited. Unlike other forms of affiliate, retargeting affiliates are not concerned with introducing new traffic or customers to merchants. Rather, they're concerned with improving returning customer conversion rates. They do this by advertising products to consumers who have reviewed but not bought them and try to entice them to return and complete their action. This is the reason why many retargeting ads also carry discounts or vouchers as this provides an extra incentive to the consumer to return. Retargetting now comprises 5 per cent of all online display media. Organizations such as **www.struq.com** lead the way in this space.

- **Social networking specialists** – we're all familiar with Facebook and Twitter, and recent studies show that some people spend more than an hour per day using them. It was therefore only a matter of time before both platforms introduced a way to monetize the traffic they receive. Facebook and Twitter have both introduced advertising options and affiliates were among the first to utilize these new features. These affiliates, particularly on Facebook, operate in much the same way as paid search affiliates in that they pay Facebook per click and hope to earn rewards from merchants that are greater than their costs. The challenge with social media is that advertising on these platforms is essentially interrupting the consumer while they're busy doing something else. Consumers aren't looking for products, nor are they in a buying mood. But they are looking to be social and it is this fact which has seen a rise in the number of merchants paying rewards to affiliates for increasing communities rather than sales. So next time you 'like' that page on Facebook, you may be helping an affiliate earn their living.

- **Voucher code/discount sites** – the late noughties saw most of the Western world enter a recession. Times were tough, consumers didn't have the expendable income they used to and online sales were slowing down. It was during this time that vouchers and discounts saw a substantial rise in popularity, which has continued well past the recession. Affiliates quickly saw the value in this channel and set about building the large numbers of voucher code sites which many of us recognize today. MyVoucherCodes.com and Vouchercodes.co.uk are two sites which many consumers would be familiar with. The concept is simple: Why pay full price when we can offer you a discount? Merchants have become a little more savvy when using voucher code affiliates to drive sales (and in this instance it is almost always a sale) as they begin to push high-margin items or end-of-range clearance items as a priority.

What are the benefits?

There are a number of benefits to using affiliate marketing, which can be loosely divided into hard and soft benefits. Hard benefits are those which are tangible and measurable. The soft benefits may be a little more difficult to quantify but are no less important.

Hard benefits

- **Reduced risk** – possibly the most important benefit of affiliate marketing is the reduced risk to the merchant. As merchants only pay per action, and only actions they define, the possibility of not receiving a return on investment is vastly reduced. In general, the upfront costs of affiliate marketing are negligible, meaning that merchants only incur costs for actions undertaken by consumers. This is in stark contrast to other forms of digital marketing where most, if not all, of the risk lies with the merchant, and upfront costs are the name of the game.

- **Channel access** – as you can see from the previous section, which explained some of the different affiliate types, affiliate marketing allows merchants to access a wide variety of digital media through one centralized campaign. Merchants, who may not be in a position to fully utilize these channels on their own, now have the ability to explore opportunities which may have been out of their reach previously.

- **Accountability** – no blind faith, no broken promises. It sounds refreshing, doesn't it? This is the cornerstone of why affiliate marketing is so popular with merchants, from the biggest brands to the smallest start-ups. The simple fact that all activity, from impression to action, is tracked means that merchants can rest assured that their campaigns are genuinely delivering according to their requirements. Whether a merchant uses its own tracking or utilizes the services of an affiliate network, each party is accountable for their actions, resulting in better-quality traffic, better communication between parties and, in general, better results.

Soft benefits

- **Free branding** – all the consumers referred by affiliates have to come from somewhere... the affiliate site. However, not every customer who visits the affiliate will click through to a merchant. So what about all of those that choose not to click? Well, they are still exposed to the merchant's advertising and, as such, the merchant has increased their brand exposure. The beauty of affiliate marketing is that this brand exposure is free as merchants only pay for actions.

- **Healthy competition** – we've already established that affiliates operate in a wide variety of channels. In some cases, their activity can overlap with other marketing channels, resulting in some healthy competition. In many instances, non-affiliate companies are loath to have affiliates playing in their sandbox as affiliates force them to up their game. Since affiliates only get paid per action, they are extremely focused on driving consumers through to merchants and ensuring those actions take place and conversions are maximized. There have been many instances where affiliate conversion rates have far exceeded those of the more traditional digital marketing companies and, as a result, merchants have begun to demand increased performance from their other marketing channels.

- **Standardized content** – if you've ever been in a situation where you get asked the same question repeatedly, you'll understand that providing the same answer time and again can get tiresome. Likewise, if you keep pushing the same message online, to numerous partners, eventually your delivery of that message will portray your tiredness. This is where your affiliate programme comes to the fore as you are able to provide standardized marketing collateral to hundreds of partners simultaneously, each time relying on your affiliate network or tracking interface to provide a pitch-perfect delivery of what your company is about. Add to that the advice you'll receive from your network regarding best practice for your industry and there is the potential to provide much more than the sales pitch. Creative, price lists, content copy and more can be delivered to industry standard, to hundreds of partners, thereby maximizing compatibility and increasing conversions.

Our top affiliate marketing tips

- **Do your homework** – knowing your industry, your company and your competition is one of the most important steps in making affiliate marketing work for you. While, as the name suggests, affiliate marketing is a marketing function, the basis for a profitable campaign lies in analysing statistics. Identifying the action required and the acquisition cost of that action are just two important pieces in the puzzle. Benchmarking your findings against your competition will highlight areas where you have a competitive advantage and it's these areas that need to be communicated to your affiliates.

- **Be a people person** – let's not forget that affiliate marketing is about connecting merchants with affiliates who have sites or activities relevant to promoting that merchant's business. Let's also not forget that this promotion takes place on a voluntary basis and affiliates will promote the 'best' merchant. 'Best' is a relative term but often it is determined by whether the affiliates feel they can communicate with you effectively. Relationships are at the core of a successful campaign and, as we all know, people buy people.

- **Pick your partners** – picking your partners extends outside your affiliate base to include your network or tracking provider. Contrary to popular belief, there are some major differences between networks and tracking platforms. Some may be purely technical in nature and these will need to be weighed to determine the true impact on what you're trying to achieve. More important, especially if choosing to use a network, is ensuring that you choose a network with a solid track record in your industry or one that can confidently display proficiency in what you're looking to achieve. In the main, you're going to be relying on your network to introduce you to affiliates, at least initially, so it is best to ensure that your chosen network has the right contact list.

Common affiliate marketing pitfalls

Everyone makes mistakes. New entrants into affiliate marketing are no different and, as with anything digital, what works for one company may not work for another, so there is bound to be a bit of trial and error involved in establishing your affiliate programme. However, there are a few common pitfalls which we'll hopefully help you avoid:

- **Focusing on actions rather than costs** – or 'Bambi syndrome', as some in the affiliate industry like to call it. This sometimes happens when a new entrant into the market realizes the true power of affiliate marketing. They see the number of sales rocketing, but forget to stay focused on the bottom line. It is not uncommon for a new programme to offer huge commissions to get off the ground by attracting top affiliates, but at some point commission rates will need to come down or the campaign will run at a loss.

- **The 'Our message is timeless' effect** – you've worked hard, your launch content is outstanding, your creative elements are top notch and affiliates flock to your campaign. Success! But don't sit back. The hard work is only just beginning. You'll need to keep the various elements of your campaign fresh to keep affiliates interested and recruit new partners. A common mistake is for companies to take their eye off the ball when their collateral is working for them. By the time they realize performance is slipping it's too late to come up with something new and their hard-won affiliates have moved on to the new 'best' merchant in the space.

- **If I brand it, they will come** – being a big brand doesn't guarantee success in the affiliate market. In fact, being a huge brand, the biggest brand, doesn't guarantee success. Your brand strength will help you to be recognized by affiliates, but don't get lulled into relying on your brand equity. Affiliates won't feel obliged to promote you – they'll assess your offer on its merits, and will only choose to partner with you if your offer stacks up.

CASE STUDY Personalized retargeting and affiliate marketing increase conversion

FIGURE 9.2 By combining personalized retargeting with their existing affiliate programmes, Maximuscle increased conversion of repeat visitors by 362 per cent

The affiliate channel saw month-on-month uplifts of over 40 per cent, whilst year-on-year sales were up by 94 per cent. By utilizing the myThings retargeting service via our affiliate programme, using a CPA model, it allows us to successfully retain customers that leave our site in a manner that is cost effective to the business.

Chris Wiseman, Affiliate Marketing Manager, PineSolutions.

The challenge

According to some sources, around 98 per cent of visitors to e-commerce websites leave without making a purchase. Online merchants are allocating significant time and resources to generate higher levels of traffic to their sites, and yet are still unsuccessful at securing enough buyer interest to convert those visitors into customers.

Two of the UK's leading online retail brands were searching for a solution that could analyse and leverage anonymous user intent to promote improved conversion and return on investment.

Retailer overview: Maximuscle

Maximuscle is the UK leader in sports nutrition, operating an e-commerce site that provides a range of specialized sports nutrition supplements, protein powders, weight-loss products, diet plans, calorie counters and more.

Retailer overview: PineSolutions

PineSolutions is the UK's largest online furniture retailer, offering quality and competitively priced wooden furniture delivered fast.

Action

The myThings personalization engine aims to increase website conversions by delivering content optimized to be more relevant to the individual site visitor. Affiliate Window's partnership with myThings makes this level of personalization technology accessible to online retailers through their existing affiliate programmes.

Both Maximuscle and PineSolutions elected to use the new myThings personalization solution to microtarget web visitors with individualized product recommendations based on previous interactions with their websites. myThings then used the data to make informed decisions, in real time, about the user's propensity to buy (ie whether the user should be retargeted or not), and then selected the product recommendations, banner placement and promotion most likely to result in a conversion of that individual user.

Predicted product and promotion relevancy was calculated based on advanced algorithms taking data on product and categories browsed, stage in the predefined sales funnel and other parameters.

For example, if a viewer on the Maximuscle website showed interest in an arm-strengthening product last week, on the return visit myThings would optimize content to present similar strengthening supplements predicted to deliver an increased probability of conversion.

Results

- Both merchants experienced much higher click-through rates than they had previously, and benefited directly from increased conversation rates and a subsequent boost in their ROI.
- Maximuscle reported that the return conversation rates for visitors exposed to the myThings retargetting were up by 362 per cent.
- PineSolutions tracked a consistent uplift of over 40 per cent per month on their Affiliate Window campaigns, resulting in a 94 per cent increase in sales.
- Following the success of the campaign, Maxinutrition, parent company of Maximuscle, intends to extend the personalized retargeting campaign to other websites in the group, including Maxitone and Maxifuel.

Credits

Clients:	● Maximuscle; PineSolutions
Geographical scope:	● United Kingdom
Strategic partners:	● Affiliate Window; myThings
Campaign contact:	● Shachar Radin, myThings.com

Your marketing in your prospect's pocket

10

> **“** Whatever the device you use for getting your information out, it should be the same information. TIM BERNERS-LEE

> **“** Mobile is about people and people are mobile.
> PETER VESTERBACKA, ROVIO (CREATORS OF ANGRY BIRDS GAME)

> **“** There was a time when we reached in our pocket to jingle our change. Today, it's our pocket that jingles us... as we reach not for change, but for our mobile devices. DAN HOLLINGS (WWW.DANHOLLINGS.COM)

OUR CHAPTER PLEDGE TO YOU

When you reach the end of this chapter you'll have answers to the following questions:

- What is mobile marketing?
- What is the potential for mobile marketing?
- How do I go about setting up a mobile marketing campaign?
- What can mobile marketing do for my business?
- What are the top tips for building a successful mobile marketing campaign?
- What role do mobile apps play in an increasingly mobile marketing world?
- How significant are location-based apps and mobile gaming?
- What are the privacy issues surrounding mobile?

Mobile: market size and rate of growth

In November 2009, the Mobile Marketing Association updated its definition of Mobile Marketing to the following:

> Mobile Marketing is a set of practices that enables organizations to communicate and engage with their audience in an interactive and relevant manner through any mobile device or network.

Over the past decade or so, mobile marketing has gone from being a fairly broad advertising term to referring to a rather specific type of marketing. Once used to describe any form of marketing that made use of a moving (mobile) medium (things like moving billboards, road shows and other transportable outdoor advertising), today it refers to a completely different form of advertising: reaching out to connect and interact with consumers through their mobile electronic device of choice.

As with other forms of online marketing, mobile marketing in its various guises has evolved rapidly in a relatively short space of time, fuelled by consumers with a hunger for anything that can help them streamline their congested, hyper-connected lives. As lifestyles evolve to become ever more generic, global and portable, the lure of the 'always connected' mobile device gets ever stronger.

According to a Gartner study published in June 2011, mobile ad spend worldwide is predicted to reach US\$3.3 billion in 2011, jumping to a massive \$20.6 billion by 2015, more than doubling each year and continuing to grow thereafter.

'Mobile advertising is now recognized as an opportunity for brands, advertisers and publishers to engage consumers in a targeted and contextual manner, improving returns,' said Stephanie Baghdassarian, research director at Gartner. 'For that reason, mobile advertising budgets are set to increase tremendously across the various categories and regions, growing from 0.5 per cent of the total advertising budget in 2010 to over 4 per cent in 2015.'

While Gartner cites the growth in smartphone adoption and mobile media tablets as a major driver in the growth of mobile advertising budgets, there's no getting away from the fact that, for now at least, the vast majority of mobile users don't currently own a smartphone.

In October of 2010 the International Telecommunication Union (ITU) estimated that there would be 5.3 billion mobile handsets in circulation by the end of 2010, covering a staggering 77 per cent of the global human population. Estimates suggest that so-called 'feature handsets' (non-smartphones) still outnumber smartphones by a ratio of 4:1.

A Portio Research study from January 2011 revealed that a total of 6.9 trillion SMS messages were sent in 2010, and estimated that SMS traffic would break through the 8 trillion barrier in 2011. Those are ludicrously big numbers.

'Messaging is still king,' states Portio. 'We want to be absolutely clear about this. Messaging still dominates [mobile operators'] non-voice revenues worldwide.' Estimates predict that the mobile messaging market will be worth over US$200 billion in 2011 (with SMS messaging accounting for $127 billion), and will reach US$334.7 billion by 2015.

But what does that mean in mobile marketing terms?

Another study, this time by Juniper research in May 2011, shows that by 2016 application to person (A2P) messaging will overtake person-to-person messaging (SMS texting), in a market worth more than US$70 billion. What is A2P messaging? It's simply automated messages from an application rather than a person. It's widely used in financial services, advertising, marketing, business administration, ticketing, television voting, etc. When your mobile operator sends a text to your phone to say your latest bill is available online, or your credit is running low, that's an A2P message.

Despite all the hype surrounding mobile web access, search, apps, smartphones, tablets, location-based services and everything else, for the time being at least messaging is very much at the heart of the mobile marketing industry. But things change quickly, more so in mobile than perhaps any other branch of digital marketing, and marketers around the world would do well to prepare for a future dominated by mobile access to online information and services.

The steady rise of mobile has become *the* main event in the digital marketing arena over recent years. Mobile has, of course, been the 'next big thing' for what seems an eternity, but with the continued growth of smartphone adoption (increasing by more than 30 per cent year on year), the convergence of mobile computing, improved connectivity and development of the cloud, it seems that mobile is finally rising to realize at least some of its latent potential.

Mobile internet adoption is increasing at a rate that is eight times that of the equivalent for desktops 10 years ago. More than half of all new internet connections now originate from mobile devices. We're in the midst of another fundamental shift in the way people access digital information and services – when most marketers are still reeling after the last one.

Don't ring the death knell of desktop, laptop and netbook computers just yet, though; for many things (writing this book, for example) a 'proper' computer is always going to be a better choice than a mobile device. But there's little doubt that as people get used to accomplishing more and more with the devices in their pockets, they'll turn to their computers less and less.

As marketers, we need to adapt to this shift in communications technology and learn once more to connect with our audience through their current medium of choice.

Mobile: Web2.0[2]

The widespread adoption of internet-enabled mobile devices gives consumers access to timely, relevant information and services wherever they happen to be. It lets them interact with their network of online contacts and share experiences, images and content any time, any place, anywhere. That takes the paradigm shift that is the interactive Web 2.0 and raises the bar to another level entirely.

With mobile you have to deliver personalized, relevant and exciting content, participate in two-way conversations rather than one-way messaging, and really listen to and engage with your customers. When you reach out to a person's mobile, you essentially reach into their personal space. There's something immediate and intimate about it. That's a powerful combination for the marketer, but it's one that comes with a lot of responsibility. It's a position that's easy to abuse, and the potential repercussions for your brand reputation could be huge.

From the consumer's perspective, if you're delivering marketing-related content to their personal mobile device, then you'd better 'wow' them. Give them a flawless user experience, efficiency and convenience, and respect their privacy and personal preferences. Make it *relevant*, make it *useful*, make it *entertaining*. As with the rest of digital marketing, the days of using mobile as a one-way broadcast medium for spammy one-way marketing messages are coming to an end.

We're entering mobile's next generation, and it's time to engage! (Apologies for the Star Trek reference; we couldn't resist.)

Mobile marketing: a game-changing channel or just another conduit?

Mobile marketing *is still* marketing on the internet.

The net *is still* the net, regardless of the device you use to access it. Social media *is still* social media no matter what device you use to share your content; the world wide web *is still* the world wide web, whether you're accessing a mobile-optimized version of a site or belt-and-braces desktop version; e-mail *is still* e-mail no matter how you choose to pick up your messages.

That's good news. It means that all of the information you've read so far in this book – by and large – also applies to marketing for mobile devices! The real differentiators with mobile today are the immediacy of having access to information and services wherever you are, the additional functionality afforded by the hardware in modern mobile devices (like GPS sensors, motion sensors and touch screens), and the way these combine to alter user perception, expectation and ultimately the potential utility of your marketing message.

As with everything in digital it's the human element of the mobile equation that makes it so powerful; the technology is the bit in the middle that helps that human connection to happen in new and more interesting ways. You may recall earlier in the book – way back near the beginning – we mentioned that digital marketing has little to do with understanding technology, and everything to do with understanding people. Well, it's the same thing with mobile.

Mobile works because it makes people's lives easier, it's portable, it's accessible, it's always on and it lets people tap in to the information they've come to rely on 24/7. It's in our pockets, it's the last thing many of us check before we go to sleep at night and the first thing we reach for in the morning.

If you understand people – specifically your customers – and how they integrate their mobile devices into their lives, then you already know how your business can reach out to them across the mobile internet. Making it happen is just logistics.

'Show and sell' is dead; welcome to the world of 'utility and entertainment'

A great example of a brand embracing the 'utility and entertainment' aspect of mobile to maximum effect was the 'Axe Wake-Up Service', a campaign that ran in the mobile marketing capital of the world: Japan.

Research showed that 70 per cent of Japan's urban male youth (the brand's target market) used their mobile phones as alarm clocks. All Axe did was use this generic consumer behaviour as a platform and build a campaign around it.

Axe simply launched a service that allowed the consumer to visit Axe online, enter their mobile number and set a wake-up call time. A young, attractive woman would then make the wake-up call, even appearing by videophone if the customer desired. Naturally, the campaign reminded the customer to spray on a little Axe to smell great. The brand took an existing consumer behaviour and offered a useful and entertaining solution that built upon it in a fun and engaging way. The result: a runaway success!

So what can mobile marketing be used for?

The answer to that question could take up an entire book... and then some. Because mobile is essentially a new, exciting and convenient way for people to access online information and services, elements of your mobile marketing can be employed to achieve many of the same business goals as any other form of digital marketing. You can use mobile to:

FIGURE 10.1 The Axe Wake-Up Service campaign – entertaining and useful... the essence of effective mobile marketing

- build awareness of your brand, product or service;
- foster and nurture conversation with your online community;
- gather valuable insight into consumer behaviour;
- take iterative customer engagement to the next level;
- harness the wisdom of the crowd;
- drive lead generation and new business;
- establish loyalty programmes, competitions and rewards;
- build a deeper and more personal brand experience;
- target your market more effectively based on demographics, geography and behaviour;
- retain more customers and reduce 'churn';
- listen and learn.

The list could go on and on, but you get the idea.

With massive uptake of internet-connected mobile devices accelerating all the time, marketers need to start taking mobile seriously as a fundamental component (if not the principal component) of their digital marketing strategy. The potential of mobile is profound... and the impact of mobile marketing is only going to grow.

Mobile: evolution on steroids

Innovation and the very human desire for something newer and better are driving the rapid evolution of the mobile device. We're never content with the status quo. Last month our all-singing-all-dancing smartphone was the bee's knees… but today – well, today we really *need* that shiny new tablet. You know, the one that's so achingly cool we don't even need to turn it on to impress our friends. Next month a new version of our phone will hit the shelves – sleeker, brighter, faster…

It's all happening so damned quickly.

When you break it down it's not really that different from the evolution of biological systems – it just happens much, much faster. Darwin's survival of the fittest theory still applies, but instead of waiting hundreds of thousands of years for new species to evolve, in the mobile ecosystem we have new mobile devices evolving in a matter of months.

Manufacturers introduce new features and form factors in their mobile devices all of the time in a bid to capture and retain a share of this burgeoning new market. If those features resonate with people (are truly useful, fun or ideally both), then the positive selection pressure of people handing over hard-earned cash pushes the retention and enhancement of those features; if not, they die. Over time this leads to the iterative refinement and development (the evolution) of devices that are ideally suited to their particular niche in the digital ecosystem.

Full circle: from tablet to tablet

In the beginning there was the stone tablet: Flintstone marketing at its best. Today the tablets we have to play with are a bit more functional and weigh substantially less. But are tablets here to stay, or are they a passing fad?

Tablets are interesting because they're not really portable in the way that your mobile phone is portable. They're still mobile – but they're not something people have with them 24/7 like their phones.

They're also not fully fledged computers in the more 'traditional' sense of the word. You still won't find many people sitting down to write a 10,000 word business report or create a complex financial spreadsheet on their iPad.

Tablets sit somewhere in the middle ground. The bigger screens and intuitive touch interface mean that tablets excel as media consumption devices: watching online video, catching up with a TV show you've missed, accessing blogs, websites, social media, video-calling your gran, playing games and running apps are all quick, convenient and intuitive on a tablet. Tablets are also fantastic for doing simple online tasks quickly: things like online banking, ordering a birthday gift for your mum on Amazon, subscribing to a new podcast, quickly checking your e-mail or discussing a TV show you're watching with your peers on Twitter.

FIGURE 10.2 Apple's iPad is leading the charge in tablet innovation, but for how long? The company's flagship device faces stiff competition from a swathe of new devices based on Google's Android platform as the tablet wars hot up

For more complex tasks you'll typically boot up the laptop... but for convenience and instant gratification, you'll reach for a tablet every time if there's one available. There's little doubt tablets are here to stay, and with competition hotting up the constant pressure to innovate will drive their continued evolution. Tablets are going to become more capable, and as more of us acquire the habit of using them we'll do more things online with them. Which, of course, means that as marketers we have to factor the rise of the tablet into our online strategy.

How big are tablets going to get?

No, we're not talking screen size; we're talking market size.

Various reports from industry behemoths like IBM, Ericsson and Cisco suggest that there could potentially be up to a trillion (yes, you read that right) internet-connected devices by 2015. To put that number into perspective, we passed the five-billion device milestone in late 2010 and the number keeps growing apace.

Gerd Leonhard, from the aptly named Futures Agency in Switzerland, concludes that 'tablet devices will become the way many of us will read magazines, books, newspapers and even attend live concerts and kick off an era of mobile-augmented reality with content being bundled into mobile service contracts to be consumed on any mobile or tablet device'.

However the future of mobile marketing evolves, tablet devices are likely to play a significant role in that evolution. They span the divide between mobile phones and full-blown computers, are already the quintessential device for multimedia consumption and are getting more capable with each iteration. Tablets are here to stay.

The rise and rise of mobile advertising

Stefan Adamczyk,
Managing Director of Mobile Ventures

Those of us working in the media industry have heard for years now that this year will finally be the year of the mobile. So are we there yet? It has been building for years and finally, thanks to the likes of Steve Jobs, the mobile phone is so versatile it's frequently named by people as the one item they couldn't live without.

Whether you're sitting in your lounge, commuting or out and about, mobile devices are proving more popular than many thought possible for accessing the internet – just think about the number of commuters you see 'playing' with their phones on every bus, train and plane you travel on.

Let's look over some of the facts:

- In September 2009, just 0.2 per cent of all UK web traffic originated from a mobile device, compared to January 2011, when the figure was a staggering 8.09 per cent (representing a growth of over 4,000 per cent). If growth continues at this rate, as it did for the latter part of 2010, by the end of 2011 over 20 per cent of UK web traffic will be of mobile origin.

- The huge market penetration of smartphones in the UK (32 per cent at December 2010, forecast to be 43 per cent by December 2011), better connectivity through increased wi-fi networks and 3G services, unlimited data plans and the roll-out of 4G networks throughout 2012 to 2015 are the key drivers behind this growth.

- Mobile advertising in the UK has experienced a staggering 116 per cent year-on-year growth between 2009 and 2010. For example, advertisers spent £83 million on mobile advertising in 2010 and this is growing annually.

- Growth will be between 100 per cent and 150 per cent in 2011. This at a time of the world's biggest financial crisis since the 1930s.

- The UK's internet advertising market is now worth over £4 billion in 2010, a 25 per cent share of the overall UK advertising spend. Mobile advertising in comparison, with £83 million, is only 2 per cent of this figure.

What is clear to all is the disparity between the percentage of web traffic viewed from mobile devices and the percentage of advertising spend on mobile media. Everyone knows that where the people are, advertisers are sure to follow (just look at the success of social media over the past three or four years).

So, for advertisers, why are mobile media so powerful?

Let's look at the device. A smartphone is the owner's mini personal computer in their pocket, so always with them and always connected. It allows them to send and receive e-mail, instant messages, surf the web, find out the weather, play games, watch TV, even make phone calls and text too! Built in sat nav means they will never get lost and will always find a place nearby which caters for their needs. Whether it is looking for a bite to eat or how to repair a puncture, there's always an app for that. Utilized in the right way, this is hugely powerful for advertisers. Mobile advertising allows advertisers to target people on the move or at home and capture them when they're most receptive.

In a nutshell, advertising to consumers via their mobile device is the future and brands that are quick to learn how to use this highly innovative medium will be the ones to win the mind share of the public.

In 2011, for the first time, standardized key metrics for measuring advertisements have been established for the mobile interactive industry. Developed in a joint effort by the Interactive Advertising Bureau (IAB) and the Mobile Marketing Association (MMA) and with the assistance of the Media Rating Council (MRC), the 'Mobile Web Advertising Measurement Guidelines' have just been established in 2011 to provide a framework to govern how ad impressions are counted on the mobile web.

The guidelines will help marketers accurately assess the delivery of ads within mobile websites and offer a clear way to count ad impressions, assuring them that their advertising messages are reaching mobile consumers.

More than anything, the guidelines demonstrate the mobile industry's commitment to its marketing partners to create a transparent and consistent business environment for buying and selling ads. Brands and their agencies will be further encouraged to devote resources towards marketing campaigns unique to the mobile web – reaching customers at critical times in the purchase cycle, enhancing brand relationships or providing critical information through mobile marketing.

The objectives of the Mobile Web Advertising Measurement Guidelines include:

- defining the mobile web ad impression;

- creating a common methodology that will be widely adopted globally for counting mobile web ad impressions;

- encouraging mobile web ad servers to have their impression counts audited by an independent third party;

- providing marketers and agencies with greater clarity and certainty (via the auditing process) that key metrics used for buying mobile web ads are methodologically sound and meet the highest standards available to the media industry;

- reducing levels of discrepancies and spurring the industry's growth by offering internet publishers and ad servers a consistent, rigorous way to count the delivery of ad impressions.

The IAB's Mobile Advertising Committee is comprised of over 140 member companies who are dedicated to developing and expanding the mobile space as a viable advertising platform. This committee now sits under the newly created IAB Mobile Marketing Centre of Excellence, a new unit within the organization that will serve as an industry-wide resource for innovation in mobile advertising.

These kinds of developments are encouraging. We still have a long way to go but there are exciting times ahead for everyone involved in the mobile advertising industry today.

Case study – Accor Hotels

Accor is a world leader in hotels and services. Accor's free iPhone application allows users to find their ideal hotel, leveraging geo-localization and intuitive map search. Users can add the hotel contact details to their contact lists, find current promotions, book their hotel and check their current reservations.

With the introduction of their iPhone app, Accor and their agency turned to Google's AdMob to help them boost downloads on the launch of their app and increase the number of mobile bookings. Accor's priorities for their campaign were threefold:

- Reach target audiences in core markets, including Australia, Germany, France, Italy, the UK and the United States.

- Maximize the ranking of their app within their target App Stores in both the travel and overall categories.

- Drive cost-effective downloads of the app.

Solution

Accor used geo-targeting to reach the millions of iPhone and iPod Touch users in AdMob's network globally. Their ads appeared in many of the most popular local iPhone apps and sites. AdMob's cost-per-click iPhone ads enabled easy discovery and downloads of the app by consumers, taking users from the ad directly to the App Store download page with just one click.

Accor worked with PureAgency, who managed the campaign on their behalf. Monitoring cost per acquisition in real time through AdMob's robust reporting and with their own download measurements, PureAgency was able to ensure optimal results.

Results

The campaign achieved their objectives in each of their target markets. Within the travel category, the app moved up to become one of the highest-ranking apps in each App Store; highlights include France becoming the number-two app, Italy number four, UK number 11, and the app reaching numbers 29 and 30 in the overall App Stores in France and Italy respectively. Accor firmly believes that if they had continued their advertising spend it would have pushed them into the top 10 rankings in these markets as well.

Throughout the two-week campaign, Accor was extremely pleased with the results that their campaign received:

- click-through rates of 1.30 per cent on average;

- conversion rates (clicks resulting in app downloads) of 5 per cent on average;

- approximately 300,000 visits to their apps download page.

Some conclusions

To deliver on this continuing growth, we need to overcome many of the existing challenges to mobile advertising uptake. Delivering the tools, capabilities and features that guarantee greater transparency, measurability, relevance and, crucially, profit will be the trigger that brands need to fully embrace mobile.

As consumer adoption of smartphones and tablets reaches critical mass, brands now realize they need to move beyond using mobile as just another channel for consumer engagement and develop a fully comprehensive mobile strategy around marketing, advertising and increasingly around mobile commerce. This is where many in the industry believe the true tipping point in driving these predicted volumes of growth will lie.

As consumers spend more time engaging with smart devices, their willingness to purchase through these devices will increase. Yet the availability of transactional m-commerce sites and apps still needs to catch up with consumer demand. As m-commerce technology evolves and delivers an increasingly seamless user experience, the propensity of consumers to buy through mobile will be instrumental in persuading brands to spend greater chunks of their budgets on the channel. This is the real opportunity for marketers to get their heads around.

The realization of the importance of having a mobile strategy, the right tools and appreciation of delivering measurable consumer engagement and ever more sophisticated mobile technology will mark the coming years as a turning point for mobile advertising.

Stefan Adamczyk is Managing Director of Mobile Ventures, a leading mobile advertising sales company.

Stefan has over 10 years' digital advertising experience working within both media agencies and commercial teams. He was responsible for the first mobile advertising campaign in the UK back in 2000 (for VNU.net on XY Networks' WAP portal).

On the media agency side he has held positions at Media21 (acquired by Grey Group) and PHD, where he was responsible for online strategy, planning and trading for key advertising brands which included COI, First Direct and HSBC.

Location, location, location

The fact that your mobile *always* knows where you are can be a bit disconcerting, but there's no denying that it's also an incredibly useful feature. Using maps to quickly find out where you are, how to get to where you want to be, locate a nearby Thai restaurant your friends recommend or find the nearest cinema showing the movie you want to see always comes in handy.

But what about taking the utility of knowing *where* people are and using it to help them make the most of what's available around them, discover cool new locations, locate friends who happen to be nearby or avail them-selves of the latest offers from local businesses? Welcome to the world of location-aware applications and location-based services. These apps read your mobile's built-in GPS or triangulate your position based on data from the mobile phone masts your device is connected to, and use that data (with your permission, hopefully) to do all sorts of clever things.

The real opportunity with location-aware applications from a marketing perspective is that they offer businesses with bricks-and-mortar premises the opportunity to deliver real-time information, offers and incentives to people *who are physically in the area*. Location information is something marketers can leverage to make the information they provide to prospects more useful and relevant than ever... and that is always going to drive higher conversion rates.

Checking out the check-in

For now, stand-alone location-based applications, like those of industry pioneer FourSquare (**www.foursquare.com**) and those built into existing social net-works, like Facebook Places, rely on users making a conscious decision that requires action: they need to physically 'check-in' at locations using soft-ware on their mobile device. They can typically choose from a list of nearby locations, or add new locations on the fly, and choose whether or not they want to share their check-in location with their network of online contacts.

Over time, check-in profiles build up. Users are awarded points, badges and 'mayorships' as their 'status' grows and they check in to locations regu-larly. Slowly they start climbing their local leader board. All of this, of course, is designed to reward repeated use of the service, encouraging people to check in wherever they go, and ultimately establish a habit that will endure beyond initial experimentation with the shiny new toy of location-based social media.

Applications like FourSquare turn routine life events like going to the supermarket or visiting your favourite restaurant into an elaborate location-based game. They blur the lines between the real and virtual worlds courtesy of your mobile phone. Businesses are in on the game too, of course, offering specials for first-time check-ins, discounts for regular visitors or free coffee for the 'mayor', and so on.

Location-based services and networks like FourSquare, Gowalla, Facebook Places and others (there are more players entering this fledgling space all the time in a bid to cash in on the next big thing) are very much in their infancy, and there's some debate surrounding how they're likely to evolve and grow. Ultimately one of the big challenges current location-based models face is the very premise the services are based on: the act of checking in.

Check-in fatigue is a very real problem for location-based services based around a check-in model, because there is no intrinsic value to the process of checking in.

Digital agency Beyond (**www.bynd.com**) did some research that they released as an informative infographic (see Figure 10.3) revealing some of the figures and trends behind location-based check-in hype in the run-up to the Social Loco (**www.socialloco.net**) conference in May 2011. Here's what they found:

- Privacy is still a huge barrier to adoption for any application that asks a user to disclose his or her physical location.
- Both Facebook and Groupon are well placed to exploit the opportunity presented by the current convergence of the social web, mobile and local business through Facebook Places and GrouponNow respectively.
- Discounts and coupons are far and away the biggest motivation for a user to disclose their location. Status rewards, like badges and mayorships don't really resonate with mass consumers.
- While the focus to date has been very much on small local businesses benefiting from location-based technology, there is a huge opportunity for big brands to connect with people at a local level.
- In the future, consumers are more likely to check in at a friend's house than they are at cafes, restaurants or bars.

Some of the key statistics to emerge out of the research were:

- 17 per cent of the US population have checked in using an app on their mobile device.
- 49 per cent of the population didn't feel there was any real motivation to check in.
- 48 per cent have never checked in, due to privacy concerns.
- 90 per cent of all the people who have checked in have done so using Facebook Places, 31 per cent have disclosed their location on Twitter and 22 per cent using Foursquare.
- 55 per cent of people who said they have never checked in would be most likely to use Facebook Places, while 40 per cent said they would check in using Groupon. Only 6 per cent said they would consider using Foursquare.

Why people would check in:

- 54 per cent of early adopters and 41 per cent of consumers revealed that deals and discounts were the biggest draw for them to check in.
- For people who currently check in, the next biggest check-in motivators were meeting up with friends (33 per cent), learning about a new location (32 per cent), promoting a favourite location (30 per cent), followed by winning a badge or becoming mayor (21 per cent).
- For the mass consumer, after discounts, the next biggest draw was learning about a location (19 per cent).

FIGURE 10.3 The truth behind the check in – cutting through the location-based hype, courtesy of Beyond (**www.bynd.com**)

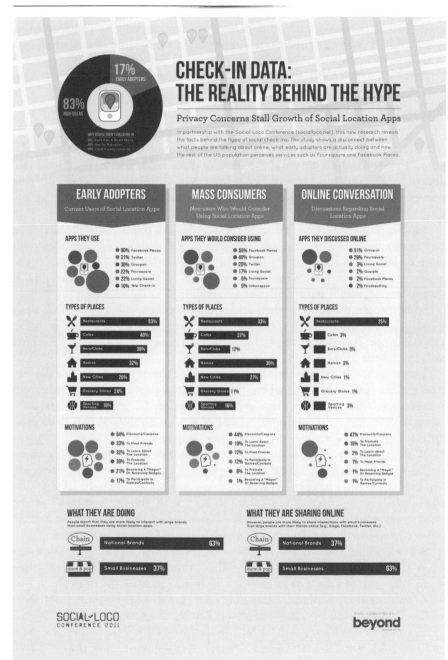

- 99 per cent of consumers do not view badges and mayorships as sufficient motivation to check in.

Whether or not location-based services offer a potential avenue for you to connect with local customers will depend very much on your audience, your goals and, of course, your business. For many it has a lot of potential, and is an area of mobile marketing that's well worth looking at.

Mobile gaming

Mobile gaming has been described as the wide-open battleground of the entertainment industry. While the likes of Facebook and Zynga dominate social games and big publishers such as Xbox, Sony and Nintendo rule console games, the global smartphone games market is still patently up for grabs.

Mobile games are huge because mobile devices are... well, mobile! You have your mobile with you 24/7. Sitting in a doctor's waiting room with time to kill? Waiting for the bus home from work? Waiting in line at the supermarket checkout? What are you going to do? Almost invariably, if you have one, you'll whip out your smartphone.

Some people will update their social media status, some will check their e-mail, others might read their favourite blog, and even check in using their location-based service of choice to check out local offers. But many will fire up the latest and greatest mobile game.

There are millions of mobile games spanning the gamut of mobile devices and mobile platforms. And where there are games there's an audience, and where there's an audience there are opportunities to promote. Brands are already delivering promotional messages *within* mobile games and even sponsoring entire games to drive consumer engagement.

With potentially billions of users in the mobile market, mobile gaming could well grow to become the single largest gaming market of them all. Smartphone games have been growing fast since 2007, when the iPhone was introduced, and tablet games followed suit with the introduction of the iPad in early 2010. As of July 2011 the fastest-growing mobile game market is based around devices running Google's Android operating system.

Successes like that of Rovio's now legendary 'Angry Birds', which has been downloaded more than 200 million times, mean that mobile game companies can attract tens of millions of dollars in investment capital.

According to Tim Merel, Managing Director of Digi Capital, publishers of the Digi-Capital 2011 Global Video Games Investment Review, mobile games alone could be worth US$13 billion in 2014. Taken together with online games, you have a $44-billion market, or 50 per cent of the estimated global $87-billion games market for 2014.

The games market today is dominated by consoles, with mobile games accounting for a relatively small but rapidly expanding slice of the pie. Few doubt that the growth will continue, as emerging digital markets in Asia embrace the smartphone revolution, and mobile devices become the primary connectivity and entertainment device of choice for a massive chunk of the human population.

But it's not all a bed of roses in mobile gaming. Established mobile game developers such as Digital Chocolate have warned that a glut of games being released on major smartphone platforms means that game developers will find it very hard to make money. They point out that in many cases average revenue per game doesn't even cover development costs. A rash of poor games can ruin the market for everyone, making it more difficult for consumers to find what's 'good' and generally tainting the gaming experience on mobile platforms for everyone. At the time of writing there were 64,048 games in the App Store, and they were being joined by around 300 new games daily.

But it's not just about the numbers either. Savvy mobile marketers need to remain neutral in their assessment of the market and, of course, platform agnostic. The winning platform for your business isn't necessarily the one with the most apps, it's the one that retains and engages the attention of your particular target market.

Kiip: virtual gaming – real-life rewards

Two hundred million minutes a day. By now, that's an extremely conservative estimate of the amount of time that people spend flinging birds at pigs.

In many respects, Angry Birds has become the flagship title and the single biggest story in the app ecosystem to date. However, it is just one game among thousands that are attracting people's attention during their downtime.

Mobile gaming is massive – and with it come numerous opportunities for brands to connect with a new, engaged audience. Kiip is one new company with a unique twist on mobile advertising. They offer real rewards for virtual achievements. In an era where up to 80 per cent of traditional mobile ads are clicked through by accident, Kiip offers a new way to get an audience's attention in a good way.

Rewards are tied to achievement moments – finishing a level, completing a task, levelling up or getting a new high score. Their algorithm learns how good you are and tailors rewards accordingly. Most importantly, it doesn't disrupt the gaming experience – the rewards are delivered using a simple HTML5 overlay that disappears if you don't want it and never pulls you away from the game. By tying in with achievement moments, which provide a natural break in game play, Kiip ensures that they don't annoy developers and gamers alike.

So far, the results have been impressive. The official launch came in April 2011. Kiip is already working with major US brands like Dr Pepper, Popchips, Sephora, 1-800 Flowers and many others. An EMEA launch is planned for autumn 2011. To date, campaigns have achieved double-digit redemption rates across the board.

Perhaps more surprisingly, Kiip has yet to hear a single complaint from a gamer or developer – while brands are reaping the rewards associated with developing quality engagement with their customers by rewarding them rather than simply pushing a banner ad at them.

A combination of quality offers, smart behavioural economics and partnerships with established and up-and-coming games developers should ensure that gamers start to see a lot more real-life rewards for their in-game achievements over the coming months and years.

Mobile applications

Mobile applications are quite a simple concept. They are just pieces of software that are pre-installed on your mobile phone or are available to download from the internet. They are nothing new. There have been mobile applications available for multiple handsets for years now – ranging from games to currency-conversion tools to more complicated applications allowing you to broadcast live video and audio from your phone.

As technology advances rapidly we are moving from a push model to one of pull. People no longer want information they don't really need shoved down their throats. Today's consumers want to be in control; they decide what they want, when they want it and how they want it delivered… and the result is modern mobile apps.

App stores and the explosion of mobile applications has been little short of revolutionary.

'I've never seen anything like this in my career in software,' was how Apple founder and CEO Steve Jobs described the initial success of the iPhone App Store – and once again it seems Mr Jobs was right on the money.

Every major media outlet in the world has run pieces on the success of the App Store. The statement 'There's an app for that' peppers headlines and conversations around the world. The *New York Times* heralded the revolution in mobile applications as a 'new gold rush'.

There are now more than 425,000 applications in the App Store (and counting) – with hundreds of thousands more available across Android, Blackberry, WebOS, Windows 7, Symbian and myriad alternative operating systems in the market. In early 2011, Apple announced they had powered past 10 billion application downloads since the launch of their store.

The subsequent launch of a variety of tablet devices has generated yet more app-related hyperbole, and with the imminent launch of Chinese-made sub-$100 handsets running Google's Android operating system in the offing, and a serious push from Microsoft/Nokia, Blackberry and all of the other major smartphone manufacturers, we live in interesting times for mobile marketers.

The hard reality is that there are a significant number of different application platforms available to brands, agencies and marketers. Choosing the right platform, talking to the right audience and breaking through the noise generated by the sheer volume of applications released on a daily basis is an incredible challenge. At the time of writing, Apple's App Store is the strongest marketplace for many brands. While Google's Android Market grew by 196 per cent in 2010, Apple's App Store still accounted for a massive 86 per cent of all app download activity during that time.

Over the last few years, we've seen apps released by nearly every brand on the planet. Users like branded apps. Research by AdMob, one of the biggest mobile advertising networks in the world, found that 70 per cent of iPhone users surveyed had downloaded a branded app.

Some of the download figures for branded applications are enormous. Barclaycard released a Waterslide app which tied in with a recent UK television ad campaign. To date, it has been downloaded more than 9.5 million times. Lighter manufacturer Zippo was one of the first companies to release an app – a simple interface that allows you to 'flick' a lighter on your screen and produce a flame. That simplicity has been rewarded with more than 6 million downloads. Audi's A4 Driving Challenge, where players take a new Audi A4 round a track, has topped 4 million downloads.

The difficulty for brands and developers is how to measure the success of these applications (see the measurement section later in the chapter). Download numbers are a possible metric, but they don't tell the whole story. Engagement is key.

FIGURE 10.4 Apple's phenomenally successful App Store is home to more than 425,000 downloadable applications for the company's iconic iPhone and iPad (viewed early August 2011)

Research by New York-based app analysis company Pinch Media has shown that only 20 per cent of users return to a free application after one day. After 30 days, fewer than 5 per cent are engaging with the app.

The key seems to be giving people something that adds a level of value or engagement. North Face, the outdoor equipment manufacturer, had more than 300,000 downloads of its snow report app in 2009. The app is simple enough: it gives people the weather forecast for multiple ski resorts world-wide, along with details of what time lifts open at, webcam feeds and more. While the headline figure of 300,000 downloads may not be as impressive as Zippo's or Barclaycard's, North Face brand manager Nate Bosshard has said that users 'utilize the service several times a day, sharing reviews, check-ing weather, and updating Twitter feeds regularly'.

The outcomes can be impressive as well. Audi generated more than half a million visits to the A4's website from its iPhone driving application. Kraft's iFood Assistant carries recipes and how-to videos, and not only does it generate revenue for the company (it costs $0.99), but it is also respon-sible for a sizeable mailing list, with 90 per cent of app users registering at Kraftfoods.com.

The real key for brands and agencies is not to get caught up in the idea of building an application for the sake of building one. Surely it is far better to follow the lead of pioneering companies like North Face (or Smirnoff Vodka, who, rather than build their own mobile applications, opted to sponsor the Time Out London application): build something useful, promote it using all available channels, and you could find your app being hailed as the next big success story.

Top tips for building a successful app

- Plan, plan, plan – scope the app out well in advance.
- Do your research.
- Understand the business model around the app (free/paid).
- What problem is it addressing?
- How will the app be marketed? Who are the target profile/demographic?
- How will you measure success (not just downloads)?
- Focus on design, UI (user interface) and UX (user experience) – the best, most popular applications are simple, effective and look good.
- Think about content – are you building an entertainment app that will amuse people for 30 seconds before being deleted? Or are you building a utility that people will use on an ongoing basis – like the North Face example above?
- Think about the device – problems occur when brands try to shoehorn existing content onto a mobile device. Instead of thinking about the limitations presented by screen size, think instead about the options open to you in terms of the device you're targeting.

Measuring mobile

The old adage 'You can only manage what you measure' certainly rings true for most marketers in this ROI-driven world. A number of recent White Papers have tried to shed light on the measurement of mobile marketing, customer loyalty and engagement. Surprise, surprise: the overriding message is that, when it comes to evaluating the success (or otherwise) of your mobile campaign, there's really no substitute for timely, accurate and independent tracking and measurement.

While we're still some way off a standardized set of metrics for measuring mobile campaign success, White Papers and the introduction of guidelines by organizations like the IAB and MMA help offer a consistent overview of the mobile marketing landscape, and facilitate knowledge transfer in terms of measuring mobile campaigns across the industry. Together they offer some pretty good signposts that help us decide what we need when choosing our mobile analytics solution.

What insights do mobile analytics deliver when measuring mobile marketing?

Mobile KPIs

We looked at KPIs for general web-based analytics in Chapter 5, and the basic premise with mobile is exactly the same: a KPI gives an instant snapshot of how your campaign is doing. As with other elements of your digital marketing, measurement and analysis of your mobile metrics are invaluable. They allow you to instantly gauge how well your mobile strategy is working, and to adapt it to deliver better results.

Some examples of popular KPIs for mobile campaigns might include:

- total downloads;
- total app users;
- new users;
- frequency and duration of visit;
- bounce rates;
- segmentation by device type;
- CTRs.

Successful digital marketing is all about iterative refinement – constant tweaking based on interpretation of real data to deliver more effective marketing creative that drives conversion. It's exactly the same with mobile campaigns. By using real data and the insight it provides we can focus our efforts (and our finite marketing budget) where they will yield maximum results.

Some of the variables to watch in your mobile campaigns might include:

- User segmentation – it's important to understand which users are interacting with your campaign and taking the actions you want. Are there trends or patterns based on the user's country, device type, platform or other variables?

- Timing – look at the timing of your campaigns in different regions. Do some times yield better returns than others? Understand what times of day are likely to deliver higher conversion rates with your particular audience.

- Advertising channel – based on your analytics you can identify which advertising channels deliver the best results across your mobile portfolio, and reinvest your budget accordingly. The key here is to ensure an independent and viable comparison across all your mobile advertising channels.

According to research carried out by specialist UK-based mobile analytics company Bango, 83 per cent of brands do not use mobile-specific analytics tools, and 27 per cent of brands failed to implement any sort of analytics for their mobile campaigns. That's throwing away a massive opportunity to improve the return on investment they see from their mobile spend.

We know from the statistics presented at the beginning of this chapter that mobile marketing is growing fast, yet the Bango survey shows that brands are missing a beat when it comes to utilizing real data to enhance the performance of their mobile campaigns. Accurate and comprehensive data and effective reporting help to keep campaigns focused, deliver enhanced ROI, and ultimately drive brands to achieve more success with their mobile marketing campaigns.

Mobile privacy

If the holy grail of mobile marketing is accurate and effective measurement, then its arch-nemesis must surely be privacy. Privacy concerns are rife across the web, but they're more prevalent than ever when you're talking about a device that most of us carry around with us all day, every day: a device that knows exactly where we are, when and for how long.

How much data do consumers *really* want to share with marketers anyway?

From a marketer's perspective, the more data we have about a prospect, the more effectively we can deliver useful, relevant, timely information to them exactly when and where they need it. That all sounds great for the consumer too... and it is, as far as it goes. That old chestnut 'When advertising becomes useful it ceases to be perceived as advertising' was never truer than when somebody's mobile phone helps them find a local Italian restaurant that six of their friends recommended over the last few months.

There are plenty of win–win examples like that. Essentially that's what mobile marketing at its best is all about. But things are intensely competitive in the mobile arena, and there's a line in the ever shifting sands of the digital marketing landscape beyond which mobile marketing becomes intrusive rather than informed. Defining exactly where that line is – that's the tricky bit.

Most responsible marketers realize that sending mobile advertising without the relevant permission or consent causes more harm than good. The mobile equivalent of e-mail spam is only going to turn consumers off in an era when you really need to be engaging in a productive and enduring relationship with them.

For mobile marketing to work, consumers need to have confidence that their privacy will be protected. If they don't, it doesn't really matter how well crafted, imaginative or cool your next mobile campaign is. Without consumer consent and buy-in it's really not going anywhere. Successful mobile marketing needs to be permission based, it needs to be relevant and useful (or entertaining) and it needs to be part of a broader mobile engagement strategy that extends beyond the initial 'blip' of campaign-based marketing.

As with many other areas of digital marketing, the legal framework in which we operate has struggled to keep pace with innovation and change. The law is playing catch-up as it tries to deal with issues like unsolicited mobile advertising, behavioural targeting and the use of personal identification and location-based information without the user's explicit consent.

Many mobile telecommunications regulations across the developed world are woefully outdated, particularly when it comes to unsolicited commercial communications. The result is a flood of fast-tracked legislation and regulation aimed at assuaging consumers' fears that governments around the world aren't taking their privacy seriously. The danger, of course, is that rapid-fire reactive legislation is often poorly thought out and ends up stifling innovation and simultaneously disrupting the user experience – which is bad for marketers and even worse for consumers.

What impact all of this legislation and regulation will have on the evolution of mobile marketing remains to be seen, but when the dust settles, if privacy concerns of users have been allayed, at least somewhat, then that's good news for mobile marketers. While regulation and legislation by their vary nature give us more hoops to jump through, ultimately this has to be better than the anarchy that would otherwise prevail. If unscrupulous marketers are allowed to fuel consumer paranoia about their privacy, then people will simply stop engaging with *any* form of mobile advertising, no matter the source. That would be bad news for everybody.

There are undoubtedly some very serious consumer protection issues that marketers need to be aware of as mobile takes off. Some of the key legal elements mobile marketers should consider carefully include the following.

Disclosure

Marketers should clearly disclose the terms of any offer. With the growth of mobile applications, the spotlight is on how transparently mobile marketers disclose the terms of things like in-app purchases. The limited space on mobile screens can present challenges when it comes to full disclosure, but marketers need to find creative ways to make sure consumers see material terms before they part with their money.

Privacy

Mobile companies are increasingly coming under fire for not adequately disclosing their mobile data collection practices to consumers. As we've already discussed, there's a huge push around the world to bring legislation up to date in the mobile privacy arena. Now is the time for marketers to put their house in order in terms of mobile privacy. Keep an eye on legal developments in your jurisdiction and those of your customers, and pay attention to how new mobile privacy proposals may ultimately affect your mobile strategy now and into the future.

Consent

Consent or permission is another key area, and one that's likely to become more critical as mobile commerce and payments take off. Issues like how to ensure that the person making a mobile transaction is in fact authorized to do so will be at the forefront.

Many companies using mobile as a direct communications channel to their customers have been caught out for failing to get consent before sending promotional text messages. In some cases settlements reached into the millions. Make sure you get the consumer's permission before contacting them on their mobile.

Mobile data

As with privacy, a lot of interest is now being paid to our behaviours and the data trail we're leaving behind on a daily basis from all our activity on mobile devices. One such study is the Allot Mobile Trends Report that collected data from 1 January to 30 June 2011 from leading mobile operators worldwide with a combined user base of 250 million subscribers.

According to the Allot report, mobile data usage grew by 77 per cent for the first half of 2011 and YouTube accounted for 22 per cent of that growth. Video streaming to mobile devices grew by 93 per cent during the reporting period, and unsurprisingly it consumes the single largest chunk of mobile bandwidth worldwide at 39 per cent of the total. File sharing takes up 29 per cent of mobile bandwidth, while web browsing accounts for another 29 per cent.

Though video takes the lion's share of bandwidth, it isn't the fastest-growing activity in mobile. Voice over Internet Protocol (VoIP), led by Skype, grew by 101 per cent and Twitter and Facebook use grew by 297 per cent and 166 per cent, respectively. VoIP only accounts for 4 per cent of mobile bandwidth, according to the report.

Futurists (now there's a job title we'd love…) are also predicting that new 'open' environments will lead to a new generation of mobile devices with even more sensors capturing ever-increasing streams of data about our movements in the physical world – including things like temperature, noise, location and even smell!

Add sensor data to user data, voice data and other data sources and it's easy to see how that data could be used to build a picture of individual behaviour that's scarily close to the mark. It poses some tough questions. How will all this potentially valuable and personal data be filtered? Who is going to own it? Where is it going to be stored? How is it going to be secured?

The mobile cloud

Having weathered the economic storm of the last few years, mobile network operators are now eagerly seeking out new revenue opportunities, and they're looking to the cloud. There is a lot of energy and investment currently flowing into 'mobile cloud' projects and mobile companies and other players in the mobile ecosystem are betting heavily on the trend of services and applications being hosted in and delivered from the cloud.

The proliferation of smart mobile devices of all types fuels massive demand for data to power social networking, sensor-based interaction and video and digital entertainment. This demand is resulting in an exponential need for computational muscle, storage and bandwidth, which in turn is driving the development of new cloud-based applications and platforms.

A Morgan Stanley study from September 2010 found 41 per cent of mobile peak-hour traffic is due to 'real-time entertainment', most of which is video. Considering that YouTube adds approximately 35 hours of video to its archive every minute, that's hardly a surprising statistic, but when it comes to coping with that ever-increasing demand it does present significant challenges.

Behind the scenes the industry is moving from a rigid model of individual servers or designated banks of servers towards a much more scalable and dynamic model that can respond almost instantly to changes and shifts in computational demand. The dynamic scalability of cloud computing is essential to modern mobile developers as they strive to improve user experience through lower latency, increased throughput and reduced costs.

How is the mobile cloud different from 'the cloud'?

Ask 10 different tech experts that question and you'll get 10 different answers. Often, the term 'mobile cloud' is simply used to indicate that the most common device being used to access a particular service is mobile, although as the mobile cloud evolves you can expect subtle differences in terms of security, back-end infrastructure, application design and other variables tailored to the particular demands of mobile access.

A recent report from Yankee Group analyst Brian Partridge entitled 'The mobile cloud: unlocking new profits from 2011' sheds some light on possibilities and challenges for the mobile cloud and suggests that it has the potential to change how we work, transact, socialize and entertain ourselves in every conceivable way. Yankee Group defines the mobile cloud as a 'federated point of entry enabling access to the full range of capabilities inherent in the mobile network platform', which sounds very grand, but essentially means that you can access every available mobile service from a single point: your mobile device of choice.

Many solution providers in the mobile space have been actively working on assembling the networks, skilled people and real-world experience they're going to need to deliver new and exciting managed services. Essentially these operators are looking to offer a one-stop shop for enterprises, brands, mobile marketers, content and application owners, network owners, solution providers and developers. Their services aim to seamlessly integrate multiple networks into one convenient commercial offering, bringing the world of the internet and mobile together and unlocking the potential of the operators' entire networks, including infrastructure and, of course, customer data.

Downstream, all of this impacts the end user experience. As network operators strive to improve the overall experience for developers, brands and service providers (their customers), that in turn filters down, allowing them to make more relevant, engaging and affordable services available to consumers. It's another one of those win–win situations that seem to crop up constantly in digital.

The mobile cloud is the future – that's something most experts agree on – but at the moment the reality for many of us still falls far short of the promise. Always-on, always-connected devices tapping into the boundless capacity of the amorphous cloud only work when you actually have a high-speed data connection. If you live in the middle of a major city you're probably fine, but venture a bit further afield and that all-promising cloud quickly becomes an impenetrable fog as your device switches to a legacy mobile connection and everything slows to a crawl.

'There's no point having beautiful shiny products or the best content playing on the best mobile device or tablet if you have intermittent connectivity,' cautions Torsten de Riese, Digital Director for CNBC in EMEA. 'That's still the case even in developed countries, not just in the developing countries. I live in London and struggle to connect to my iPad in many areas.'

de Riese warns that we shouldn't get ahead of ourselves. No sooner are we adjusting to the latest tranche of mobile products and services, powered by mobile cloud solutions, than the rapidly evolving industry heaps another dollop of innovation on our heads. 4G connectivity is being dangled as a tantalizing carrot, with the promise of better coverage and higher bandwidth, but it's important for marketers to remember that not everybody has access to the same connectivity, products, experience or expectation.

It's vital to keep your particular audience and the technology and platforms they use in mind as you develop your mobile strategy. 'Mobile devices are going to create a different working "sensation" for individuals,' de Riese predicts. 'When you can do things like connect your social network to your car, all sorts of behaviours will change. There will be a different paradigm for how we use and think of mobility.'

Further exploration

We have only really scratched the surface, and looked at a high-level snapshot of the mobile marketing landscape. Getting into the detail would go far beyond the scope of this volume. The years ahead promise to deliver more innovation, change and rapid development in the mobile space.

Mobile marketing is finally coming of age. With the gradual introduction of sophisticated new technologies, marketers are beginning to track results and manage mobile metrics in ways similar to those used for the web. Some critics argue that the medium is still not reaching its full potential: of course it's not – even in terms of digital marketing it's still a baby – but it's growing up fast. In this chapter we hope we've shared some of the boundless scope and potential that makes mobile marketing so exciting. Mobile is already a significant layer in the digital marketing mix, and over time will grow in importance as more people turn to their mobile devices for the information, answers, products and services they need every day.

Whether mobile marketing is a good fit for your business is up to you to decide... but the potential of mobile is certainly worth exploring.

Some other areas of mobile that fall beyond the scope of this chapter but may be worth a quick 'Google' include:

- SMS and short-code mobile marketing;
- mobile payments;
- mobile commerce;
- QR codes;
- augmented reality;
- mobile mapping;
- mobile banking;
- mobile health.

CASE STUDY Helping women beat breast cancer
with an innovative mobile app

FIGURE 10.5 The iBreastCheck iPhone app – an innovative guide to self-examination for women

I am enormously impressed by the Breakthrough phone app, iBreastCheck. It is a
very skilled piece of work.

> King's College London professor

Campaign budget

£12,000.

The challenge

Breast cancer is the most common cancer in the UK. Nearly 48,000 women are diagnosed
each year. The earlier the onset of the disease is recognized, the better the chances of
beating it, yet less than 50 per cent of women regularly check their breasts.

Lots of leaflets and posters exist promoting the importance of breast-checking, but
research told the charity Breakthrough Breast Cancer that women wanted access to more
practical information on how to check their breasts, what to look for, and a gentle periodic
nudge prompting them to check regularly.

Target audience

Women over 30 years old.

Action

Working with agency TorchBox, iBreastCheck commissioned a smartphone application called iBreastCheck, the UK's first digital app designed to encourage women to be more breast aware. Market research showed that the target demographic skewed towards Apple's iPhone platform, so that was selected as the initial channel on which to launch the new app.

The aims of the app were to improve understanding of the signs and symptoms women should look out for, build awareness of the risk factors associated with the disease (and what women could do to help mitigate them), and provide a practical reminder service.

The app uses a combination of content, including informative video, a 'What to look for' slide show, a questionnaire that helps women determine their personal risk factor, and a handy 'Set it and forget it' reminder that sets a repeating alert on the iPhone to remind women to check regularly.

Ultimately this application and the associated content could save lives.

Results

The campaign received a great response across all digital and traditional media channels. Using the release of the app as a hook, Breakthrough Breast Cancer successfully delivers timely and newsworthy content across multiple media channels, driving awareness, message amplification and subsequent app downloads.

Lorraine Kelly (a popular morning television presenter in the UK) demonstrated the app live on her morning show on ITV, and the charity secured a strong editorial presence across a wide range of broadcast media, women's consumer magazines and national print titles. High-profile Tweeters and bloggers were also targeted – with a single tweet from BBC Radio One DJ Sara Cox driving an additional 500 downloads of the app!

- App downloads: the app was downloaded by more than 20,000 people in the first six months, beating pre-campaign targets by 70 per cent.

- Media coverage: independent media evaluation estimated media exposure secured as a result of the app launch at £2.6 million, providing 66 million opportunities to see and reaching 46.79 per cent of women in the UK over the age of 24, beating pre-campaign targets by 87 per cent.

- Public perception: the campaign received an overwhelmingly positive response from the general public, celebrities, media commentators, eminent health professionals and leaders in the field of health promotion.

- iTunes rating: iBreastCheck achieved a five-star rating in iTunes, and has regularly topped the App Store 'health and fitness' chart.

Link to campaign creative

- http://www.ibreastcheck.com

Credits

Client:	• Breakthrough Breast Cancer
Geographical scope:	• United Kingdom
Agency:	• Torchbox
Campaign contact:	• David Barker, Director of Communications, Breakthrough Breast Cancer

What's next?

11

For marketing to service the new needs of business, and for it to profit from rather than suffer from the changing world of media, it will have to adapt in a radical way.
CHRIS WARD, MICROSOFT MSN, 'THE FUTURE OF DIGITAL MARKETING'

Get your head out of the television space and into the video space... everything on video and video on everything.
OVERHEARD AT THE LAUNCH OF 'THE BEST DIGITAL MARKETING CAMPAIGNS IN THE WORLD', LONDON, 19 JULY 2011

I look to the future because that's where I'm going to spend the rest of my life. **GEORGE BURNS (1896–1996)**

OUR CHAPTER PLEDGE TO YOU

When you reach the end of this chapter you'll have answers to the following questions:

- What are the key trends that are shaping the digital marketing landscape of the future?

- How is the relationship between consumers and marketers evolving?

- What are the main challenges digital marketers will face over the next three years?

- What can you do to future-proof your business?

The future's bright: head towards the light

If the last five years have taught us anything in the digital marketing space, they've taught us to expect rapid and unprecedented change. In a few short years digital marketing has gone from talent show wannabe to a headlining Broadway act, emerging from the wings of cyberspace to take the centre-stage spotlight.

Spending on online advertising continues to grow rapidly, poaching budget from more 'traditional' channels as businesses realize that the future is online – and so are their customers. In 2007 US internet advertising revenues totalled $21.2 billion, 26 per cent higher than in 2006, which was itself a record year (Interactive Advertising Bureau (IAB)/Pricewaterhouse-Coopers (PwC) '2007 Internet Advertising Revenue Report'). That pace has continued. A recent survey by Zenith Optimedia predicted US ad spend on display media to be worth $25 billion in 2011 and that it was set to grow by 36 per cent to $34 billion in 2013. More meaningful still is the figure for US total online spend, which includes search and classified. This looks likely to hit $72 billion in 2011 and will grow to a whopping $94 billion in 2013. What that means is that online will soon represent *one-third of all advertising spend*. That's some feat for a medium that's only turned 20! (Sir Tim Berners-Lee created the first placeholder page for the world wide web on 6 August 1991.)

And this is only the beginning. Mainstream business is just starting to understand and tap into the rich vein of potential that digital marketing represents. Right at the start of the book we mentioned that this is an incredibly exciting time to be involved in the digital marketing space. We're now beyond the tipping point. Digital channels have entered the mainstream: the crazy, lawless, 'wild frontier' days of the pioneers are behind us.

As digital marketing continues to mature and evolve, we're entering a new and exciting era of opportunity, accountability and sustainable growth. It is quite simply the biggest revolution in marketing history. And we can all be a part of it.

Word of mouth: savvy consumers control the future

Technology continues to evolve at a startling pace – getting faster, more capable, easier to use and affordable – and that trend doesn't look set to slow any time soon. But the technology itself is a very small part of the digital marketing story: what's really exciting for the digital marketer is the way technology is enabling people. It's the way people are adopting and using technology that is a catalyst for rapid and enduring change. Consumers are using technology to redefine their consumption of media, their relationships with brands and marketers, and their relationships with each other. It's changing the nature of the game – and marketers either have to adapt or be left behind.

All the wonderful new things technology makes possible for media is really the driver of this new marketing era. Two things immediately spring to mind that perhaps aren't covered elsewhere in this book:

Collaborative consumption

Not the easiest trend to pronounce after a few pints but nonetheless a key trend for the future of marketing and media. What's it all about? People being enabled by technology to save money and hassle through co-ownership and co-consumption. Think about **www.streetcar.co.uk** – why bother owning a car in London when you can share with others who don't want to be bothered either?

Where can this go to? Well, think about all the things we own or want to own and how much we get to use these things – some things obviously don't suit the co-consumption concept (eg your bed, your laptop, your fridge,

FIGURE 11.1 The collaborative home: how people are already making and saving money through collaborative ownership and consumption; infographic courtesy of Collaborative Fund in partnership with Startup America (**www.collaborativefund.com**)

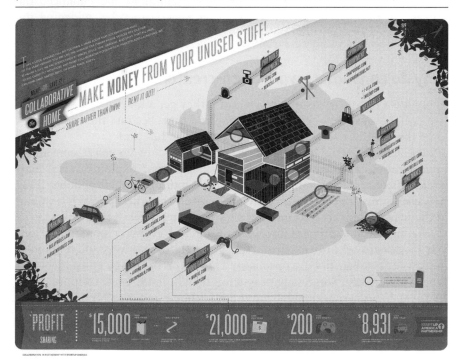

your mobile) but others certainly do (eg ladders, properties, lawnmowers, etc) – think about the reduced cost and the reduced wastage of *sharing* these items.

Today's consumers are more than happy to share pretty much every aspect of their lives through social media, but before long that propensity to share will extend to include real-world 'things' too. It's yet another example of the blurring lines between the virtual world and the real one, and how else could this collaborative ownership be managed other than through the use of innovative connected technology to power the process?

Take a look at **www.collaborativeconsumption.com** – this story is going to feature strongly in the years ahead.

Co-creation

We covered this to some extent earlier in the book, and there are examples of it in action to varying degrees in *The Best Digital Marketing Campaigns in the World*, but this baby still has a long way to go. The rise of social media coupled with the pursuit of the purest forms of customer engagement have lent themselves to co-creation. What is it? Simply a brand working and engaging with consumers to improve and innovate their product or service.

The crux of it is that people really don't mind being sold to if what is on offer is relevant, required and competitive. Technology has enhanced the process of refining the products and services we can offer, widening the field for more to play.

Why do consumers want to co-create?

There are a few possible answers: because they get a kick out of authorship (we do!), because they get to save money and time, because they don't want to be the same as everybody else and because it's fun too!

'The reality is communication technology has always made consumers savvier, more educated and amplified their diversity,' explains digital marketing visionary Jonathan Mendez in his Optimize and Prophesize blog (**www.optimizeandprophesize.com**). 'We will all agree that power has shifted in the marketplace to consumers as they take on an ever-active voice in the marketing and the ultimate success of products. Reviews, recommendations and social networks necessitate factual and helpful messages and marketing that quantifies benefits to consumers. This is the only way consumers will accept your voice. Some might say straight talk lends itself to more direct response-focused marketing – and it does – but it can also become the best friend of a brand builder.'

There's little doubt that as the population of digital savvy consumers continues to grow around the world, so too will the imperative for marketers to engage with them online: listening to and learning from them, and including their input in the evolution and development of brands. Some forward-thinking companies, like Dell and Procter & Gamble, are already embracing this consumer-driven trend, and it's something that will continue to grow.

As marketers, our biggest challenge is how we manage that transition from broadcasting a message to entering an ongoing dialogue: how do we make sense of this plethora of new communications tools, and use them to connect with customers who are ever more fragmented and dispersed? How can we engage in a way that adds mutual and enduring value? The answers demand a paradigm shift in the marketing mindset – a change that's proving painful for a lot of old-school marketers and agencies – but which opens up a whole new world of opportunity to those nimble enough to adapt.

We need to harness the power of digital media to talk with our customers, not at them, and to recognize that in the online space the consumer really is controlling the conversation. Someone once said that 'if I engaged with my friends like most advertisers engage with me they'd probably punch me in the face'!

That's not to say that message-based advertising will die out – it almost certainly won't – but to be effective the message will need to become more targeted, focused and relevant. Advertising will have to add tangible value through delivering useful information, entertainment or a practical tool or application in exchange for the user's attention.

We're in a period of transition: broadcast-style interruptive advertising will continue to co-exist with more engaging formats for some time yet. Ultimately though, engagement-based marketing delivers more all-round value. As more marketers start to understand and accept that fact, we'll see engagement becoming the dominant model in digital marketing.

Search: a constantly evolving marketing powerhouse

Because search is so central to the online experience it can be difficult to believe that, as an industry, it is still very much in its infancy. People who predict that search marketing has peaked (and there are some out there) are fundamentally underestimating both the power of search engines to innovate and adapt, and the overwhelming desire of a continually expanding user base to find relevant, valuable information on an increasingly cluttered web.

At the time of writing, Google, by far the dominant player in search, is only a little more than a decade old. The technology underpinning search, while it has developed extraordinarily quickly, is still very young. It has a lot of growing up to do over the coming years.

Blended search is already with us, and will be refined and developed over the coming years; search engines will continue to hone their ability to understand context in search queries – to divine exactly what users are looking for and to deliver ever more relevant results. Personalized search based on both profile information and preferences we explicitly provide (or give permission for search engines to collect) is already part of our individual search experience, and that personalization will be refined further, combined with information inferred from aggregated search history and other anonymous user data to deliver more relevant search results for each and every one of us.

The method search engines use to rank pages is constantly evolving. At the moment, inbound links are still a dominant factor in determining the quality, authority and relevance of a page for search rankings; over time though, as search engines get better at evaluating the actual content of a site, and introduce a more human measure of quality, perhaps through the integration of signals from across the social web, the emphasis will shift away from link-based ranking.

How the ranking algorithms will evolve is anybody's guess. But they will evolve, and search marketing will continue to evolve alongside them. At the forefront of these developments, for the foreseeable future at least, will be Google, and despite the best efforts of leading competitors it's difficult to see how anyone in the current search marketplace can seriously challenge the wily incumbent for the top spot over the next few years. That's not to say they won't try, or that others won't emerge with a whiz-bang new search technology that will ultimately topple Google. This is an incredibly disruptive arena, as Google itself has proved, and there are any number of search start-ups out there, working frantically on what they believe to be Google-killing search technologies. Watch this space!

Humanizing and personalizing search

Introducing a human recommendation element into search makes all sorts of sense. Human-powered search engines like Mahalo (**www.mahalo.com**) present results that have been screened and recommended by a real, live editorial team rather than a computer program. Obviously this approach can and does deliver more relevant and useful search results for popular search terms... but even adopting a social media, wiki-esque model of co-creation and collaboration, it's difficult to see how purely human-powered search will ever scale to become a real contender as a comprehensive and universal internet search engine.

Social search – taking things a step further

In an interview with VentureBeat in early 2008, Marissa Mayer, Google's Vice President of Search Products and User Experience, defined social search as: 'any search aided by a social interaction or a social connection... Social search happens every day. When you ask a friend "What movies are good to go see?" or "Where should we go to dinner?" you are doing a verbal social search. You're trying to leverage that social connection to try and get a piece of information that would be better than what you'd come up with on your own.'

While social media sites allow us to connect with our 'friends' and find out what they recommend, to see what they consider 'hot-or-not', delivering social search in a web search engine context introduces a variety of complications – not least of which is privacy. Think about it – do you really want the stuff you enter into a search engine to influence the search results of all your online social connections? Do you want your search results influenced based on what they've been searching for in turn? Some may; many more will not.

So, just how our online social connections and interactions might influence our personal search results in the future is unclear, but there's no doubt that leading search engines are looking into the possibility, and that social elements will feature in determining the ranking and relevance of search results for specific individuals in some way.

'If we look at a search engine 10 years from now, we know it will be better than Google is today,' said Mayer. 'Google itself gets better every single day because we're constantly making changes to the relevance... I think one way it will be better is in understanding more about you and understanding more about your social context: who your friends are, what you like to do, where you are. It's hard to imagine that the search engine 10 years from now isn't advised by those things.'

What all this means for marketers

In marketing terms, search is the biggest platform in the digital marketing space but display is fast on its heels. All of the developments in search – universal search, human-powered search, social search, etc – are ultimately being driven by a single universal goal: the prime directive we mentioned back at the start of Chapter 4. Search engines need to deliver the most relevant, authoritative results to their users if they want to maintain and expand their user base. By giving users what they want, search engines attract more users, which in turn attract more advertisers... and that means more money for search engines.

More relevant, focused search results, as we've mentioned, is great news for marketers – because as long as you're targeting the right keyword phrases in your SEO and paid search campaigns, it means the traffic coming your way will be more qualified and more likely to convert. Search marketing looks set for continued and sustainable growth, both in terms of organic SEO and paid search campaigns.

While paid search has to date attracted the lion's share of the search marketing dollar, we'll probably see more of that spend drifting towards display, social media and SEO over the coming years as businesses feel the pinch of rising costs per click in their paid search campaigns, and realize the ongoing value of organic rankings to deliver traffic for their targeted keyword terms.

Overall, more businesses are going to realize the benefits of establishing coordinated search marketing campaigns, running paid search and SEO in tandem, choosing their keywords wisely to garner the most valuable traffic from both.

Mobile: whoah... it's finally here!

Mobile marketing – it's hard to ignore this monster now, particularly since the advent of smartphones. Just take a look at our chapter on mobile marketing!

It feels as if it's taken forever; it was so incredibly obvious to everyone in the business; there must have been at least 12 years in a row which were anointed 'the year of mobile' by a range of self-confessed experts with varying degrees of stakeholding in mobile marketing agencies and content providers. But (sharp intake of breath) it's official, guys – mobile is here now!

Let's dial it down a bit and see where things came from before we ring the changes once more.

The first mobile phone call was made in 1973 by Dr Martin Cooper in New York City. Comedian Ernie Wise made the first UK mobile phone call some 12 years later from Vodafone's HQ in Newbury.

Around the same time, Sir David Brown, Chairman of Motorola, re-counted a tale when mobile industry analysts forecast a global mobile phone market of just 900,000 units by the year 2000. Their prediction fell a little short. As we rolled into the new millennium, the global mobile industry was selling 900,000 handsets every nineteen hours (**www.bbc.co.uk** 'Mobiles still ringing in New Year', December 2006).

By the end of 2007 there were a staggering 3.3 billion active mobile phone subscriptions in the world – that was about one phone for every two people.

Also in 2007, over 798 million people around the world accessed the internet using a mobile phone rather than a personal computer.

Mobile data bandwidth then increased to the sort of levels that make accessing the internet on the move practical. It also became more affordable, and devices started to emerge which took advantage of this increased band-width and innovative user interface design to deliver a rich and engaging mobile internet experience.

The trigger for this refinement of the mobile device was the introduction in 2007 of Apple's iPhone and iPod Touch – both of which featured the same outstanding multi-touch user interface and a fully functional web browser capable of displaying full-fledged web pages, rather than the dumbed-down mobile web typical on other devices.

The impact: more people are using them to access the web than any other mobile device. How many more? On 13 February 2008, Vic Gundotra, head of Google's mobile operations, told the *Financial Times* that the search company was getting 50 times more search traffic from Apple's iPhone than from any other mobile handset on the market. The gap was so big that Google got their engineers to re-check the server logs to make sure they were accurate. When you consider the relatively small number of iPhones out there compared to other web-enabled mobile devices, the figure became even more astonishing.

What it proved was that people are willing to use the internet extensively on mobile devices, as long as the experience is rich enough. People want to be connected all the time – just try taking away a teenager's mobile phone and internet access and watch their reaction – but they're not prepared to compromise on user experience: they demand something seamless and intuitive.

Other manufacturers quickly followed Apple's lead, and a number of mobile devices with slick, easy-to-use interfaces, fully functional web browsers and feature-rich web-enabled applications entered the marketplace.

In January 2011 sales of smartphones exceeded the sale of desktop PCs in the UK. Peach Digital has predicted that 42 per cent of the UK's population will have a smartphone by the end of 2011. The same firm also predicts that by 2014 users accessing the web from mobile devices will overtake those using desktops.

All of the ingredients are in place for mobile internet usage to explode – it's not a question of when; it's now about the sheer size of growth. The implications for digital marketers will be profound, in terms of the scope and reach of our digital campaigns, and the ability to target and connect with consumers wherever they are and whatever they're doing.

At the moment we have the standard web and the mobile web – essentially a minuscule subset of the web that's been shoehorned to fit the constraints imposed by today's mainstream mobile devices. In the not too distant future, widespread adoption of much more capable devices will herald the demise of the 'mobile web'. What we'll be left with is just the web we know and love, complete with search, rich media, video, graphics, engagement and everything else, all seamlessly accessible, wherever we happen to be and using whichever device we choose.

Knowing where you are and who's nearby

Another aspect of mobile technology that's something of a hot topic, especially in relation to mobile, is geo-location – or the ability to work out exactly where the device is at any given time. Many high-end devices now have built in GPS (global positioning system), but even for those that don't, software can triangulate the phone's position based on its proximity to the nearest mobile operator masts.

Combine the ability to accurately place your phone on the map with the software's ability to use your phone's capability to detect other devices (and hence people) nearby, and you have all the ingredients for enhanced real-life networking in the palm of your hand. The possibilities are mind boggling.

Feel like eating Mexican food? Your mobile will serve you up all the spicy details of places nearby, complete with reviews, ratings and menus. Theoretically it could even take into account the fact that it's lunchtime and suggest where you might like to eat based on your past preferences, such as location, time of day, places you've frequented recently, etc.

At a party, but don't know anyone? No problem... a quick look at your mobile will tell you that three of the people in the room are friends of friends in your online social networks, and that two of them have similar interests to you. Recognizing them is easy – you've seen their profile picture – and with a bit of background to help break the ice, you're soon chatting away about those common interests.

Or perhaps you're attending a business conference, and are on the look-out for a new job? Your mobile lets you know there are four CEOs scheduled to be at the conference whose companies are looking to hire someone with your skill set. It can show you their online profile information, and tell you that one of them is standing approximately 10 metres away. That evening, when you get back to your hotel, there's a record of everyone you've met that day waiting for you on your tablet computer, complete with links to their online profiles. You check your social network and see that three of your friends are in town (based on geo-location data from their phones), so you contact them. Instead of dining alone on room service you spend a social evening at a local restaurant with friends – all thanks to your mobile.

While there are still some fairly large hurdles to overcome before all of this comes to pass – issues relating to privacy, security and data protection, to name a few – all of it is technically possible right now. It will take a little time for it to permeate into the mainstream, but it is literally just around the corner. From a marketing standpoint the possibilities are staggering, and will help businesses to engage with customers more effectively, and deliver timely, valuable, focused, location-specific content to them as and when they need it.

SMS for life

Before we head off this small section on mobile we'd like to take a look at an extraordinary mobile project called 'SMS For Life'. It's an amazing example of mobile engagement which is saving lives and changing the world we live in, one text at a time.

The SMS for Life initiative is a new 'public–private' project that harnesses everyday technology to eliminate stockouts of and improve access to essential malaria medication in sub-Saharan Africa.

Maintaining adequate stocks of anti-malarial medicines at local health facilities across rural sub-Saharan Africa is a major barrier to effective management of the world's biggest killer. Lack of visibility of anti-malarial stock levels at rural health facilities is a significant contributor to the problem.

'It's simple. If there are no malaria treatments, someone will die. It is very likely to be a child. Reducing stockouts saves lives,' said Professor David Mwakyusa, former Minister for Health and Social Welfare in Tanzania, speaking in April 2010.

Tanzania was selected as the pilot country for the scheme, and 20 regional managers from PSI and ministry IT personnel were trained in how to implement the system.

The SMS for Life approach

The 21-week pilot study, 'SMS for Life', was undertaken during 2009–10 in three districts of rural Tanzania, involving 129 health facilities, covering a population of 1.2 million. Undertaken through a collaborative partnership between Novartis, the Roll Back Malaria Partnership, IBM, Vodafone and the Ministry for Health of Tanzania, SMS for Life used mobile telephones, SMS messages and electronic mapping technology to facilitate provision of comprehensive and accurate stock counts from all health facilities to each district management team on a weekly basis.

The system covered stocks of the four different dosage packs of artemether-lumefantrine (AL) and quinine injectable. The data captured through the SMS stock count messages was available through a secure reporting website. The website was then accessed via the internet on a computer or a Blackberry or other smart mobile phone. Access to the website was granted through a unique user ID and password allocated at the group level and was granted to the following groups:

- the district medical officer and his staff in each district;

- the regional medical officer and his staff in each region affiliated with the chosen districts;

- the project team;

- The National Malaria Control Programme in the Ministry of Health;

- The medical stores department (including the zonal stores affiliated with each district).

Results

Stock count data was provided in 95 per cent of cases, on average. A high response rate (≥93 per cent) was maintained throughout the pilot. The error rate for composition of SMS responses averaged 7.5 per cent throughout the study; almost all errors were corrected and messages re-sent.

Data accuracy, based on surveillance visits to health facilities, was 94 per cent. District stock reports were accessed on average once a day. The proportion of health facilities with no stock of one or more anti-malarial medicine fell from 78 per cent at week 1 to 26 per cent at week 21. In Lindi rural district, stockouts were eliminated by week 8 of the pilot, with virtually no stockouts thereafter. During the study, AL stocks increased by 64 per cent and quinine stock increased by 36 per cent across the three districts.

Conclusions

The SMS for Life pilot provided visibility of anti-malarial stock levels to support more efficient stock management using simple and widely available SMS technology via a public–private partnership model that worked highly effectively. The SMS for Life system has the potential to alleviate restricted availability of anti-malarial drugs or other medicines in rural or under-resourced areas.

Overall, the SMS for Life system was built to be a generic and highly scalable solution that can be leveraged to support any medicine or product, and can be implemented in any country with minimal tailoring. Additionally the system could also be utilized for disease surveillance.

'I'm grateful for what you are doing for my country – I lose a child every five minutes, which is a waste from a disease that is completely preventable. This is a great project and an innovation that I support very much. It's exciting to me,' commented Professor Mwakyusa, when he was presented with the SMS for Life pilot results.

Tracking and measuring human behaviour

Tracking, measurement and accountability in the digital marketing space have come a long way in a few short years. Now powerful web-based analytics tools are available for free, and even small businesses can track and measure their ROI with some degree of confidence over much of their online marketing investment. We can track everything from impression, through clicks to conversion, we can even analyse exactly where the process is breaking down and take steps to remedy the problem. With a little bit of effort we can establish what's working and what's not, we can test, make changes and refine our campaigns in real time. All of this measurement makes marketers more accountable for the investment they make – and that's a great thing.

Web analytics and measurement will continue to grow, and if anything will become even more important to digital marketers over the coming years. The model of delivery may change, with more online agencies developing their analytics capabilities and offering the service as a value-added option for their clients – an option many may opt for in preference to in-house teams and external consultants. Regardless of the model that emerges, measuring and tracking performance online (and we're including mobile analytics under that umbrella) are going to be critical to success and will involve tracking new and fairly unconventional metrics.

With standard analytics we can measure what people are doing and when. Where things tend to fall down is when it comes to pinpointing the one thing people really want to know: why. Why are people abandoning their shopping cart at stage X? Why aren't people who click on ad Y going on to sign up for our newsletter? Why aren't visitors clicking through to deeper content pages on our website? Why won't people engage with our latest social media campaign?

Analytics are great for collecting, aggregating and reporting on the where and the when – the quantitative empirical data of online transactions. Clicks, impressions, visits… all straightforward, all measurable: observable actions where one equals one, two equals two, etc. However, quantitative data alone can never truly describe the subtleties of human behaviour.

And therein lies the problem – because the brave new world of conversational marketing that we've described, where consumer engagement reigns supreme, is all about identifying and responding to the subtleties of human behaviour and interaction. But how do you accurately measure qualitative concepts like engagement, influence, trust and authority in a repeatable and comparable way? How do you consistently and comparably measure the evolution of online conversation?

There are already plenty of speculative suggestions, theories and formulae out there, but little consensus to date. Over time, gradual consensus will emerge on how and where to measure these qualitative online metrics, and how they can best be used in conjunction with existing analytics solutions to help us improve both our relationship with consumers and our ROI.

In-game advertising

Computer and video games have become fertile ground for advertisers over recent years. Since Sony launched its first Playstation back in 1995, the games console market has exploded. Video games are one of the fastest-growing areas of entertainment, and are perfect for hitting the desirable 18–34-year-old male demographic. Predictions vary wildly, but estimates suggest that in-game advertising could be worth between US$800 million and just shy of US$2 billion in 2012.

With the advent of always-on broadband internet connections, modern games consoles can connect players with each other – and crucially allow advertisers to connect with the games. In-game advertising is a particularly attractive proposition, because unlike most other media, gamers tend to welcome the presence of real-world brands within games. It brings an added sense of realism to their gaming experience. In fact, a study by Nielsen Interactive Entertainment found that some 70 per cent of gamers respond positively to the presence of real brands and advertising in their games, as long as they remain contextually relevant and serve to enhance rather than disrupt their game-playing experience.

Static billboard-style advertising in games is rapidly being replaced by dynamic ads served up in real time over the internet by specialist in-game advertising networks. Ads can be geo-targeted and contextual, and can be modified at will by the networks – offering changing and ongoing advertising opportunities throughout the lifetime of the game. There are also product placement opportunities in games, in much the same way as there are in feature films – but in games the gamer gets to actually interact with the placed product, making for a more engaging experience. Because these ads are served over the internet, their performance can be tracked in much the same way as any other form of online advertising.

A little further down the track there are also likely to be opportunities to link in-game purchases to online stores. For example, buying a pair of jeans or sunglasses for your in-game character could generate a corresponding purchase for the same items with an online retailer. Brands will also be able to sponsor specific sections or 'challenges' within gaming environments, and offer real-world rewards and incentives for gamers to complete the challenge, generating brand engagement and positive online and offline publicity.

As the in-game advertising market continues to mature and grow it will become an increasingly dynamic and imaginative arena for marketers... definitely one to watch.

Video; two screens; wrappers

Where do we start with this one? Online video advertising is already a massive, game-changing and high-growth sector. According to the official YouTube blog, the leading online video service adds a staggering 35 hours of new video content to its database *every minute*. To put that figure into context, here's a quote from the aforementioned blog post:

> Another way to think about it is: if three of the major US networks were broadcasting 24 hours a day, 7 days a week, 365 days a year for the last 60 years, they still wouldn't have broadcast as much content as is uploaded to YouTube every 30 days.

In terms of advertising figures, an eMarketer report from May 2010 estimated that in the United States online video advertising would hit US$2.15 billion in 2011, rising to US$5.52 billion by 2014. Advertising spend is currently dominated by Google through its ownership of YouTube. However, YouTube is far from the only game in town. Other website and mobile publishers are waking up to the power of video. Our friends in Peach Digital predict that 66 per cent of all mobile data traffic will be video by 2014.

Advertisers are slowly wising up to the fact that transplanting television ads as online video ads (dubbed pre-rolls) is perhaps not the smartest thing to do. It's the same old story: online consumers have more control, they can turn ads off just in the same way they can fast-forward through ads using their Tivo or Sky+. This presents a challenge for advertisers and publishers. How can the power of video advertising be harnessed without becoming intrusive? In other words, how can video advertisers engage rather than enrage their audience?

One London-based organization, **www.inskinmedia.com**, has solved this problem by creating 'wrappers' which sit in a frame around a piece of video giving users the option to find out more about the product or service being advertised. It's clearly a better and more practical way to engage an audience than forcing them to sit through a 30-second slot for something they don't want. As the next few years unfold we expect ad formats like wrappers to grow in popularity and 'forced' viewing of TV-style ads to fall off markedly. In fact, IMDB (**www.imdb.com**), the world's largest movie database site, has recently announced it is moving away from the pre-roll ad format because it finds it is losing audience.

We're also seeing a new marketing challenge arrive in the form of two-screen or multiscreen environments. We have all sat in front of the television with our laptop open and the smartphone on, right? Okay, well, that's what we're talking about. How do we start to use this 'multi-screen/device environment' to engage more productively with audiences?

Companies like Monterosa (**www.monterosa.co.uk**) in the UK are meeting this challenge already on popular shows such as Channel 4's *Million Pound Drop*, a TV show where the audience can join in at home on their laptops or mobiles. Watch out for a lot more activity in this space as digital media empowers consumers to take real charge of what they see on television, rather than just being armed with the remote control!

Holistic marketing: blurring lines and integrating media

Digital marketing is a big part of the future, for sure... but it's important to remember that it's not the only option. In fact, even thinking of media in terms of digital and traditional is becoming an increasingly invalid position. The lines are blurring as traditional media are used to drive traffic online and increasingly start to embrace digital channels to deliver 'traditional' content on consumers' terms. TV, radio, newspapers, magazines – all of these traditional media are embracing digital channels through necessity; consumers demand it, so they deliver it, and they're getting better at it all the time. In their favour, of course, is their content. People know their content, and trust their brands. The success of initiatives like the BBCs on-demand TV service, iPlayer, is ample testament to the fact that traditional media can learn to 'play' the digital game.

So we're not forecasting the death of traditional media advertising here; rather the continued evolution and diversification of media as a whole. For marketers, that diversification presents both significant challenges and boundless opportunity. Fragmentation of the market into ever-smaller niche groups across an array of different media means that each potential marketing channel reaches a smaller audience – but it also means your campaigns can be more targeted, relevant and engaging than ever before.

Technology is also helping marketers to address fragmentation by providing us with ever more sophisticated tools to track multiple, integrated campaigns that span numerous channels and audiences. As mentioned earlier in the book, digital marketing, uniquely, allows us to both broaden our scope and narrow our focus at the same time.

Over the next five years or so we'll see a much more holistic view of the marketing landscape emerge: a view with less emphasis on 'traditional versus 'digital', and more focus on integrating campaigns to span not just the different elements of digital marketing – search, display, e-mail, affiliate, social media, etc – but also a seamless integration with offline channels.

Thought leaders predict the future

In the first edition of *UDM* (written in 2007–08) we asked some of the industry's leading lights to give us their views on the future landscape for digital marketing. It was really quite prophetic looking back on their answers as they had accurately predicted 'digital marketing in 2011'. In particular they were resoundingly correct about the rise of mobile, the continued importance of analytics and the spectacular growth the digital sector would experience during this time.

Our thanks go to Richard Eyre, (Chairman of the UK IAB), Alain Heureux, (CEO of IAB Europe) and Martin Murray of Google for their important contributions to this discussion.

But it can't stop there, can it?

This time around we asked Scott Seaborn of Ogilvy, Justin Cooke of Fortune Cookie, Colin Lloyd, former Chair of CAM, and Jonathan Forrest of Cybercom to gaze into the crystal ball and predict the future. Here's what they shared.

Scott Seaborn, Head of Mobile Technologies, Ogilvy Group UK

Q. *What do you feel are the greatest challenges facing the digital marketing industry between now and say 2015?*

A. Education. There are so many people around that still do not really understand digital – and we have moved into a mobile age! Sometimes there are incredible ideas that we must get across – the skill is in making them simple.

Q. *Which tools or channels do you think will show the greatest level of growth and why (ie social media, mobile, something else)?*

A. Mobile will, of course, show the greatest growth. In the UK, mobile already accounts for 20 per cent of all internet traffic. From a global perspective, mobile internet will eclipse the PC web in the short-to-medium term. The growth curve for mobile is set to dramatically outstretch PCs, social and offline media.

Q. *Do you expect the top sites to be more or less popular by 2015 (ie Google, Facebook, YouTube, Wikipedia)?*

A. By 2015 I expect them to be more popular from a global perspective, but there will be markets (mainly in the developed world) where popularity will decline. By 2020 I would expect things like Facebook to have either diversified or declined.

Q. *Digital currently represents about 25 per cent of all marketing spend (UK) – how do you see this evolving by 2015?*

A. I think that digital will come back into the fold of the large (traditional) agencies. It will simply be part of the DNA in understanding and managing a brand, it won't stand alone for much longer. With that in mind, budgets might merge into each other. Also, there might be new metrics governing price.

Justin Cooke, CEO, Fortune Cookie

Q. *What do you feel are the greatest challenges facing the digital marketing industry between now and say 2015?*

A. Our industry faces three significant challenges: managing an enormous channel shift while still delivering quality, relevant, engaging communications and recruiting new and re-educating existing talent.

Q. *Which tools or channels do you think will show the greatest level of growth and why (ie social media, mobile, something else)?*

A. The greatest level of growth will undoubtedly come from the increasing convergence of social media platforms, the mobile channel and location-based services. We have already reached massive levels of adoption for both mobile and social media and yet only just begun to understand the possibility of providing new products and services by combining the three. I think this opportunity is so great that it may be worthwhile revisiting Metcalfe's law and changing the impact from squared to cubed. Perhaps we could call it Cookie's law?

Q. *Do you expect the top sites to be more or less popular by 2015 (ie Google, Facebook, YouTube, Wikipedia)?*

A. I think we are fast moving to a world where sites are no longer a way of measuring significance. We are already becoming very comfortable using the average number of active users and/or subscribers as a metric. Therefore it will be the brands that can provide content and services from a platform to multiple channels that will thrive.

Q.   *Digital currently represents about 25 per cent of all marketing spend (UK) – how do you see this evolving by 2015?*

A.   If you exclude digital TV, then I would be confident in predicting that at least 60 per cent of all marketing spend will be digital by 2015. If you include digital TV, then I would predict more like 90 per cent of all marketing spend being digital in all its various guises.

Colin Lloyd, Former Chair of CAM Foundation

Q.   *What do you feel are the greatest challenges facing the digital marketing industry between now and say 2015?*

A.   Ensuring that the 'craft' skills of traditional marketing and in particular direct marketing that have stood the test of time are not lost in the rush for digital adoption.

Q.   *Which tools or channels do you think will show the greatest level of growth and why (ie social media, mobile, something else)?*

A.   I fear that social media will become over-commercialized and lose its raison d'être. We have already seen defections from Facebook, and there is a danger that it might be just another passing fad. I don't think so, but marketers need to be cautious in risking brand reputation. The lessons of test, test and test again come to mind. A substantial investment has been made in mobile marketing technology. However, to date the revenues are very small by comparison to other channels. The number of apps is reaching biblical proportions and no marketing campaign worth its salt runs without one. Whether they get the impact that a 30-second commercial still gets for the same cost, I remain unconvinced. However, I have no doubt that the plague will continue.

So, what's coming? I believe a more harmonious marriage between traditional and new media as they lose their silo mentalities. Digital is nearly mainstream and will get there in four years.

Q.   *Do you expect the top sites to be more or less popular by 2015 (ie Google, Facebook, YouTube, Wikipedia)?*

A.   Unless someone out-Googles Google, which I doubt, Google will continue to dominate search and related services. I can see, however, an overarching site that brings together all of the front runners under a single digital umbrella. I am not sure quite what I mean by this – just a gut feeling. The lawyers, however, will have a field day with IP, content and privacy.

Q.   *Digital currently represents about 25 per cent of all marketing spend (UK) – how do you see this evolving by 2015?*

A.   Forty per cent.

Jonathan Forrest, MD of Cybercom

Q. *What do you feel are the greatest challenges facing the digital marketing industry between now and say 2015?*

A. Growing into a leadership role. There is no such thing as digital marketing any more, just good marketing with digital technology at its core. The greatest challenge for digital marketing over the next four years is to mature and step into this industry-leading role.

Remaining flexible. As the stakeholders of digital marketing become more established and corporate, our greatest challenge as organizations is to retain the ability to adapt to the ever-evolving digital environment.

Determining comparable ROI. The single greatest challenge for all digital channels remains the ever-elusive ROI model for measuring quality of engagement comparably against other media.

Changing the way we think. It is not in the nature of the marketing manager to design for gaps. The traditional mindset is to plan out every element of a campaign but people will take what a brand has put out there and mould it into their own. We must learn to leave gaps in our planning that will lead to new and enhanced ways of consumer participation.

Q. *Which tools or channels do you think will show the greatest level of growth and why (ie social media, mobile, something else)?*

A. Mobile and m-commerce. The evolution of m-commerce will see people shift from using smartphones to purchase music and apps to use smartphones as a replacement for credit cards or cash. We will see a decline in the use of plastic credit and debit cards as a result. In particular, the integration of near-field communication (NFC) devices into smartphones will exponentially explode the role of mobile in retail marketing.

Social TV. TV will be socialized. Consumers will participate in live TV and engage in personalized media experiences. With the advent of high-speed broadband and the right technical infrastructure, more and more homes will enjoy a more personalized and social TV experience on their TV, mobile, tablet or laptop. Screen ubiquity will become more prevalent.

The internet of things. The next four years will see the emergence of a new and ubiquitous channel. Every object will essentially be connected to the internet. 'We are moving from an era where the network will evolve from a network of connected human beings to one where a majority of the nodes on it will be devices: printers, cameras, monitoring devices, domestic appliances – even the humble toaster.' John Naughton, *Observer*, March 2011.

Two forces are driving this new channel. Sensors and actuators are increasingly being embedded in physical objects. We now have enough internet addresses to assign a unique address to every object on the planet.

Q.   *Do you expect the top sites to be more or less popular by 2015 (ie Google, Facebook, YouTube, Wikipedia)?*

A.   With their expansive suite of products (Docs, Reader, Calendar, Chat, Mail, Apps, Plus), Google has an unrivalled digital omnipresence, posing a strong threat to the social behemoth Facebook.

Facebook is already losing fans in developed countries like the United States and the UK (globally numbers are still rising but its growth rate is slowing) who are most likely bored and/or reverting to a more private life. Google+ membership figures have risen to over 25 million since its June launch – the fastest digital innovation to reach such numbers. As Google puts more investment into the social web, it's likely that its increasingly social web packages will lure more participants.

Driven by faster broadband speed, video creation and viewing are also on the rise and likely to rise exponentially in the next few years as web users increasingly look to 'watch the web' rather than read it. Yes, numbers to YouTube will continue to rise, but more interestingly video will have a stronger presence across the entire web.

With the rise of visual search, people will be delivered instant search results on taking a photo. Direct visits to Wikipedia will likely fall although Wikipedia content will most likely be integrated into visual search results.

Online sharing sites like Spotify will continue to gain traction if the positive consumer reaction to its recent US launch is anything to go by.

Always expect the next big thing and never underestimate its ability to disrupt and eclipse today's top sites.

Q.   *Digital currently represents about 25 per cent of all marketing spend (UK) – how do you see this evolving by 2015?*

A.   Digital marketing and advertising are experiencing explosive growth at the moment and are likely to continue that way into the future. In fact, a recent study by PwC forecast a compound interest growth of 11.2 per cent in internet marketing. This will be the only segment of the UK market to experience double-digit growth.

Technology is going to become a serious differentiator of competitive advantage within advertising agencies. Technology is going to *become* the business.

Investment will skew in favour of owned digital media content versus paid content – ie we will build things that people find interesting, useful and inspire collaboration and creativity, rather than spending all our messaging in broadcasting a brand message.

Also, investment in social media monitoring and moderation services will rise as companies realize that an absence of such services can lead to unprecedented PR/reputation damage.

Dynamic, unpredictable, exciting... and essential

Digital marketing is going places. Of that there's no doubt. Where exactly it's going, and how it's going to get there are all part of the adventure. In this chapter we've offered just a few suggestions of what might lie in store... but finding out for yourself is all part of the fun.

Looking further ahead

When we laid out this chapter we thought it would be worthwhile to get some input from industry experts as you have seen above but we also wanted to use our imagination too. It's one thing predicting what might happen by 2015 but we thought we should go the whole hog, and try to think a bit further out. What might things look like, for example, in 2050? It's amazing the insight you can get pondering the evolution of digital over a few pints in a bar in the southwest of Ireland!

Simply put, technology will continue to find ways to make our lives easier. It's certainly believable that we could soon have devices that will respond to our spoken commands instead of needing keystrokes and mouse clicks.

For example, you utter the instruction 'Flight, Dublin, Sunday'. Instantly your voice-activated device is off into the web, ferreting out the best deal it can find on your favourite airline. It buys the tickets, books the cab, collects relevant offers from the shops at the airport, who now know that you'll be walking past later in the week, and whispers back the magic word: 'Sorted'!

That's where we are heading – into a world of permission-based engagement, full of value-for-money and *value-for-time* experiences where personal repetitive actions are outsourced to your 'sidekick' digital device of choice.

It's a world where the media we know now will be transformed yet again. There will be no place for paper media. Consumers will *build* their own personal media the way early adopters already do today, but in an infinitely refined way. We'll see further commoditization of products and services, and co-creation and collaborative consumption will lead the way towards a society where only the most responsible and 'truthful/trusted' brands will be allowed to compete for access to a new customer base. Consumers will essentially control the profitability of those brands based on their behaviour and demonstration of social responsibility.

The winning marketer will be the one who continues to invest in the latest technology while observing Colin Lloyd's words of wisdom – test, test, test.

In this dynamic and unpredictable place, fortune favours not just the brave... but also the nimble. Your organization has to be able to adapt quickly to change, recognize the opportunities it presents and capitalize on them quickly. If you build a digital marketing strategy and team that can give you that flexibility, you'll find plenty of opportunity opening up for you as digital marketing continues its stellar evolution.

So stick around for the ride... it's shaping up to be a very interesting one indeed.

GLOSSARY

Throughout the book we've avoided technical jargon wherever possible and have tried to present information in plain, clear English. Where specific digital marketing terminology was unavoidable we provided a brief definition in the text itself. To supplement the definitions in the text and to give you a handy reference for digital marketing terms, we've included the following glossary, reproduced here with permission from the UK's Internet Advertising Bureau (**www.iabuk.net**).

abandon   When a user does not complete a transaction.

ad impression   An advertisement impression transpires each time a consumer is exposed to an advertisement (either appended to an SMS or MMS message, on mobile web (WAP) page, within a video clip, or related media).

ad serving   Delivery of online adverts to an end user's computer by an ad management system. The system allows different online adverts to be served in order to target different audience groups and can serve adverts across multiple sites. Ad technology providers each have their own proprietary models for this.

ad unit   Any defined advertising vehicle that can appear in an ad space inside of an application. For example for the purposes of promoting a commercial brand, product or service.

advertiser   Also called merchant, retailer, e-retailer, or online retailer. Any website that sells a product or service, accepts payments, and fulfils orders. An advertiser places ads and links to their products and services on other websites (publishers) and pays those publishers a commission for leads or sales that result from their site.

affiliate marketing   An affiliate (a website owner or publisher) displays an advertisement (such as a banner or link) on its site for a merchant (the brand or advertiser). If a consumer visiting the affiliate's site clicks on this advertisement and goes on to perform a specified action (usually a purchase) on an advertiser's site then the affiliate receives a commission.

algorithm   The set of 'rules' a search engine may use to determine the relevance of a web page (and therefore ranking) in its organic search results. See also *organic search results* and *search engine optimization*.

application service provider (ASP)   An online network that is accessible through the internet instead of through the installation of software. It is quickly integrated with other websites and the services are easily implemented and scalable.

avatar   A picture or cartoon used to represent an individual in chat forums, games or on a website as a help function.

bandwidth   The transmission rate of a communication line – usually measured in kilobytes per second (kbps). This relates to the amount of data that can be carried per second by your internet connection. See also *broadband*.

banner   A long, horizontal, online advert usually found running across the top of a page in a fixed placement. See also *universal advertising package, embedded format*.

BARB   Broadcasters' Audience Research Board is responsible for the measurement of TV viewing.

behavioural targeting   A form of online marketing that uses advertising technology to target web users based on their previous behaviour. Advertising creative and content can be tailored to be of more relevance to a particular user by capturing their previous decision making behaviour (eg: filling out preferences or visiting certain areas of a site frequently) and looking for patterns.

blog   An online space regularly updated presenting the opinions or activities of one or a group of individuals and displaying in chronological order.

broadband   An internet connection that is always on and that delivers a higher bit rate (128 kbps or above) than a standard dial-up connection. It allows for a better online experience as pages load quickly and you can download items faster.

buffering   When a streaming media player saves portions of file until there is enough information for the file to begin playing.

button   A square online advert usually found embedded within a website page. See also *universal advertising package, embedded format*.

cache memory   Used to store web pages you have seen already. When you go back to those pages they'll load more quickly because they come from the cache and don't need to be downloaded over the internet again.

call to action (CTA)   A statement or instruction, typically promoted in print, web, TV, radio, on-portal, or other forms of media (often embedded in advertising), that explains to a mobile subscriber how to respond to an opt-in for a particular promotion or mobile initiative, which is typically followed by a notice (see *notice*).

click-through   When a user interacts with an advertisement and clicks through to the advertiser's website.

click-through rate (CTR)   Frequency of click-throughs as a percentage of impressions served. Used as a measure of advertising effectiveness.

click to call   A service that enables a mobile subscriber to initiate a voice call to a specified phone number by clicking on a link on a mobile internet site. Typically used to enhance and provide a direct response mechanism in an advertisement.

commission   An amount of income received by a publisher for some quantifiable action such as selling an advertiser's product and/or service on the publisher's website.

content sponsorship   Advertiser sponsorships of content areas (eg entire website, home page or a specific channel) to include the total value of the package including any embedded or interruptive formats. This category also includes revenue related to e-mail advertising or prioritized listing of results in search engines that are included as part of the sponsorship deal.

contextual advertising   Advertising that is targeted to the content on the web page being viewed by a user at that specific time.

conversion rate   Measure of success of an online ad when compared to the click-through rate. What defines a 'conversion' depends on the marketing objective, eg: it can be defined as a sale or request to receive more information, etc.

cookie   A small text file on the user's PC that identifies the user's browser and hence the user so they are 'recognized' when they re-visit a site, eg: it allows usernames to be stored and websites to personalize their offering.

cost per action (CPA)   A pricing model that only charges advertising on an action being conducted, eg a sale or a form being filled in.

cost per acquisition (CPA)   Cost to acquire a new customer.

cost per click (CPC) The amount paid by an advertiser for a click on their sponsored search listing. See also *PPC*.

cost per mille (CPM)/cost per thousand (CPT) Online advertising can be purchased on the basis of what it costs to show the ad to 1,000 viewers (CPM). It is used in marketing as a benchmark to calculate the relative cost of an advertising campaign or an ad message in a given medium. Rather than an absolute cost, CPM estimates the cost per 1,000 views of the ad. (Wikipedia definition)

CRM Customer relationship management.

deep-linking advert Linking beyond a home page to a page inside the site with content pertinent to the advert.

display advertising on e-mail Advertising that appears around the unrelated editorial content of e-mail newsletters. This can take the form of embedded formats like banners, or as sponsorship, and includes both opt-in (sent to customers specifically requesting it) and opt-out (sent to customers with the option to be removed at their request) e-mails.

domain name The unique name of an internet site, eg **www.iabuk.net**.

downloading the technology that allows users to store video content on their computer for viewing at a later date. Downloading an entire piece of media makes it more susceptible to illegal duplication.

D2C Direct to consumer.

DRM Digital rights management is a set of technologies used by publishers and media owners to control access to their digital content. Access can be limited to the number of times a piece of content is accessed from a single machine or user account; the number of times access permissions can be passed on; or the lifespan of a piece of content.

dynamic ad delivery Based upon predetermined criteria, dynamic ad delivery is the process by which a mobile advertisement is delivered, via a campaign management platform, to a publisher's mobile content.

e-commerce (electronic commerce) Business that takes place over electronic platforms, such as the internet.

e-mail bounced Those e-mails sent as part of a mailing distribution which did not have a valid recipient e-mail address and so generated a formal failure message. (ABC Electronic jargon buster definition)

electronic programme guide (EPG) Is the electronic version of a television schedule showing programme times and content on the television screen or monitor. In the case of VOD, an EPG displays the content of all of the services available to a subscriber.

embedded format Advertising formats that are displayed in set spaces on a publisher's page. See also *banner, skyscraper, button*.

emoticons Emoticon symbols are used to indicate mood in an electronic mode of communication, eg e-mail or instant messenger. :-)

encoding The conversion of an analogue signal to a digital format.

EPC (average earnings per one hundred clicks) A relative rating that illustrates the ability to convert clicks into commissions. It is calculated by taking commissions earned (or commissions paid) divided by the total number of clicks times 100.

expandable banner/skyscraper Fixed online advertising placements that expand over the page in the response to user action, eg mouseover. See also *rich media*.

firewall software   Provides security for a computer or local network by preventing unauthorized access. It sits as a barrier between the web and your computer in order to prevent hacking, viruses or unapproved data transfer.

flash   Web design software that creates animation and interactive elements which are quick to download.

flash impression   The total number of requests made for pages holding flash-based content by users of that site in the period being measured. (ABC Electronic jargon buster definition)

geotargeting   The process of only showing adverts to people on a website and in search engines based on their physical location. This could be done using advanced technology that knows where a computer is located or by using the content of the website to determine what a person is looking for, eg someone searching for a restaurant in Aylesbury, Buckinghamshire.

GPRS   General Packet Radio Service or '2.5G' is an underlying mechanism for the networks to deliver internet browsing, WAP, e-mail and other such content. The user is 'always connected' and relatively high data rates can be achieved with most modern phones compared to a dial-up modem. Most phones default to using GPRS (if capable), and Incentivated is able to develop services that utilize this delivery mechanism.

graphic banners   A graphic mobile ad represented by a banner featuring an image. Similar to a web banner but with lower size constraints. (See *banner*.)

GSM   Global Standard for Mobiles. The set of standards covering one particular type of mobile phone system.

hit   A single request from a web browser for a single item from a web server.

hot spotting   The ability to add hyperlinks to objects in a video that enable viewers to tag a product or service. Hot spotting can be used as a direct response mechanic in internet video.

HTML   Stands for HyperText Markup Language, which is the set of commands used by web browsers to interpret and display page content to users. (ABC Electronic jargon buster definition)

image ad   An image on a mobile internet site with an active link that can be clicked on by the subscriber. Once clicked the user is redirected to a new page, another mobile internet site or other destination where an offer resides.

impressions   The metric used to measure views of a web page and its elements – including the advertising embedded within it. Ad impressions are how most online advertising is sold and the cost is quoted in terms of the cost per thousand impressions (CPM).

instant messaging   Sending messages and chatting with friends or colleagues in real time when you are both online via a special application.

Integrated Services Digital Network (ISDN)   High-speed dial-up connections to the internet over normal phone lines.

Internet Protocol TV (IPTV)   The use of a broadband connection to stream digital television over the internet to subscribed users.

internet service provider (ISP)   A company which provides users with the means to connect to the internet. Eg: AOL, Tiscali, Yahoo!

interruptive formats   Online advertising formats that appear on users' screens on top of web content (and sometimes before the web page appears) and range from static, one-page splash screens to full-motion animated advertisements. See also *overlay, pop-up*.

interstitial ads   Which appear between two content pages. Also known as splash pages and transition ads. See also *rich media*.

IPA   Institute of Practitioners in Advertising is the trade body representing advertising agencies in the UK.

IP address   The numerical internet address assigned to each computer on a network so that it can be distinguished from other computers. Expressed as four groups of numbers separated by dots.

keyword marketing   The purchase of keywords (or 'search terms') by advertisers in search listings. See also *PPC*.

LAN (local area network)   A group of computers connected together, which are at one physical location.

landing page (jump page)   The page or view to which a user is directed when they click on an active link embedded in a banner, web page, e-mail or other view. A click-through lands the user on a jump page. Sometimes the landing page is one stage upstream from what would ordinarily be considered the home page.

lead   When a visitor registers, signs up for, or downloads something on an advertiser's site. A lead might also comprise a visitor filling out a form on an advertiser's site.

link   A link is a form of advertising on a website, in an e-mail or online newsletter, which, when clicked on, refers the visitor to an advertiser's website or a specific area within their website.

location-based services (LBS)   A range of services that are provided to mobile subscribers based on the geographical location of their handsets within their cellular network. Handsets do not have to be equipped with a position-location technology such as GPS to enable the geographical trigger of service(s) being provided since the location of the cell-site can be used as a proxy. Assisted GPS combines cell-site information with satellite positioning for a more accurate read. LBS include driving directions, information about certain resources or destinations within the current vicinity, such as restaurants, ATMs, shopping, movie theatres, etc. LBS may also be used to track the movements and locations of people, as is being done via parent/child monitoring services and mobile devices that target the family market.

locator   An advertisement or service through which an advertiser's bricks-and-mortar location can be identified based on proximity of the consumer or their preferred location (can be LBS or user-defined postal code).

log files   A record of all the hits a web server has received over a given period of time.

meta-tags/-descriptions   HTML tags that identify the content of a web page for the search engines.

micro-site   A sub-site reached via clicking on an ad. The user stays on the publisher's website but has access to more information from the advertiser.

MMA   The Mobile Marketing Association (MMA) is the premier global non-profit association that strives to stimulate the growth of mobile marketing and its associated technologies. The MMA is an action-oriented association designed to clear obstacles to market development, to establish standards and best practices for sustainable growth, and to evangelize the mobile channel for use by brands and third-party content providers. The MMA has over 500 members representing 40-plus countries.

mobile data services   Includes SMS, MMS, WAP, LBS and video.

mobile internet advertising   A form of advertising via mobile phones or other wireless devices (excluding laptops). This type of mobile advertising includes mobile web banner ads, mobile internet sponsorship and interstitials (which appear while a requested mobile web page is loading) as well as mobile paid-for search listings. Mobile internet advertising does not include other forms of mobile marketing such as SMS, MMS and shortcode.

MP3   A computer file format that compresses audio files up to a factor of 12 from a .wav file.

MPEG   File format used to compress and transmit video clips online.

MSISDN   Mobile Subscriber Integrated Services Digital Network. The mobile phone number of the participating customer.

multiple purpose units (MPU)   A square online advert usually found embedded in a web page in a fixed placement. Called 'multiple purpose' as it is a flexible-shaped blank 'canvas' in which you can serve flat or more interactive content as desired. See also *rich media, universal advertising package*.

natural search results   The 'natural' search results that appear in a separate section (usually the main body of the page) to the paid listings. The results listed here have not been paid for and are ranked by the search engine (using spiders or algorithms according to relevancy to the term searched upon). See also *spider, algorithm, SEO*.

notice   An easy-to-understand written description of the information and data collection, storage, maintenance, access, security, disclosure and use policies and practices, as necessary and required of the entity collecting and using the information and data from the mobile subscriber.

NVOD   Near video on demand service is the delivery of film and television programming from a server via a cable network or the internet. Like VOD these services are nonlinear and navigated via an EPG. Programming must be downloaded and the majority of existing services require the same amount of time to download as the duration of the selected programme.

OB   Outside broadcast unit known as a 'production truck'. In the United States an OB unit is a truck containing a mobile TV production studio.

off-portal   Point of sale/access on the mobile network, but outside of the operator's 'walled garden'/portal/deck, where consumers can access/purchase information and mobile products/content/utilities.

online HD   Is the delivery of high-definition streamed video media. This typically conforms to 720p standards where 720 represents 720 lines of vertical resolution and p stands for progressive scan.

online video advertising   Video advertising accompanying video content distributed via the internet to be streamed or downloaded onto compatible devices such as computers and mobile phones. In its basic form, this can be TV ads run online, but adverts are increasingly adapted or created specifically to suit online.

on-portal   Point of sale/access within the operator's 'walled garden'/portal/deck, where consumers can access/purchase information and mobile products/content/utilities.

opt-in   An individual has given a company permission to use his/her data for marketing purposes.

opt-out   An individual has stated that they do not want a company to use his/her data for marketing purposes.

organic search results   The 'natural' search results that appear in a separate section (usually the main body of the page) to the paid listings. The results listed here have not been paid for and are ranked by the search engine (using spiders or algorithms) according to relevancy to the term searched upon. See also *spider*, *algorithm*, *SEO*.

overlay   Online advertising content that appears over the top of the web page. See also *rich media*.

paid-for listings   The search results list in which advertisers pay to be featured according to the PPC model. This list usually appears in a separate section to the organic search results – usually at the top of the page or down the right-hand side. See also *organic search results*, *pay per click (PPC)*.

paid inclusion   In exchange for a payment, a search engine will guarantee to list/review pages from a website. It is not guaranteed that the pages will rank well for particular queries – this still depends on the search engine's underlying relevancy process.

paid search   See *PPC*.

pay for performance program   Also called affiliate marketing, performance-based, partner marketing, CPA, or associate programme. Any type of revenue-sharing programme where a publisher receives a commission for generating online activity (eg leads or sales) for an advertiser.

pay per click (PPC)   Allows advertisers to bid for placement in the paid listings search results on terms that are relevant to their business. Advertisers pay the amount of their bid only when a consumer clicks on their listing. Also called sponsored search/paid search.

pay per lead   The commission structure where the advertiser pays the publisher a flat fee for each qualified lead (customer) that is referred to the advertiser's website.

pay per sale   The commission structure where the advertiser pays a percentage or flat fee to the publisher based on the revenue generated by the sale of a product or service to a visitor who came from a publisher site.

pay per view (PPV)   Is an e-commerce model that allows media owners to grant consumers access to their programming in return for payment. Micro-payments may be used for shorter programming whilst feature films may attract larger sums.

personal video recorder (PVR)   Is a hard-disc-based digital video recorder (most use MPEG technology) and enables viewers to pause and rewind live TV. PVRs also interact with EPGs to automatically record favourite programmes and have led to an increase in the number of consumers watching 'time sifted' TV and skipping advertising breaks.

pharming   An illegal method of redirecting traffic from another company's website (such as a bank) to a fake one designed to look similar in order to steal user details when they try to log in. See also *phishing*.

phishing   An illegal method whereby legitimate looking e-mails (appearing to come from a well-known bank, for example) are used in an attempt to get personal information that can be used to steal a user's identity.

placement   The area where an advertisement is displayed/placed within a publisher's mobile content.

podcasting   Podcasting involves making an audio file (usually in MP3 format) of content – usually in the form of a radio program – that is available to download to an MP3 player.

polite loading   Fixed online advertising placements that load and display additional flash content after the host page on which the advert appears has finished loading. See also *flash*.

pop-under   An ad that appears in a separate window beneath an open window. Pop-under ads are concealed until the top window is closed, moved, resized or minimized.

pop-up   An online advert that 'pops up' in a window over the top of a web page. See also *interruptive formats*.

portal   A browsable portal of links to content, pre-configured usually by the network operator, and set as the default home page to the phone's browser.

post-roll   The streaming of a mobile advertising clip after a mobile TV/video clip. The mobile advert is usually 10–15 seconds.

pre-roll   The name given to the adverts shown before, or whilst an online video is loading. There can be more than one and, although they all vary in length, they average 21 seconds in duration.

PSMS   Premium SMS. A text message that is charged at a premium over the standard rate.

publisher   Also referred to as an affiliate, associate, partner, reseller or content site. An independent party, or website, that promotes the products or services of an advertiser in exchange for a commission.

query string formation   In a search engine, a query string is the set of words entered into a search engine by an individual. For example, a search for 'search engine marketing information'. Query string formation is simply the process of thinking of the correct query string to get the results required.

reach   The number of unique web users potentially seeing a website one or more times in a given time period expressed as a percentage of the total active web population for that period.

real time   No delay in the processing of requests for information, other than the time necessary for the data to travel over the internet.

really simple syndication (RSS)   Software that allows you to flag website content (often from blogs or new sites) and aggregate new entries to this content into an easy-to-read format that is delivered directly to a user's PC. See also *blog*.

rich media   The collective name for online advertising formats that use advanced technology to harness broadband to build brands. It uses interactive and audio-visual elements to give richer content and a richer experience for the user when interacting with the advert. See also *interstitial ads*, *superstitials*, *overlay* and *Rich Media Guidelines*.

Rich Media Guidelines   Design guidelines produced by the IAB for effective use of rich media technologies in all forms of internet advertising. They aim to protect user experience by keeping them in control of the experience, eg: encouraging clearly labelled close, sound and video buttons.

sale   When a user makes a purchase from an online advertiser.

sales house   An organization which sells advertising on behalf of other media owners. These sales houses typically retain a percentage of the revenue they sell in exchange for their services. These organizations may combine a number of websites together and sell them as different packages to advertisers.

search engine marketing (SEM) The process which aims to get websites listed prominently in search engine results through search engine optimization, sponsored search and paid inclusion. See also *PPC, SEO* and *paid inclusion.*

search engine optimization (SEO) The process which aims to get websites listed prominently within search engines' organic (algorithmic, spidered) search results. Involves making a site 'search engine friendly'. See also *organic search results.*

serial digital interface (SDI) Is a dedicated digital video interface used to carry broadcast quality video content.

server A host computer which maintains websites, newsgroups and e-mail services.

session The time spent between a user starting an application, computer, website, etc and logging off or quitting.

SIM Subscriber identity module. A removable part of the mobile phone hardware that identifies the subscriber.

simulcast Watching an existing TV service over the internet at the same time as normal transmission.

site analytics The reporting and analysis of website activity – in particular user behaviour on the site. All websites have a weblog which can be used for this purpose, but other third-party software is available for a more sophisticated service.

skyscraper A long, vertical, online advert usually found running down the side of a page in a fixed placement. See also *universal advertising package.*

SMPP Short Message Peer-to-peer Protocol – used for exchanging SMS messages.

SMS Short Message Service.

SMSC Short Message Service Centre. A network switch for routeing SMS traffic.

sniffer software Identifies the capabilities of the user's browser and therefore can determine compatibility with ad formats and serve them an advert they will be able to see/fully interact with (eg: GIF, flash, etc).

Solus e-mail advertising Where the body of the e-mail is determined by the advertiser, including both text and graphical elements, and is sent on their behalf by an e-mail list manager/owner. Solus e-mail advertising is conducted on an opt-in basis where the recipient has given their consent to receive communications.

spam Unsolicited junk mail.

spider A programme which crawls the web and fetches web pages in order for them to be indexed against keywords. Used by search engines to formulate search result pages. See also *organic search results.*

sponsored search See *pay per click (PPC).*

sponsorship Advertiser sponsorships of targeted content areas (eg entire website, site area or an event) often for promotional purposes.

SS7 Signalling System 7. A worldwide standard for telecommunications hardware to talk to each other.

stickiness Measure used to gauge the effectiveness of a site in retaining its users. Usually measured by the duration of the visit.

streaming media Compressed audio/video which plays and downloads at the same time. The user does not have to wait for the whole file to download before it starts playing.

superstitials A form of rich media advertising which allows a TV-like experience on the web. It is fully pre-cached before playing. See also *rich media, cache memory.*

tenancy The 'renting' out of a section of a website by another brand who pays commission to this media owner for any revenue generated from this space. Eg: dating services inside portals or bookstores inside online newspapers.

text ad A static appended text attached to an advertisement.

text link Creative use for mobile advertisements – represented by highlighted and clickable text(s) with a link embedded within the highlighted text. Usually limited to 16–24 characters.

traffic Number of visitors who come to a website.

UMTS Universal Mobile Telephony Service or '3G' offers comprehensive voice and multimedia services to mobile customers by providing very high data rates and new functionality such as data streaming. 3G phones are backward compatible and can access all the services that 2 and 2.5G phones can, except that in this case data can be transferred a lot quicker. This means that any service that Incentivated can currently provide will work on the newer phones whose experience can be enhanced specifically based on handset type.

uniform resource locator (URL) Technical term that is used to refer to the web address of a particular website. For example **www.iabuk.net**.

unique users Number of different individuals who visit a site within a specific time period.

universal advertising package A set of online advertising formats that are standardized placements as defined by the IAB. See also *banner*, *skyscraper*, *button*, *MPU* and *embedded format*.

universal player Is a platform-agnostic media player that will allow video and audio to be played on any hardware/software configuration from a single source file.

user-generated content (UGC) Online content created by website users rather than media owners or publishers – either through reviews, blogging, podcasting or posting comments, pictures or video clips. Sites that encourage user-generated content include MySpace, YouTube, Wikipedia and Flickr. See also *blog*, *podcasting*.

video on demand (VOD) Allows users to watch what they want, when they want. This can be either 'pay per view' or a free service usually funded by advertising.

viral marketing The term 'viral advertising' refers to the idea that people will pass on and share striking and entertaining content; this is often sponsored by a brand which is looking to build awareness of a product or service. These viral commercials often take the form of funny video clips, or interactive flash games, images, and even text.

VMNO (Virtual Mobile Network Operator) A company that uses the infra-structure of an existing (licence-owning) telecoms network operator. Tesco and Virgin are two of the largest VMNOs in the UK.

Voice Over Internet Protocol (VOIP) Technology that allows the use of a broadband internet connection to make telephone calls.

WAP (Wireless Application Protocol) Standard for providing mobile data services on hand-held devices. Brings internet content such as news, weather, travel, etc to mobile phones and can also be used to deliver formatted content such as wallpapers, ringtones, video, games, portals and other useful links.

Web 2.0 The term Web 2.0 – with its knowing nod to upgraded computer applications – describes the next generation of online use. Web 2.0 identifies the consumer as a major contributor in the evolution of the internet into a two-way medium. See also *user-generated content*.

web based   Requiring no software to access an online service or function, other than a web browser and access to the internet.

web portal   A website or service that offers a broad array of resources and services, such as e-mail, forums, search engines, and online shopping malls.

whitelist   An e-mail whitelist is a list of contacts that the user deems are acceptable to receive e-mail from and should not be sent to the trash folder. (Wikipedia definition)

Wi-Fi (Wireless Fidelity)   The ability to connect to the internet wirelessly. Internet 'hotspots' in coffee shops and airports, etc use this technology.

wiki   A wiki is a type of website that allows the visitors themselves to easily add, remove, and otherwise edit and change some available content, sometimes without the need for registration.

wilfing (What Was I Looking For?)   Seven in 10 of Britain's 34 million users forget what they are looking for online at work and at home. Wilfing is an expression referring to browsing the internet with no real purpose.

Wireless Markup Language (WML) aka WAP 1.0   Where the mobile internet started many years ago. Hardly supported any more.

XHTML (Extensible Hypertag Markup Language) aka WAP 2.0   The language used to create most mobile internet sites.

XML (Extensible Markup Language)   Language used by many internet applications for exchanging information.

INDEX

NB: page numbers in *italic* indicate figures or tables

Also available from **Kogan Page**